Poverty and Wealth

Other Books by the Author

Poverty and Wealth

Why Socialism Doesn't Work

RONALD H. NASH

RICHARDSON, TEXAS

DISTRIBUTED BY WORD PUBLISHING

DALLAS • LONDON • VANCOUVER • MELBOURNE

Copyright	©1986 by Ronald H. Nash
Library of Congress Cataloging-in-Publication Data	Nash, Ronald H. 　　Poverty and wealth : why socialism doesn't work / Ronald H. Nash. 　　　　p.　cm. 　　Originally published: Westchester, Ill. : Crossway Books, c1986. 　　Includes bibliographical references (p.　　) and indexes. 　　　　1. Economics—Religious aspects—Christianity. 2. Capitalism—Religious aspects—Christianity. I. Title. 　　[BR115.E3N29 1992] 　　261.8'5—dc20　　　　　　　　　　92-14204 　　　　　　　　　　　　　　　　　　　　　　CIP
ISBN	0-945241-16-X (pbk.)
Place of Printing	*Printed in the United States of America*
Design	Cover concept/design by John M. Henderson III/ JMH III Designs.
Cover photograph	©1991 Josh McDowell Ministries, used by permission.

95 96 97 98 99 / 10 9 8 7 6 5 4 3

This book is dedicated to our two children

—Jeffrey and Jennifer—

What is Probe?

Probe Ministries is a non-profit corporation whose mission is to reclaim the primacy of Christian thought and values in Western culture through media, education, and literature. In seeking to accomplish this mission, Probe provides perspective on the integration of the academic disciplines and historic Christianity. The members and associates of the Probe team are actively engaged in research as well as lecturing and interacting with students and faculty in thousands of university classrooms throughout the United States and Canada on topics and issues vital to the university student.

In addition, Probe acts as a clearing house, communicating the results of its research to the church and society.

Further information about Probe's materials and ministries may be obtained by writing to Probe Ministries, P.O. Box 801046, Dallas, Texas 75204 or by calling Probe at (214)480-0240.

Contents

1

The Christian War Against Economics

everal years ago, I began a different book by talking
about the two faces of Christian social concern.[1] I
drew attention to the extent to which theologically
conservative Protestants, long known for their relative indifference
to cultural and social issues, were becoming increasingly involved in
social action. I applauded the new and growing social concern on
the part of such Christians.

However, I pointed out that while there was much that was
praiseworthy about the fact that large numbers of Christians were
becoming conscious of their need to care about things like poverty,
there was a second side to Christian social concern. Christians need
to care about the poor: that is one side of Christian social concern.
But they also need to become informed about the relevant philo-
sophical, political, and economic issues that ground wise and efficient policies to help the poor. Unfortunately, many Christians act
as though the only thing that counts is *intention*. But when good
intentions are not wedded to sound theory, especially sound *economic* theory, good intentions can often result in actions that produce consequences directly opposite to those we planned.

There is growing evidence that this is precisely what has
happened in the case of the social policies to help the poor adopted
in the United States since 1965. A number of recent studies cite
evidence that appears to show that a combination of good intentions and bad theory produced bad programs that did serious harm
to the very people they were supposed to help. About the very time
when the social programs of the Great Society were being enacted,
economist Benjamin Rogge made some comments that deserve serious attention now, twenty years later. He wrote:

[T]he typical American who calls himself a Christian and who makes pronouncements on economic policies or institutions, does so out of an almost complete ignorance of the simplest and most widely accepted tools of economic analysis. If something arouses his Christian concern, he asks not whether it is water or gasoline he is tossing on the economic fire—he asks only whether it is a well-intended act. As I understand it, the Christian is required to use his God-given reason as well.[2]

Perhaps nothing illustrates the continuing relevance of this warning better than the recent efforts of America's Roman Catholic bishops to produce a pastoral letter on the American economy. American writer Dinesh D'Souza decided to interview a number of the bishops associated with the pastoral letter in order to assess the extent of their economic knowledge. The results of his interviews have been published in an article that is both enlightening and troubling.[3] He discovered that the typical Catholic bishop whose authority is being used to support debatable economic policies knows less about economics than a college freshman in the third week of a basic economics course. The title of D'Souza's article, "The Bishops as Pawns," suggests that the real force behind the drafts of the pastoral letter are a few radical churchmen and intellectuals who are using the bishops' goodwill and general economic illiteracy to score a huge public relations victory in support of their left-wing causes. While many Catholic laypeople may think the drafts of the pastoral letter reflect the bishops' detailed grasp of the issues addressed in the letter, it turns out—D'Souza discovered—that the bishops themselves have no idea what they're talking about.

But the Catholic bishops are hardly alone in their rush to issue public pronouncements on complex social, political, and economic issues. Nor are they alone in their decided tilt towards the political and economic Left. And they are certainly not alone in the degree to which their judgments reflect a defective understanding of basic economics.

Within the Christian church today, one can find a small but growing army of Protestants and Roman Catholics who have entered into an uncritical alliance with the political and economic Left.[4] The so-called liberation theologians not only promote a synthesis of Marxism and Christianity, but attempt to ground their recommended restrictions of economic and political freedom on their interpretation of the Bible. In fact, one of the most significant developments in this whole area during the last ten years is the growing attempt to use the Bible as a weapon against capitalism. While the Catholic bishops use the Bible to show that God is a *very* liberal Democrat, the liberation theologians use the Bible to show that God is a Marxist.

Students of the subject know how often a similar bias against economic freedom appeared in the writings of theologically liberal Protestants in the 1930s and 1940s. What has taken many people by surprise is the recent appearance of similarly radical views in the thinking of a growing number of theologically conservative Christians known as evangelicals. The convictions of these politically radical evangelicals are expressed regularly in journals like *Sojourners* and *The Other Side*. Evangelical publishers like Eerdmans and InterVarsity produce a steady stream of books recommending socialism as the only economic system that is consistent with the Bible. Such views have become so deeply entrenched on leading evangelical campuses that they are often treated by their professorial advocates as though they were part of the Christian creed. Any student or colleague who disagrees is viewed as an intellectual Neanderthal or more typically as someone who obviously does not share God's loving concern for the poor and oppressed peoples of the world.

It is ironic, however, that the current obsessions of the Christian Left are surfacing at the very time when data from twenty years of War on Poverty programs is beginning to show how badly such programs have harmed the poor. For years, these Christians insisted that a rejection of their beloved ideology demonstrated a lack of compassion. But as Ben Rogge pointed out two decades ago, good intentions are not enough. Good intentions combined with bad theory have produced bad policies that have harmed the very people they were supposed to help.

Author Herbert Schlossberg had Christians like this in mind when he titled a section of a recent book "The War Against Economics."[5] He wrote:

> Having convinced themselves, rightly, that the biblical tradition has much to say about economics, the church intellectuals make theological statements serve as substitutes for economics. They enlist in what [economist Ludwig von]Mises referred to as the century-long battle against economics but without realizing what they are doing.[6]

Such Christians, Schlossberg continues, combine an attempt to induce feelings of guilt "with willful ignorance and contempt for any factual understanding of economic processes."[7] Their efforts to help people, he states, only succeed in making things worse.

Several things are clear. The number of Christians seeking to relate the concerns of their faith to economic issues is growing rapidly. Unfortunately, few of the attempts to integrate Christian concerns and economic issues evidence much understanding of basic and relatively simple economic concepts. There is an obvious need for a book that will address the large number of questions being raised by Christians who are interested in filling in the gaps in their economic knowledge.

This book is not an attempt to produce a system of Christian economics. There is no such thing as revealed economics. There is no such thing as positive Christian economics.[8] The distinction that counts is that between good and bad economics.[9] I make no effort to deduce a system of economics from the Bible. Such an activity strikes me as muddle-headed as an attempt to deduce a theory of the solar system from the Bible. But nothing that I have said in this paragraph should be taken to mean that the Christian who is studying economics should do so in isolation from the Scriptures or his Christian world view. The best way to see how I work all this out in practice is simply to read the rest of the book.

Richard Weaver once wrote that "Ideas have consequences." A major burden of this book is the claim that "Economic ideas have consequences." I have written this book in the hope that it can make some small contribution toward reducing the bad consequences that have resulted from bad economics that continue to plague our society and that continue to obstruct the initiation of policies that would make real and lasting help for the poor possible.

2
What Is Economics?

It is a mistake to think that economics deals only with the making, spending, saving, and investing of money or with the creation, development, and management of wealth. Economics per se covers a much larger territory. Economics studies the choices human beings make with regard to scarce resources. As we know, scarcity is an unavoidable feature of human existence. Since human wants and desires are always greater than available resources, we can never have everything we want. Therefore, human beings have to rank their alternatives and make choices among the available options. The human actions that are the subject of economics are conscious human choices with regard to individual goals.

Economic decisions often have nothing special to do with money. Imagine a very busy person faced with many demands on his time. Suppose further that this person is given the opportunity to do several new things that he regards as more important than some of his other tasks. Since this person can only do so much in the time available to him, he begins to rank his options. He then uses his scarce time to pursue those goals that he has ranked highest. In this example, the person is engaged in a typically economic activity. Because of scarcity (in this case, scarcity of time), he has been forced to make conscious choices.

Sometimes choices between competing alternatives involve a trade-off between time and money. Suppose I want to buy tickets to an important baseball game that fifty thousand people want to attend. I have two choices: I can either spend hours in a long line waiting to buy the tickets myself for $15 each; or I could pay someone else to stand in line for me, in which case the tickets would cost $25 each. If I value my time more than the extra $10, I will select option two. If I value the $10 more than the time required to wait in line, I'll choose the first option.

The attainment of any scarce resource involves some cost. But it is a mistake to think of cost exclusively in terms of money. The cost of obtaining some scarce resource might include physical pain or a sacrifice of time and effort that might have brought me other goods. There is an important sense in which the cost I incur to obtain any scarce resource will include everything else that my money, time, and effort might have secured had I chosen a different alternative.

It is clear then that the two main ingredients in any economic study are scarcity and choice. The conscious pursuit of goals often leads humans to exchange things they desire less (such as time or money or some possession) for things they want more.

Microeconomics and Macroeconomics

Microeconomics is the branch of economics that focuses on smaller, individual units of economic activity. It studies the economic choices of single persons, households, and businesses. As one economist explains, "Microeconomics consists of looking at the economy through a microscope, as it were, to see how the millions of cells in the body economic—the individuals or households as consumers, and the individuals or firms as producers—play their part in the working of the whole organism."[1]

Macroeconomics looks at the larger picture. Instead of studying the economic activity of individual persons, families, and businesses, it examines the aggregate of the particular economic choices. Macroeconomics studies a nation's economy as a whole. In macroeconomics, the choices of individual persons and the activities of particular businesses are lumped together.

While economists are often interested in understanding the actions of collections of individuals such as unions, societies, organizations, and nations, the actions of these groups are explained best by concentrating on the actions of the individual human beings that make up the groups. The basic unit of economic analysis is the individual human being and the choices he or she makes.[2]

Positive and Normative Economics

Positive or scientific economics is descriptive in the sense that it seeks to determine and report *what is the case*. Normative economics builds on the information supplied by positive economics and makes value-judgments about the alternative policies that can be pursued. Normative economics makes judgments about *what ought to be the case.*

Positive economics reports that under policy A one set of conditions will be followed by certain consequences, while under policy B a different set of conditions will produce different consequences. But positive economics offers no judgment as to which policy is superior. When an economist recommends policy A over policy B, he is doing normative economics. For example, someone doing positive economics will report that if the price of a particular automobile is raised above a certain level, then there will be a tendency—other things being equal—for consumers to buy a smaller quantity of that car. Or to take an example more closely related to Christian concerns, an economist might argue that if our nation adopts a particular approach towards helping the poor, then certain consequences will tend to follow. These consequences might include lessened initiative on the part of many of the poor to seek employment, a rise in the rate of illegitimate births, and an increase in the number of one-parent families.

The claims made by someone doing positive economics are verifiable or falsifiable, at least in principle. Therefore, two economists who disagree about the anticipated consequences of a particular poverty program could examine the data over a period of time to see if the predicted consequences show up in the empirical evidence. When people are engaged in normative economics, they go beyond the question of whether a certain set of conditions will lead to a particular set of consequences. They are involved in making judgments about whether those consequences are good or bad. The judgments of normative economics cannot be falsified by empirical data; they cannot be tested.

Some economists object to the distinction between positive and normative economics.[3] They do not deny that economists often make value judgments about economic matters. But, they argue, when an economist makes such value judgments, he has in effect taken off his economics cap and is functioning in some other capacity—for example, as a moralist. For people who hold this view, all economics is positive economics. Whenever an economist begins to insert value-judgments into his work, on this view, he is doing so in some capacity other than that of an economist. An example may help to make this clearer. Albert Einstein was, as everyone knows, a very good scientist. But at any point when Einstein began making claims about the actual origin of the universe, he was doing something other than physics; he had stopped functioning as a scientist and had begun doing theology or metaphysics.

Many contemporary Christians who evidence an interest in economic questions appear to be most interested in normative economics. They are concerned to pass judgment on the moral suitability of one policy over another. They often insist that economic policies should be evaluated in light of their probable impact upon the poor.

The dispute over whether normative economics is a legitimate concern of economists insofar as they function as economists is not really critical so far as the contemporary Christian concern about making normative judgments about competing policies is concerned. Even those economists who reject normative economics as a legitimate concern of economists agree that most economists make normative judgments. Whether we choose to say that they make those normative judgments in their capacity as economists or make them in some other role—as moralists, for example—seems to be a technical point that economists can quarrel over in advanced seminars. The important point is that in one capacity or another, human beings are going to make normative judgments about economic subjects.

The distinction between positive and normative economics has relevance for another distinction: that between good and bad economics. Economic judgments may be said to be good or bad in two senses depending on whether one has positive or normative economics in view. In the context of positive economics, an economic judgment may be said to be an example of good economics if the means or policies that an economist endorses will in fact produce the anticipated consequences. The economist is asked to come up with a policy that will help bring about a particular end. All that is necessary for this economic theorizing to be good *in the positive sense* is for the policy to work.

Two examples may help make this clear. Consider a business that sells a possibly harmful or immoral product. If that business seeks advice about ways of increasing its sales and that advice works, the recommendation qualifies as good economics (in the positive sense) even though many people might find the end result unfortunate. Or consider a nation whose economic advisors recommend a program that is supposed to help the poor. To be more specific, we could consider any one of a number of welfare programs instituted in the United States in the last twenty years.

Suppose that the evidence shows that a particular program or set of programs designed to help the poor actually harmed them. In this case, the ends or goals were good enough. But the failed policies must be judged to be examples of bad economics.[4]

When we turn from positive to normative economics, the question of what constitutes good versus bad economics is answered on different grounds. In the context of normative economics, we are concerned less with the success of certain means in bringing about a goal than we are with the whole picture of means and ends. It would be a mistake to pronounce an economic judgment or proposal as good in the framework of normative economics exclusively on the desirability of its ends. Even in the case of normative economics, good intentions are not enough. Policies recommended on the best of intentions can hardly qualify as good economics if they actually produce consequences quite different from those that were anticipated. Recommendations about how to increase the profits of a business specializing in pornography will strike many people as bad simply because they judge the end or goal to be bad. Policies designed to help poor people that end up actually harming them are examples of bad economics both in a positive sense (the recommended means did not produce the desired consequences) and in a normative sense (the actual end result was injury to poor people).

In the case of certain poverty programs, certain politicians and their advisors assured us that their ends were noble; they wanted to help the poor. But we now know that if those same politicians had set out to reach a different goal (harming the poor), they could hardly have adopted a set of policies that would have realized that second goal any more efficiently than the poverty programs of the past twenty years. Therefore, such programs can be judged to be examples of bad economics both in a positive and normative sense.

It would be unfortunate if we concluded that the only reason two people reach different conclusions in the area of normative economics is because one person's views are more properly Christian than the others. It is certainly true that a Christian's values should affect his judgments in normative economics. But even Christians have a way of bringing other values to bear on their normative economic judgments. Two Christians may disagree about a particular policy because one of them is a Socialist and the other a non-Socialist. One Christian may believe that economic and political freedom are important values in the Christian world view, while the other Christian may believe that "helping the poor" should take priority even if this requires constraints on economic and political freedom. The serious disagreements over economics that are reflected in the writings of various Christians are not simply expressions of varying degrees of faithfulness to the Biblical revelation. These disagreements also reflect disputes over matters that may have little or nothing to do with Scripture, even though the disputants may believe that all elements of their positions are derived from Scripture.

The effect that ideological considerations may have on one's conclusions about normative economics should not extend into scientific economics. There is a basic core of economic concepts and theories in positive economics that applies to all nations and to all economic systems. A nation that adopts institutions and legal frameworks to support communism does not negate a basic economic principle such as the principle of supply and demand. A move from one economic system to another does not abrogate such basic economic notions as opportunity cost, diminishing marginal utility, and comparative advantage. These concepts do not apply exclusively in capitalist systems, for example. But while a basic core of economic theory does exist, different ways of organizing a society economically can have a significant effect on the incentives to which workers and managers respond.

Economics as a Way of Thinking

Some economists have pointed out the value of viewing economics not so much as a set of doctrines or conclusions, but as a distinctive way of thinking.[5] The principles that underlie the economic way of thinking are not difficult to grasp; they are often matters of common sense. But anyone who is unaware of these principles will have difficulty understanding why some things are true in economics.

The Importance of Incentives

The economic way of thinking begins by recognizing the importance of incentives. The greater the benefits people expect to receive from an alternative, the more people are likely to choose that option. The greater the costs expected from an alternative, the fewer people are likely to select it.

If we understand what makes human beings tick, we can make general predictions as to how individuals or groups of individuals will respond to changes in their economic situation—in particular, how they will respond to new incentives. If a society establishes programs that provide unemployed people with cash and noncash benefits that approximate or even exceed what they would earn working (after taxes), one can safely predict that many of these people will choose to remain unemployed. If a welfare program is set up in such a way that it provides incentives for unmarried women who become pregnant to remain unmarried, we should not be surprised when the rate of illegitimate births begins to increase. In economics, you get what you pay for. If you give people incentives to do A rather than B, the number of people who choose A— all other things being equal—will increase.

Everything Has a Price
Because human beings live in a world marked by scarcity, nothing is free.[6] Every economic good has a price in the sense that before anyone can obtain it, something else must be sacrificed. It is impossible to get A (some economic good) without giving up B (some other economic good). The economic principle in view here is often expressed in such folk sayings as: "You can't have your cake and eat it too" and "There is no such thing as a free lunch." The unavoidable fact of scarcity forces us to make choices in which we sacrifice some things in order to obtain others.

Scarcity, Choice, and Personal Value
In a world of scarcity, choice and sacrifice are unavoidable. People's economic behavior is simply a reflection of, first, their need to make choices, and, second, the relative value they place upon their options. In cases where it is impossible for someone to have both A and B, the choice that a person makes will reflect the relative value he places upon A and B. People's actions, then, are a reflection of their value scales. Their choices are made in order to help them secure the alternatives that accord more closely with their values.

The value that different people place upon different economic goods varies from person to person. People's value scales are personal and different. It would be highly unusual ever to find two people who ranked every economic good in precisely the same way.

Economic Uncertainty
We seldom know enough about individual persons, even people especially close to us, to predict with total certainty what choices they will make among various economic goods. We may know that a particular friend ranks tickets to Chicago Cubs baseball games very high in his personal scale of values. But we may not know how

smitten he has become with the young lady he met yesterday and how suddenly the prospect of a picnic at the beach with his new friend has become more important than watching the Cubs play the Cardinals. Human value scales are more than intensely personal; they are always changing. Because people's economic choices reflect their ever-changing value scales, predictions about human economic choices will always be characterized by uncertainty.

The Importance of Long-Range Consequences

Economic theories are testable in terms of their success in predicting and explaining what takes place in the real world. One way of assessing any economic proposal is to ask what its long-range consequences will be. It is a mistake to notice only the short-run or immediate consequences of economic activity. Any proposal or policy can affect the way people view a situation and thus can alter their incentives in ways that change their choices. Such a change in incentives often produces other effects that become noticeable only in the long run.

Many economic policies have been enacted because they appeared to produce desired consequences *in the short run*. This has often been true of policies designed to help the less fortunate people in society. But measures that appeared beneficial when viewed in the short-term often look quite different after a few years. One reason this happens is because the policies produce incentives that lead people to modify their behavior in ways that turn the short-run success into a long-term disaster. Many recent proposals made in the name of Christian compassion or "Christian economics" are bad economics in the sense that they are counterproductive. A number of important recent studies document the claim that antipoverty programs in the United States have actually increased poverty.[7] According to economist James Gwartney:

> Seeking to promote the welfare of the poor, the disadvantaged, the unemployed, and the misfortunate, well-meaning citizens (including a good many evangelical Christians) have inadvertently supported forms of economic organization that have promoted the precise outcomes they sought to alleviate. For too long, socially concerned Christians have measured policies by the intentions of their advocates, rather than the predictable effectiveness of the programs. Put simply, in our haste to do something constructive, we have not thought very seriously about the impact, particularly in the long-run, of

alternative policies on the well-being of the intended beneficiaries.[8]

Gwartney's quote is only one statement of many in which economists allege that America's welfare programs of the recent past
contradict several basic principles of the economic way of thinking.

Many programs to help the poor are like heroin addiction.
The unfortunate person who begins to experiment with the drug
feels immediate satisfaction. A want he may not have known before
is satisfied in ways he may not have thought possible. But while the
newly-found want fosters the need for continuing satisfaction, the
drug begins to take control. Soon the person cannot function without the drug; he has become an addict. In a similar way, various
programs to help the poor may seem to provide some immediate
relief. But as soon as people see what the new rules are, they change
their behavior to reflect the new incentives or disincentives. When
the unfortunate long-term effects of the policy finally become rec-
ognizable, it is often too late. Too many people are hooked. Any
threat to the policies is viewed with the same dread the addict has
when his supply of heroin is threatened. The possibility that a
decrease in tax transfers might give people new incentives to become more self-reliant is often drowned in a sea of rhetoric about
compassion.

Minimum wage legislation is another example of economic
thinking in conflict with the economic way of thinking. Minimum
wage laws are justified as action that will help low-skilled workers
earn more money. However, such laws only force employers to lay
more unskilled workers off. The law that was supposed to help
unskilled workers earn more money has the long-range effect of
making many of them unemployed.

Sound economic thinking, then, looks beyond the present and
calculates the long-range consequences of recommended policies.
The long-term harm generated by unsound economic policies will
far exceed the limited, short-run benefits that may be received by
some special interest group.

Conclusion
Sound economics will always accord with the guideposts of the
economic way of thinking. When Christians begin to tout specific
economic views or policies, they should be careful to examine them
in the light of these principles.

3
Some Basic Economic Concepts

Understanding economics is like understanding anything else. You have to begin somewhere. It is probably best to start at the beginning, with the economic concepts that underlie the rest of the theory. None of the concepts discussed in this chapter are especially difficult. In fact, once they are understood, they often appear like matters of common sense.

Economic Goods

The word *good* is used in a number of different ways. In economics, the word refers to any desired goal or thing. If some person prefers having more of some thing to a situation in which he has less, that thing for him is a good. Some people fail to distinguish the fact that some person indeed desires something from the quite different question of whether that thing is desirable. When we say that *x is desired,* we are reporting what is the case. When we say that *x is desirable,* we are prescribing what ought to be the case. Statements about whether or not some thing is desirable are normative claims.

Failure to note that the word *good* is sometimes used with reference to what people do as a matter of fact desire—even when that thing perhaps ought not to be desired—can produce some confusion. Sometimes economists describe the fact that someone desires some thing or regards that thing as a good by saying that for such a person, the item has *utility.* It should be remembered then that when an economist says that something is a good or has utility (in this economic sense), all he means is that someone wants it, desires it, or values it. To say that something is a good (in this economic sense) does not imply that it is the sort of thing that the person ought to want.

Economists contrast *economic goods* with what they call *free goods*. A free good is something which can be obtained without any sacrifice. In more technical language, a free good is one that humans can obtain in quantities sufficient to satisfy their wants at a zero price. A free good is so readily available by nature that its quantity supplied exceeds quantity demanded.[1] There is more than enough to go around, to satisfy the quantity demanded.

In contrast to free goods, economic goods are characterized by scarcity. Something is scarce if people want more of it than they can have. An economic good is one that humans cannot obtain in quantities sufficient to satisfy their wants at a zero price. Because quantity demanded exceeds quantity supplied, an economic good always costs something. In order to obtain a quantity of any economic good, something else must be sacrificed. For people who live next to an unpolluted lake, water might be a free good. But for someone traveling through a hot desert, water (because of its scarcity) is an economic good. In fact, it is not difficult to imagine circumstances in which water might become so desired that a thirsty person faced with the prospect of dying might be willing to sacrifice almost anything to secure some. In most cases, air is a free good. But for people living in an area where the air is polluted, clean air might become an economic good for which they would be willing to make some sacrifice.

Economists point out that both free goods and economic goods possess utility. People place a value on air; it just happens that in most cases, the quantity supplied of breathable air exceeds quantity demanded. But things may be valued in two different ways. Some things like air and water are very valuable *in use,* but usually have no value *in trade.* Gold has a great deal of value in trade, but less value in use. The value that some things have in trade or in exchange reflects the personal subjective value that some person imputes to them.

Scarcity and Choice

Human wants are always greater than the available resources to satisfy those wants.[2] Economics studies the ways in which people attempt to satisfy their wants with the resources at their disposal.[3] It is concerned with how people choose to bridge the gap between what they have and what they want. Because our resources are never sufficient to supply all of our wants, we have to make choices about how to use our resources so as to satisfy the wants that we judge to be most important. The scarcity of economic goods means that people will always have to make choices among a number of alternatives.[4] Economics studies the ways in which human beings choose among their alternatives and allocate scarce resources.

Ranking Our Alternatives

As human beings seek ways to get the most out of their limited resources, they are forced to rank their available alternatives. This ranking will reflect the individual's own personal order of values. Everyone has a scale of values by which his needs, wants, and goals are ranked in order of the importance and urgency the person attaches to them. However, this scale of values is not always something of which people are conscious. But whether or not a person happens to be aware of his or her scale of values, he will always aim at whatever goal or end he regards as most urgent or important at the moment. Even though we may be unaware of the process, we all engage in a constant ranking of the relative value to us of things we want but do not possess and of things we possess that we might be willing to trade for something else.

The internal scales by which people express their preferences and rank their alternatives differ greatly. Since different people value some things more highly than others, several things follow. For one thing, if person A values x (some economic good) more highly than person B does, A will be willing to sacrifice more in order to secure an additional unit of x. Moreover, since person B values x less than A does, B may be willing to trade some quantity of x to A in exchange for something else that B desires more.

Not only do people's individual value scales differ, but the value scales of individual persons are constantly changing. As people's interests, wants, and information change, their preferences change. The things that a person puts forth the greatest effort to secure at any given moment are those that rank highest on his personal scale of preference; they will be the things that he values most highly at that time and in those circumstances.

Economic choices are geared towards maximizing benefits and minimizing costs. It should be clear that the word *cost* has more in view than an outlay of money. The more someone believes he is likely to benefit from an action, the more likely he is to act in that way. Greater benefits (utility) will make a choice more attractive; higher costs will make it less attractive and make it less likely that he will select the more costly option.

This analysis of economic choice entails neither materialism nor selfishness. It does not assume that human beings seek only their own welfare. But it is based on the observation that even in those cases where a person seeks the welfare of others, his choices reflect the fact that in those instances the well-being of others is the thing he most wants. To say that people choose in accordance with their highest ranked preferences does not imply that they always rank money or selfish wants first. As economists Armen Alchian and William Allen point out:

> Economics does *not* assume that men are motivated solely, or even primarily by the desire to accumulate more wealth. Instead, economic theory assumes that man . . . desires more of many other things as well: prestige, power, friends, love, respect, self-expression, talent, liberty, knowledge, good looks, leisure. Day to day, economic theory is usually applied to the production, sale and consumption of goods with money expenditures via the market place. But economic theory does not ignore, let alone deny, that man is motivated by cultural and intellectual goods, and even by an interest in the welfare of other people. . . .[5]

Alchian and Allen also explain that some people want more goods for the express purpose of being able to use those goods for the well-being of other people. They do not assume that such a person

> is oblivious to other people, that he is uncharitable or not solicitous of other people's welfare. Nor is he assumed to be concerned only with more wealth. If these assumptions had been made, the resultant theory would be immediately falsified by the fact that people do engage in charity, are solicitous of other people, do consider the effects of their behavior on other people, do consider the effects of their behavior on other people, and are interested in more than marketable wealth.[6]

Some people regard many things as more important than money. Some people give a higher priority to serving others than serving themselves. Their economic choices will reflect these priorities.

The analysis of economic choice provided thus far contains an implication that has far-ranging consequences. That implication is the claim that all economic value is *subjective*. The reason people choose one economic good instead of another is not grounded on any objective value inherent in the good itself. Their choice reflects the value that they impute to the good. This subjective view of economic value is easily misunderstood, a fact that accounts for the most common objections raised against it. The doctrine is especially susceptible to misunderstanding by Christians who mistakenly reject the theory because they believe it to be incompatible with their conviction that there are objective, absolute, and unchanging values. Because of the importance of the subject and the ease with which it can be made to appear inconsistent with important Christian beliefs, the theory of subjective economic value will be considered in detail in the following chapter.

Marginal Utility

The term *utility* entered economic analysis early in its history because it was thought that economic goods were useful in some sense. Even though economists continue to use *utility*, they have largely abandoned the earlier psychological connotations of the term. The utility of any thing is simply its power to satisfy some human want or serve some purpose. Suppose a person named Smith chooses A over B. Economists explain his choice by saying that for Smith A had more utility.

The word *marginal* is used with respect to any addition or subtraction that changes the status quo. Economic value should be measured not in terms of the total value (whatever this might mean) but in terms of one more or one less unit of the commodity. The marginal value of some commodity is what some person is willing to sacrifice in order to obtain one more unit or what he insists on receiving as his price for having one less unit. Marginal utility is "the usefulness or satisfaction which depends on the possession of a single unit of a particular good or service. We may determine the 'marginal utility' of any item by ascertaining what we would lose in the way of satisfaction if we had to get along with one less unit of it."[7]

We weigh our choices regarding the acquisition (or loss) of some economic good in terms of what we take to be the benefits (or costs) of one additional unit. This judgment is always made in terms of the situation that obtains at that particular time. In order to secure one additional unit of some good at one time, I may be willing to incur a particular cost. At some later time that follows my acquisition of one unit of the good, I contemplate the new cost I am willing to incur to obtain one more unit of the good. It is important to notice that the second situation is different from the first; I have just satisfied a want by acquiring one unit of the good. For this reason, the marginal utility of an additional unit of the commodity may be different in the second case. An example may help explain this point.

Imagine that I am walking around a large shopping mall and happen to spy one of the many franchise food establishments that abound in such a place. Imagine further that I am overcome by an inordinate want for a certain kind of pretzel sold by one of those places. Overcome by my want, I throw caution, economic sense, and good health habits to the wind, and plunk down $1.50 for one pretzel and a Coke. A few minutes later, the Coke and the pretzel have gone the way of all fast foods. Suppose I begin to contemplate whether I want seconds. The first thing to note here is that the situation in which I am now considering the marginal utility of the second pretzel is quite different from that in which I deliberated about the first one. I have just eaten the first pretzel. I am not as hungry as I was a few minutes before.

The second pretzel does not rank nearly as high in my personal preference scale as the first one did. In fact, it may rank low enough that I am unwilling to incur the same cost incurred for the first pretzel. I decide that the second pretzel and Coke are not worth $1.50. This portion of my example illustrates what is often called the Law of Diminishing Personal Value. As Alchian and Allen explain this law, "The personal valuation a person places on goods is not just a random variable, nor is it entirely unpredictable. While it depends on many things—such as past experience, education, general preference, and psychological traits—it is affected in a predictable way by the amounts of the goods he has." Generally speaking, they point out, "A person's valuation of any good depends on the amount he has of that good; the more he has, the lower his personal value of the good."[8] Once the initial unit is acquired and perhaps used or consumed, the desire for additional units which may be readily available tends to decline. Sometimes enough satisfaction is attained so that there is no further interest in obtaining additional units of the item.

But let us return to my deliberation about buying a second pretzel. True to the Law of Diminishing Personal Value, my consumption of the first pretzel has been followed by a decline in the level of my interest in a second pretzel. In fact, I have just decided that a second pretzel and Coke are not worth $1.50. But suppose at this very moment that the manager of the pretzel establishment walks by my table and announces that his business is running a special that day. People may buy a second pretzel and Coke for just 99 cents. Suddenly the cost of the second pretzel has dropped, as had my interest in obtaining an additional pretzel. Perhaps it has dropped low enough to match the lower value that I now place on the second pretzel. While I would not have paid $1.50 for a second pretzel and Coke, I judge the special price to be a good value. I return to the pretzel establishment and proceed to make both the franchise owner and myself a little happier.

My subjective ranking of one additional unit of some economic good at a time when I don't have one may be very high. After obtaining that one unit, my subjective ranking of the next additional unit may drop considerably. This has the effect of making me less willing to incur a cost as high as what I paid for the first unit.

Marginal utility is related in important ways to the price of anything. The price of some good does not measure the total value of some commodity or service. Price measures marginal value, what someone is willing to pay for one additional unit or demands to be paid for one less unit. One cannot determine the total value of some total quantity of a commodity by multiplying the number of things that exist times the price of a single item. Such a procedure can never produce the total value of the total stock of the commodity. Price (the rate at which things are exchanged in a market) is therefore not a measure of the total value of the total stock of something. Nor is price the measure of the intrinsic value of the commodity. Price measures only the value that some economic agent places on one more or one less small unit of the thing.

One additional application of this analysis of economic choice is worth considering. Some economists and students of public policy have extended this analysis to the political decisions made by politicians. According to this theory of public choice, politicians make their political decisions in much the same way that they make their economic choices. Imagine, for example, a politician who ranks winning his next election very high on his value scale. For such a politician, every pending vote on legislation must be evaluated in terms of its impact on the people who will vote in the next election and on the special interest groups whose money is needed to finance that election. Just as people make economic choices in ways that they believe will maximize their benefits and minimize their costs, politicians often make their political decisions on similar grounds. A politician's vote always says something about his priorities. This theory of public choice has at least one important consequence: if people do not like a particular public policy, they should attempt to discover incentives that will give politicians a reason to vote differently.

To summarize, the word *utility* is a synonym for benefit or satisfaction. Economic choices are especially concerned with marginal benefits (utility) and marginal costs—that is, the extra benefits or extra costs that people see resulting from the acquisition (or loss) of one additional unit. This marginal approach, coupled with a recognition of the subjective theory of value, was a major development in economics. Failure to grasp these important points is one reason for much misunderstanding and confusion about economics as well as other dimensions of human action such as public policy.

Opportunity Cost

In every economic choice something is gained, but something else must be sacrificed. What economists call *opportunity cost* is the subjective value of the highest valued option or opportunity that someone forgoes in order to obtain some good. Most people think of the cost of some good or service solely in terms of the money they must surrender in order to acquire it. Such thinking confuses money price with cost. If I had not used scarce resources to acquire good A, I could have used them in many other ways. Suppose in this case, that of all the available options, one alternative (call it B) is my first preference to A. But when I decide to acquire A, I forgo the opportunity to acquire B. My sacrifice of B then is the opportunity cost of my buying A. Since people's value scales differ, it follows that different people who acquire A will have varying opportunity costs. For one person, the opportunity cost of buying A might be a vacation in Monument Valley; for another person, it might be a large donation to starving children in Ethiopia. It is important therefore to recognize that the cost of anything involves more than money cost; it is actually the cost of forgone opportunities.

Imagine a person living on a limited but well-planned budget. Suppose further that this person is aware that his purchase of two movie tickets a week has the opportunity cost (to him) of a meal in a fine restaurant. If he buys the tickets, his opportunity cost is the forgone opportunity of eating in that restaurant. On the other hand, if he chooses to visit the restaurant, his opportunity cost is the two movie tickets. Of course, he might decide that he has other options. He might decide to buy just one movie ticket that week and dine instead at McDonald's. It is helpful to see the way in which the values of various economic goods are interrelated in the preference scales of particular people.

Because the opportunity cost of acquiring the same good will vary from person to person, it is impossible to predict for large numbers of people how much various individuals will be willing to sacrifice in order to secure some quantity of a good. This helps explain the general uncertainty that accompanies economic decisions. There is no way of predicting with certainty how many people will respond to a particular offer to sell a particular good or service at a particular price at a particular time. One can only wait and see.

Supply and Demand

The Law of Demand states that a relationship exists between the quantity of some good or service people purchase and its price. Demand is a relationship that shows the varying quantities of a good that people will buy voluntarily at different prices. Everything else being equal, a higher price for a specific unit of x will be followed by a lower quantity demanded. As prices decline, quantity demanded will tend to rise; as prices rise, quantity demanded will drop—other things being equal. This inverse relationship between quantity demanded and price is not precise to the extent that a ten cent increase in the price of a gallon of gasoline will be followed by a proportional reduction in the quantity of gas sold. The relationship between quantity demanded and price is not this precise. Nonetheless, for any good or service, other things being equal, some higher price will result in a lower quantity being demanded, and some lower price will result in a higher quantity being demanded. Because each person's assessment of the situation will differ, greater specificity is impossible.

We have already noted a number of factors that explain the Law of Demand. We have noticed that incentives matter. We have stated that people choose among scarce resources in ways that tend to maximize their benefits and minimize their costs. Higher prices increase the cost of choosing a good; lower prices decrease the cost. Thus higher prices will tend to reduce the consumption of a good while lower prices, all things being equal, will tend to increase consumption.

The Law of Supply states that price and quantity supplied are positively related. Other things being equal, a higher price will tend to result in a larger quantity being supplied. A lower price will tend to result in a smaller quantity being offered.

Unfortunately, governments have a way of forgetting or ignoring the laws of supply and demand. When a shortage of a particular good occurs, market forces will quickly become operative in ways that will relieve that shortage, unless the government takes actions that hinder the operation of the market. In the first place, the shortage will lead to higher prices which will reduce quantity demanded and increase quantity supplied. As the opportunity costs for acquiring units of the good in short supply increase, many prospective buyers will reduce their consumption. When actions by the OPEC nations led to a shortage of oil and then to an increase in the price of oil-related products, the Carter Administration could have allowed the market process to deal with the shortage. This would have resulted in an increase in the price of gasoline to a level where consumption would have been reduced and output would have been increased. But the Carter Administration did not wish to risk the political fallout from allowing gasoline prices to rise to a market-clearing level. It opted instead for a confusing and frustrating program of allocating scarce supplies. This resulted in long lines and shortened operating hours at gas stations across the country. American drivers incurred significantly higher opportunity costs (time spent in lines) because of the actions by the Carter Administration than they would have if gas had simply been allowed to climb to a market-clearing price.

As soon as the shortage of some good results in a higher price, other things begin to take place in an unhampered market—that is, a market not subject to governmental intervention. For one thing, the increased price results in decreased quantity demanded. For another, the increased price provides incentives for more potential suppliers to enter the market. This is precisely what has happened to the supply and demand for oil-related products in this country. People began to drive less; they found alternative means of transportation; they reduced their consumption of gasoline. At the same time, new oil suppliers responded to the incentives of higher prices and began to provide significant new quantities of oil. The nation did not need the misguided policies of the Carter Administration. It did not need the government to step in and dictate who would receive how much gasoline to sell. The nation did not need federally-subsidized industries in synthetic fuels. The government's intervention with the market process only prolonged the agony of short supplies and high prices. The fact that the price of "regular" gasoline, on the day this is written, is below 70 cents a gallon in my city is due to the economic factors noted in this chapter. It is not something for which the government need be thanked.

4

The Theory
of Subjective Economic
Value

The theory of subjective economic value is important enough to merit a chapter of its own. Until the theory is mastered, much about human economic activity will remain a mystery. The view that will be examined in this chapter did not really enter economic theory until the late nineteenth century. But when it finally caught the attention of a few economists, it started a revolution in economic thought. The theory is usually associated with what is known today as the Austrian School of economics whose leaders in our generation have included such thinkers as Ludwig von Mises, Friedrich Hayek, and Israel Kirzner.

This chapter will explain the theory of subjective economic value, draw out some of its more important implications, and seek to defend it against objections. Special attention will be given to the difficulty some Christians have in reconciling claims that economic value is subjective with their conviction that Christians are supposed to regard value as objective, absolute, and unchanging. Some Christians believe that an acceptance of economic value as subjective would commit them to believing that all values are relative and subjective. The fallacy in such reasoning should be obvious. Even if we should discover that *some* values (in one sense of the word *value*) should be subjective and relative, it would not follow that *all* values are subjective and relative. Problems that will take a bit longer to handle arise from the belief of some that the theory of subjective economic value may imply that every value-choice is as good as any other and that no grounds exist to show that some economic choices are morally wrong. But before I argue that such conclusions do not follow from the theory under consideration, I will first explain the nature of the theory.

Competing Theories of Economic Value

Throughout the history of human thought, a number of important thinkers were led to ponder the question of economic value. Simple observation of how human beings acted in economic exchanges made it clear that some things were thought to have more value than others. For such thinkers as Aristotle and Aquinas, it was natural to wonder about the nature of such value. What is it about one thing that makes it more valuable than another? Why do people want some goods and services more than others? Why are some things so valued that people are willing to make significant sacrifices in order to obtain them?

Until the late nineteenth century, these earlier attempts to understand the nature and ground of economic value regarded economic value as *objective*. This is to say, the value of the economic good was thought to be inherent in some way in that which was valued. One of the most influential of these objective theories of economic value appears in the writings of Karl Marx who borrowed the outline of his view from earlier thinkers including Adam Smith. Marx believed that the value of a good or service is determined to a great extent by its cost of production. Suppose, for example, that all of the production costs (including the cost of supplies, labor, and everything else) to make a pair of shoes amount to twenty dollars. The value of those shoes (while new) then can never be less than twenty dollars. Its value is objective in the sense that a number of factors having nothing to do with human preferences and wants have given those new shoes that value.

As many readers will know, Marx went on from this point to develop his famous theory of surplus value. He believed that the true value of the new shoes was a function of the socially necessary labor that produced them. But, Marx observed, the capitalist sells the shoes for more than this cost. This extra "value" that he keeps for himself is "profit." While it is difficult to find any economist who thinks Marx's notion of surplus value has any merit,[1] most critics of his doctrine still agree with Marx that economic value is objective—that is, inherent in the good or service. If the subjective theory of economic value is correct, Marxist economics is flawed on an even more basic level.

A simple example may help make this clearer. Consider two

diamonds of equal size and quality. Imagine that one is simply found on the ground by chance; no effort or danger was involved in its discovery. Imagine that the second diamond comes out of a diamond mine where an enormous investment has been made building and operating the mine. The men who work in such mines have a difficult and dangerous job. And so we have two diamonds: one cost little or nothing, while the second was produced at enormous cost. Imagine next that our two diamonds happen to be offered for sale at the same auction. The two diamonds might easily sell for similar prices. What this shows is that the value of the two diamonds bears no relation to their respective "costs."

At this point, someone might raise an objection to the subjective theory of economic value. The example illustrates the fact that value and cost are not necessarily related. But does it not show that value still bears a relationship to the objective properties or characteristics of the thing? Our example stipulated that the two diamonds were similar in size and quality. Does it not follow that their similar "value" reflects the fact that their objective characteristics are so much alike? It is true that the two diamonds had similar objective properties. It is also true (in our example) that they sold for prices that reflect a similar value. In this particular case, the closely related prices that reflect the fact that two buyers placed much the same value on them might well have been a function of the objective characteristics of the diamonds. After all, if two things are practically the same, they can be substituted for each other. The quarter pounders I can buy at the McDonald's on the north end of town are similar to those I can buy from the McDonald's at the south end of town. Because they are so much alike, most potential buyers will treat them as equal in value. But the economic value is not inherent in the hamburgers any more than it is in the diamonds. The value is imputed to the article by an individual valuer. Obviously, people take the objective characteristics of things into account when imputing such value.

One more thing needs to be said about our two diamonds. It would be a mistake to assume that just because two diamonds sell for the same price, they must therefore be equal in "objective value." What two buyers are willing to exchange for an article reflects their separate personal valuation of that good. It is possible that two diamonds of different size and quality might well sell for the same price. Any number of personal, subjective considerations might lead two buyers to offer the same price for goods with different properties.

Before the example of the two diamonds was introduced, the subject at hand was Marx's particular use of an objective theory of economic value. His claim that economic goods have an objective value that reflects what they cost to produce is mistaken. It is important to remember that there was nothing original in Marx's objective analysis of economic value. In this regard, he was simply following the lead of earlier thinkers. Even Adam Smith approached economic value objectively.[2] It was not until the late nineteenth century that a few economists began to question the objective theory of economic value. These critics of the objective approach included the Austrian economists Carl Menger (1849-1921) and Eugene von Böhm-Bawerk (1851-1914).

Following the lead of these men and others like Jevons and Walras, a growing number of economists began to argue that economic value is entirely subjective; it exists in the mind of the person who imputes value to the good or service. If something has economic value, it is because someone values it; it is because that good or service satisfies a human want. This new approach to economic value was a significant development in economic theory.

> It represented a completely new, revolutionary approach to economics. For the first time, the *individual actor* himself became the unit with which economics was concerned. His actions, his responses to specific units of particular goods or services at certain places and times, were recognized as the key to explaining market phenomena. At every instance, an individual has in his mind a mental cutoff point, an invisible dividing line which separates the *units* of a good or service that he considers worth striving for from those that are not, and the units of a good or service that he wants to retain from those he is willing to relinquish. . . . Economics had been concerned previously only with *physical* goods and services and the means men used for the satisfaction of the various *material* wants. It had dealt with the relatively narrow fields of monetary transactions.[3]

However, the subjective revolution in economic theory changed all this. Once economists recognized the personal and subjective ground of economic value and the importance of thinking in terms of marginal utility, "the science of economics was broadened to encompass all human (purposive/conscious) actions.

It became a study of any and all the peaceful (non-violent) means men use to attain any and all of their various ends. . . ."[4]

These comments contain some important points for Christians to ponder. Even those Christians who may not yet see how a subjective analysis of economic value can be squared with their world view should welcome the way in which the subjective theory of economic value expanded the horizons of economics to include things other than *material* goods. Many people value such things as love, honor, friendship, virtue, and help for the less fortunate more than they value such material things as money, cars, clothes, and houses. Because such people rank things like love and honor so high in their personal value scale, their economic choices will reflect this ranking. The conscious purposive actions of such people can be explained by economists who hold to a subjective theory of economic value.[5]

An important qualification must now be made. When economists state that economic value is subjective, they do *not* restrict the subjective ground of economic value to personal tastes. In other words, the fact that Jones and Smith impute different value to the same good does not necessarily reflect their differing tastes about that good. The value that people impute to things is also related to such factors as different knowledge, different interpretations of information, different expectations, and different quantities they already possess. It may also reflect varying degrees of alertness to new opportunities. Far more is involved in the subjective approach to economic value than personal taste. But what is clear is that economic value is always imputed value.

Limited Knowledge and Subjective Value

I have said that people value things differently for a variety of reasons which include: (1) different tastes; (2) different perceptions of available opportunities; (3) different interpretations of other people's actions; (4) different interpretations of current events; (5) different expectations about future events and people's future actions; and (6) different degrees of alertness to previously unrecognized opportunities.

This section of the chapter will focus on the role that incomplete, limited human knowledge plays in subjective valuation. No human being can attain perfect knowledge about the future. While it is often possible to make some estimates of what will happen, certain knowledge about the future is unattainable. One corollary of our limited knowledge about the future is the possibility that the economic value of various things will change in unpredictable ways. Natural catastrophes may make some resource more or less valuable. Human tastes, customs, and fashions may change. New highways may change traffic flows. Huge new shopping malls may lead people to develop new shopping habits. Inner cities may decay as people move to the suburbs. In all such changes, some people will win and others will lose. The scarcity of information means that economic decisions must always be made with some degree of uncertainty. No one, not even the largest and previously most successful businesses, can be completely sure what the future holds for them.

The problems that result from limited knowledge have received significant attention in the work of such economists as Ludwig von Mises, Friedrich Hayek, and most recently Israel Kirzner. Such economists, one interpreter explains,

> work within a framework where the market is understood as a process of entrepreneurial adjustment to constant change and characterized by the piecemeal elimination of pervasive ignorance and error. Individual economic actors always operate under conditions of uncertainty, and in such an environment, error is the norm and the correction of error the raison d'être of markets. In this setting, there can be no question that subjective evaluations of cost bear little predictable relation to objectively measured outlays. Each person evaluates alternatives open to him within the context of uncertainty about the likelihood of expected outcomes, ignorance of the total realm of alternatives open to him and the possibilities of error in judgment about the value to him of the alternatives he does perceive. In such a world, it would seem to be purely happenstance if two separate individuals were to evaluate the same set of alternatives in the same ways. Thus the central problem of economic analysis in this context is to explain how millions of separate individuals with differing perceptions of reality and differing valuations and expectations about the future ever manage to achieve any kind of coordination of economic activity. With such an understanding of the purpose of economic theory, it is the very subjectivity, ignorance, error and uncertainty confronting man that helps to explain the development and persistence of markets as corrective and

coordinating institutions. That is, markets enable individuals to compare their subjective judgment with the evaluations of others in a continual process of giving and receiving information relevant to economic decision making.[6]

The ideas being presented here differ significantly from what has previously been regarded as the economic mainstream. Israel Kirzner contrasts the older economic orthodoxy with the recognition of "the open-endedness of knowledge as a source of economic understanding." He writes:

> To the standard mainstream view in economics, since about 1930, the view of the world has been one in which the future is essentially known, in which the participants in markets are in effect completely informed about the relative decisions made throughout the market by fellow participants. This is a world of equilibrium, a world in balance, a world in which quantitative economic predictions are entirely feasible. Austrian economics has a quite different view of the world, and a quite different view of the way in which economic relations can be grasped.[7]

Such mainstream views led economists to believe that sufficient knowledge about the future made it possible for them to predict successfully the future effects of governmental intervention on the economy. The disastrous consequences of this kind of economic interventionism are discussed in later chapters. What is in view now are the faulty epistemological underpinnings of that theory. These same assumptions helped give rise to various forms of social engineering. Social engineering rests on the assumption that the best social order is a product of purposeful and deliberate human design rather than the result of spontaneous development. The social engineer believes that man has both the knowledge and the power to create a better social order through the state. The social engineer is never satisfied with any feature of society that comes about in an impersonal or automatic way. Human planning and centralized control, he thinks, could have always produced something better. One obvious example of an impersonal order-producing mechanism is the market, a fact that may explain the hatred that those obsessed with social engineering have towards economic freedom. It is important to notice, therefore, that social engineering and the totalitarianism that tends to accompany it have much in common with the epistemological assumptions of much mainstream economics since 1930. Both believe—in principle at least—that sufficient knowledge about the future is possible. Both believe that society is better off when those who know which buttons to push and levers to pull are running society. Both lead to the termination of important human freedoms. And, of course, both are grounded on a totally indefensible set of beliefs about human knowledge.

A Theological Objection

Before turning to a consideration of some of the more important implications of the subjective theory of economic value, the mistaken objections that many Christians have to the view must be considered and answered. As noted earlier, many Christians find it difficult to reconcile claims about subjective economic value with what they take to be important corollaries of their Biblical world view—namely, that God is the creator of all value, that value therefore has an objective ground, and that some values must be absolute and unchanging. Surely, such Christians argue, it is important for Christians to point out how some rankings of alternatives and how some economic choices are more compatible with Christian values than others. All of these Christian concerns are proper and correct. But none of them are incompatible with the subjective theory of economic value.

A problem arises at this point because the word *value* is ambiguous. It may refer (1) to that which people do in fact value or (2) to that which people ought to value. We all recognize the fact that many people value things that they ought not to value, and that they fail to value things that they ought to value.

We sometimes express the difference between these two senses of value by using the words *desired* and *desirable*. All that is required for something to be desired is for someone in fact to desire it. But just because something is desired, it does not follow that it is *desirable,* that it ought to be desired. In *economics,* value reflects the extent to which something is desired; it does not mirror that thing's desirability. Economists have ways of measuring the degrees to which people desire things; obviously, this is something quite different from attempting to measure how desirable it is.[8] No matter how desirable something may be—no matter how much people ought to desire it—the economic price of that thing will reflect only how much some individual is willing to pay for one additional unit. The price of an economic good reflects the extent to which individuals desire it; and this is something quite apart from the question of how desirable it is.

Informed Christians need to keep two things distinct. The first is the degree to which an individual may want x, a fact that reflects where x ranks in that individual's personal scale of values. The second is the need of individuals to alter the rankings in their personal scale of values to conform to what they ought to want. Christians are undoubtedly correct when they judge that their Scriptures oblige them to change the personal value scales of themselves and others in order to bring them more in line with those ultimate values that play such an important role in the Christian world view. But as important as this task may be, it is an activity that falls under a different heading than economics. Economic exchanges in the real world will mirror only the actual subjective value that individuals have imputed to the goods being exchanged. Any number of things including religious conversion may affect the way people rank things in their personal value scales. Whenever such changes in subjective value occur, it will have an obvious impact on the judgments people make about such things as marginal utility and opportunity cost.

What all this means is that the theory of subjective economic value does not imply that all economic choices are equally good in a moral or religious sense. An acceptance of the theory does not commit a Christian to believe that all values are subjective or relative or anything of the sort. A Christian—or anyone else for that matter—is within his rights, in principle, to criticize particular economic choices.[9] It seems clear, therefore, that any objection to the theory of subjective economic value on theological or moral grounds is mistaken. Positive economics does not presume to tell people that certain values ought to be ranked higher in their preference scales. That is more properly the task of the pastor, moralist, theologian, or spiritual counselor. Economics simply deals with how people do in fact make their choices with regard to the allocation of scarce resources.

Some Implications of Subjective Economic Value

The Interdependence of Economic Values

One important implication of the discussion thus far is the interdependence of economic values. People value bread because it satisfies a basic human need for food. People value flour because it is an ingredient in bread. Some economists speak therefore of the difference between a first-order economic good like bread and a second-order good such as flour. It is then possible to identify third-order goods such as farmland, seed, fertilizer, and farm machinery that have value because they help produce a second-order good such as flour. Economic goods are interdependent to the extent that some things we regard as goods are desired because they are necessary or helpful in the production of a higher-order good.

Economic goods are also interdependent to the extent that the absence of one good affects the value of others. If there is an oversupply of flour, wheat will lose some of its value. If wheat becomes less valuable, the land and other inputs needed to produce it will tend to lose some of their value, unless they can be put to alternate uses. Suppose three raw materials are valued because they are used in the production of some commodity. Should one of those raw materials suddenly become unavailable, the value of the other, complementary raw materials may decline as well, since the production of the commodity they were used in has been affected negatively.

A New Understanding of Cost

Many modern businessmen along with a number of older economists believe that the cost of some good is determined by the total outlay of money needed to produce it and make it available. According to the subjective analysis of economic value, this older view is clearly mistaken. The cost of production is determined by the subjective value of the goods that are produced. As James Buchanan explains this new understanding of cost:

> Simply considered, cost is the obstacle or barrier to choice, that which must be got over before choice is made. Cost is the underside of the coin, so to speak, cost is the displaced alternative, the rejected opportunity. Cost is that which the decision-maker sacrifices or gives up when he selects one alternative rather than another. Cost consists therefore of his own evaluation of the enjoyment or utility that he anticipates having to forego as a result of choice itself.[10]

Buchanan then carries his analysis further by noting some implications of his emphasis on opportunity cost:

1. Cost must be borne exclusively by the person who makes decisions; it is not possible for this cost to be shifted to or imposed on others.
2. Cost is subjective; it exists only in the mind of the decision-maker or chooser.
3. Cost is based on anticipations; it is necessarily a forward-looking or ex ante concept.
4. Cost can never be realized because of the fact that choice is made; the alternative which is rejected can never itself be enjoyed.
5. Cost cannot be measured by someone other than the chooser since there is no way that subjective mental experience can be directly observed.
6. Cost can be dated at the moment of final decision or choice.[11]

Buchanan is not claiming that cost exists only in the eye of the potential buyer. Prior to any voluntary economic exchange, both parties are constantly weighing cost *as they see it*. Suppose a businessman knows that he already has invested $25 in an article he wants to sell. Suppose further that the one prospective buyer he can find for that article is only willing to pay $20. In other words, the potential buyer's subjective valuation of the article weighed in terms of *his own* opportunity cost (his highest ranking alternative) results in $20 being the highest cost he is willing to incur; $20 is the magic line that separates his choosing or not choosing the article. The businessman realizes that if he doesn't exchange his commodity for the best possible deal, he will be even worse off than he is. For the businessman *at that moment of decision,* the "cost" that counts is the psychological obstacle or hurdle he must leap in reaching his decision about whether or not to accept $20 for the article. In this case, his alternative to accepting $20 is being stuck with an article he wants to sell. According to the subjective analysis, costs are forgone alternatives based on personal subjective appraisals of the value of those sacrificed options.

A New Understanding of Price
The most important way in which people can acquire objective knowledge about the subjective value that individuals place upon various economic goods is to study changing prices. Prices are determined as prospective participants in economic exchanges buy or refuse to buy (or sell or refuse to sell) in response to their

personal assessment of their opportunities. As countless individuals, each acting in line with their subjective value scales, exchange units of goods, services, and money, market prices evolve.

> In time, out of the melee of bids and asks, "higgling and haggling," competition for all goods, services and/or money among countless persons, each offering something he or she has for something he or she prefers, money prices emerge. On a free market economy—when no person or group of persons uses force or threat of force to interfere with the peaceful and moral acts of others—these money prices tend to reflect the relative importance to people of specific units of goods, services and/or money.[12]

The degree to which an individual wants some good or service will have an obvious effect on the price he will pay to acquire it. The more he wants something, the higher the price he will be willing to pay. But of course this price will always reflect not just his eagerness to acquire that good, but will also reflect his assessment of his situation and his other alternatives at that particular time.

Market Exchanges
The topic of the market is so important for the argument of this book that it will be the subject of an entire chapter. Nevertheless, the significant link between subjective economic value and the theory of the market yet to be presented should be noted in this context. The reason people exchange goods and services in a market is precisely because they place different values on them. If everyone in a market regarded a particular good or service as having the same value, there would be little or no incentive for trade. Each person in a market has gone through the mental process of appraising goods and services in terms of his own preference scale. Each has set out to find someone who has something he wants more than the good or service he is willing to trade. As people weigh their options, they sometimes find that offers are unacceptable (for example, the cost is too high), and the exchange is not made. But when two parties reach that point where their subjective appraisals of what is best for them meet, an exchange takes place. What economists call the market is the framework within which countless individuals make choices in terms of those things they value most.

Entrepreneurial Activity

Earlier in this chapter, attention was drawn to the fact that subjective economic value is not exclusively a function of personal taste. One of the other important factors that enters into the subjective character of economic valuation is knowledge—or more properly, the lack of knowledge. As Israel Kirzner points out,

> The crucial element in market competition is the circumstance that knowledge is never concentrated in a single mind—always dispersed. We never know everything. None of us. No single mind can possibly know everything. No single mind can possibly grasp the entire economic problem that tends to be solved through spontaneous market processes.[13]

But as important as human ignorance and the limitations of human knowledge are in understanding economic behavior, there is another, related notion that should be noted. The recognition of this second feature is one of the most important contributions that members of the Austrian School of economics have made to economic theory. This second insight is, in Kirzner's words,

> an appreciation for the propensity within human action to discover what was hitherto unknown—what I like to call the *entrepreneurial* propensity in human action. It is this propensity that is responsible for entrepreneurial alertness for pure profit opportunities, for entrepreneurial discovery, for bursting asunder the limits of existing knowledge. It is upon this alertness that we rely for the manner in which the market continually propels prices and decisions in the direction of greater mutual coordination. It is entrepreneurial alertness to existing errors that leads to their discovery and their eventual tendency to be corrected.[14]

An *entrepreneur* is someone who believes he sees an opportunity that others have not yet recognized.[15] The key to understanding competition is the recognition that no one knows everything; different people have different information. One thing the market process does is gather and communicate information about the most important wants of buyers and sellers. As astute entrepreneurs pay attention to the information provided by changing market prices, they often come to recognize new opportunities. These new opportunities may take the form of new products or services that consumers want or of new ways of using scarce resources.

Stephen Littlechild expresses his own appreciation for the Austrian emphasis on entrepreneurial activity:

> Austrian economics takes as its starting point the behavior of people with incomplete knowledge, who have not only to "economize" in the situations in which they find themselves, but also to be on the alert for better opportunities "just around the corner." This alertness, missing from "mainstream" economics, is called entrepreneurship. It leads to the revision of plans and forms the basis of the competitive process, which in many ways epitomizes the Austrian approach. For [members of the Austrian School of economics], the *changes* over time in prices, production, plans, knowledge, and expectations are more important than prices and output at any one time. Similarly, from a "normative" point of view (of what policy should be), the adequacy of an economic system is judged not by the efficiency with which it allocates given resources at a point in time, but by the speed with which it discovers and responds to new opportunities over time.[16]

It goes without saying that entrepreneurial ability is hard to find. Not everyone has it; and even those who seem to have it in some areas lack it in others. But it is impossible to overestimate the importance of entrepreneurial activity. As entrepreneurs recognize hitherto unrecognized opportunities and assume risks in an effort to maximize their own well-being by taking advantage of those opportunities, their actions result in significant benefits to large numbers of people through the creation of new jobs along with the provision of new goods or services.

Conclusion

The theory discussed in this chapter is difficult for many people to understand because it requires them to alter radically old patterns of thought. Unfortunately, some old patterns of economic thinking are responsible for a great deal of confusion and mischief in the contemporary world. The theory of subjective economic value, once accepted, opens new vistas to understanding economic behavior. It will also offer a new perspective from which we can evaluate capitalism and socialism.

5

The Market

The word *market* refers to an extremely important economic notion. Many people have trouble grasping that notion because of the term's ambiguity. This ambiguity results from the word being used to refer to trading in different kinds of commodities as well as to trading that goes on at increasingly general levels. For example, a mother can tell her son to run over to the market and buy six ears of corn for supper. The owner of that store can tell one of his employees to go downtown and buy twelve dozen ears of corn from the market; in this second case, the "market" means a single seller (or group of sellers) who wholesales to merchants. The wholesaler may ask someone to check how corn is doing that day on the futures market. For a single commodity like corn, there are a number of different markets in which it is exchanged.

Markets differ of course in more ways than size and general level. We speak of different markets for different kinds of things. There are stock markets and bond markets. There is the new car and the used car market. There are markets in which collectibles like coins, stamps, paintings, and even comic books are traded.

The word *market* in the title of this chapter does not refer to any of the specific markets that have been mentioned, although it encompasses them. Specific markets are places where two or more people exchange goods and services. The *market* that I'll be discussing in this chapter is the set of procedures or arrangements that prevail throughout a society that allows voluntary exchanges. In one sense, the market is the framework of customs and rules within which specific voluntary exchanges in specific markets take place.

Instead of talking simply about "the market," we could refer instead to the market system. Economist James Gwartney explains:

> At the most basic level, a market system is a form of economic organization where people help others in exchange for in-

come. Pursuit of income induces individuals to produce goods and provide services desired by others. Both buyers and sellers gain from the voluntary exchange; otherwise the trading partners would not agree to the transaction.[1]

The market then is not a specific place or thing. Neither is it simply the collection of particular markets in which goods and services are exchanged. It is a spontaneous and impersonal order of arrangements that serves as the framework within which individual human beings make economic choices. One illustration that may help to explain what I mean by a spontaneous and impersonal order is an urban traffic pattern. As a city develops and grows over a long period of time, a certain traffic pattern evolves. Anyone getting into a car in preparation for a drive across town must make numerous choices in response to such things as one-way streets, no parking zones, traffic lights, stop signs, and speed limits. Such traffic patterns are impersonal because they are supposed to apply to everyone; they were not designed for specific people in specific situations. The traffic order is spontaneous in the sense that it evolved as a result of trial and error. People learned that traffic flowed more safely and more smoothly, for example, with a traffic light at a particular intersection.

While the traffic pattern lays down rules, people still have a considerable degree of freedom as to how and where they will drive. The traffic pattern does not force them to drive down only one street, for example. Such a traffic pattern, therefore, illustrates how a spontaneous and impersonal set of arrangements can help produce order, prevent chaos and harm, and still allow for a considerable degree of individual freedom.

What we call the market functions in much the same way. It lays down certain rules that provide a context for economic exchanges. Among other things, those rules say that people should not be coerced into making economic exchanges. Economic exchange should be free from force, fraud, and theft. People should honor their contracts. The institutional arrangements that prohibit force, fraud, and theft function as an impersonal system in much the same way as the urban traffic pattern.

Economist Thomas Sowell explains that what we are calling the market "need not exist anywhere in time or space. . . . It is the set of prospective options rather than the actual retrospectively observed choice which defines 'the market.' "[2] The market can also be viewed, in the words of Ludwig von Mises, as "a process, actuated by the interplay of the actions of the various individuals cooperating under the division of labor."[3] The word "process" is significant in this connection because it points to the dynamic character of the market. The market is not static; it is in a constant state of change. To quote Mises again, "The forces determining the-continually-changing-state of the market are the value judgments of these individuals and their actions as directed by these value judgments."[4]

No one invented the market process. It is an impersonal social institution in which individual people make economic choices in accord with their personal value scales within a framework of rules. The market is a spontaneous outgrowth of people engaging freely in mutually beneficial exchanges. One of the more remarkable features of the market is the way it produces order out of apparent chaos.

> As paradoxical as it may seem, order results from the decentralized actions of individuals directed by market prices. Prices coordinate actions of both buyers and sellers. In product markets, consumers reveal their evaluation of goods by spending their limited incomes on the bundle of goods which they value most highly. In resource markets, prices direct the actions of both employers and resource suppliers.[5]

One way to see how the market produces order is to reflect on the extraordinary way in which the most ordinary wants of people in a free society are satisfied. The reader can do this by making a list of all the goods and services he wants and finds obtainable over a period of several days. My own list would begin with orange juice from Florida, coffee from Brazil, and toast made from wheat grown in Kansas, milled into flour in Illinois, and baked into bread in Tennessee. My list would include shoelaces, a razor blade, toothpaste, shampoo, my clothes, gas for my car, the paper on which I am writing these words. For each of us, the list could be endless.

Most of us lack the ability to make or provide most of the goods and services we want. How then do we persuade others to do all these nice things for us? When I go to a grocer, the things I want are there. This is just as true of the druggist and other merchants. When I need a plumber or electrician or dentist or auto mechanic, someone is there ready to satisfy my want. Do people supply all these nice goods and services because their primary goal in life is to make me happy? I think not. People do all these wonderful things for me because of the prospect of their receiving something in return, usually money. And where do I get the money I use to pay all these people? I receive it from still other people who pay me for performing some service or providing some good for them.[6]

At this stage, some very interesting points are beginning to emerge from our reflection about the remarkable ways in which our ordinary wants are satisfied in a free society. One of these points concerns the extent to which we depend upon other people. I need other people to supply the goods and services I have come to count on. But I also need people who will pay me for the goods and services that I can supply, thus providing the money I require to pay those who supply my wants.

In more primitive times, people were often forced to provide for all or almost all of their wants through their own effort. And so the same individual might have to make his own clothes, grow his own food, build his own place of lodging, and so on. A market economy permits people to specialize in those things they do best. Some people are better at plumbing than they are at teaching the philosophy of Plato. Some are better auto mechanics than cooks. This specialization enables most of us to do a better job with our time and effort. But this specialization also increases our dependence on others.

Let us return to the long list of goods and services that different people make available to us. But we'll focus now on the question of supply. While it sometimes happens that the supply of some good may be too great or too small, these occasional glitches in the system are short-lived. It is worth pondering why, in a free market system, goods and services are usually available in a supply sufficient to take care of people's wants. We all hear about people in Socialist societies being forced to stand in line for hours to secure small quantities of bread or meat. We also hear about incredible distribution blunders in Socialist societies where all the garbage cans end up in one city and the tops to the cans end up in another. How do we explain the much greater efficiency and order that we find in a free market system? Did anyone plan it this way? Is there some unknown central planner overseeing the entire process of production and distribution whose omniscient and benevolent planning results in everything being available when we want it? Since this is not the case, what accounts for the incredible order we find in a free market system that lacks any centralized coordination?

The answer, of course, is that all of this order is the product of the impersonal mechanism we call the market. When things go wrong—and they do go wrong in a market system—the impersonal mechanism soon produces results that remedy the problem. The language of this last sentence should not be taken literally, as though the market itself acted. What happens in a market system is that individual people alter their choices in response to changing incentives. For example, imagine that a commodity like gasoline is suddenly in short supply. If people continued to demand gasoline in the same quantities as before the short supply developed, prices would rise; perhaps they would rise dramatically. As the rising price of gasoline affected the way consumers evaluated the cost, the quantity demanded would begin to slacken. But the rising price of gasoline would also serve as an incentive for new suppliers to enter the market. The combination of reduced quantity demand and increased supplies would serve to remedy the temporary shortage. Paul Heyne's summary of how many different factors are coordinated in a market system is helpful:

> The manner in which we combine available resources to satisfy wants depends on the prices of these resources; and their prices reflect their relative scarcities. Thus the price system helps secure an efficient use of resources. . . . It is the market that integrates the almost infinite variety of economic activities in which people engage, that secures adjustment when imbalances arise, that creates and maintains a recognizable order in the face of a remarkably decentralized system of decision making.[7]

The market supplies important information via changes in the relative prices of goods. When the price of some good rises, the market is telling buyers and sellers that the good is less readily available relative to the quantity people wanted at its old price. A decrease in price communicates information that the good is less scarce. Increases or decreases in price can result from a number of factors including changes in people's tastes, the discovery of new supplies, or the availability of new information. As changing market prices communicate information, they also affect people's incentives. The reason people enter into market exchanges is to improve their respective situations. When rising prices raise people's perception of the cost of some option above a certain point, those who value that option less will begin to consider other alternatives.

Producers of goods and services receive information from the market by also paying attention to profits and losses. Losses tell a business person that something is wrong and that he had better stop and reevaluate things.

[L]osses serve to induce the entrepreneur to direct land, labor and capital into more profitable ventures, or at least to arrange and manage his input factors of production more efficiently. Profits, on the other hand, serve as a "green light" to the business entrepreneur. They beckon him to expand a successful enterprise; thus profits serve to attract the scarce resources of production into areas of higher economic use value.[8]

As James Gwartney explains:

[P]rofits and losses direct producers to supply the goods and services desired most by consumers. Producers who identify and supply goods that are intensely desired relative to their costs will be rewarded with profits. But the function of losses is just as vital. Losses penalize inefficient suppliers and/or those who attempt to provide goods that are costly relative to their valuation by consumers. If they are not curbed, losses will lead eventually to bankruptcy and the termination of the inefficient and unwise use of resources. Ability to bring unsuccessful experiments to a halt is one of the most important functions performed by market forces.[9]

Profits and losses give people incentives to act in ways that turn out to benefit society. Wise entrepreneurs will divert resources away from less profitable goods and services towards goods and services that more people want. A market system makes people accountable for their economic activities. When individuals or businesses act in ways that waste resources, they will be penalized by lower wages or profits (or perhaps by even larger losses). One of the major problems with an economic system that concentrates decisions in a group of central planners is that accountability too easily gets lost in the system. But in a decentralized market system,

"Market prices establish a reward-penalty system which induces individuals to cooperate with each other and motivates them to work efficiently, invest for the future, supply intensely desired goods, economize on the use of scarce resources, and utilize efficient production methods."[10]

To summarize, the subject before us is not some specific market or collection of markets but the market system, the institutional framework within which individual voluntary economic exchanges can take place. This market system is spontaneous in the sense that no one invented it. It is impersonal in the sense that it is supposed not to discriminate for or against specific individuals. Like an urban traffic pattern, it insures that countless numbers of individual drivers, all seeking their own goals, will reach their destinations in an orderly way. Without help from any group of central planners, the impersonal market system does a remarkable job of supplying the countless wants of countless numbers of people. It does this by supplying information about people's ever-changing wants and preferences through changes in prices. As buyers and sellers act in ways that they believe will maximize their own benefits and minimize their own costs, extraordinary consequences appear. Goods and services that people want are supplied in ways that many believe possible only when someone with complete and perfect knowledge is issuing orders. But as we will see in the chapter on socialism, societies that adopt a centralized economy inevitably fall far short of the efficiency of those that follow a decentralized market approach.

There are several necessary conditions without which a market could not exist, however. They include an enforced right to own and to exchange property, an enforcement of contracts, and laws forbidding the use of force, fraud, and theft. Government has several important roles to play. It must set up a stable system of rules within which exchanges can take place. Both the market system and the people who trade in the market need protection from the kinds of actions that hinder or prevent free exchange. This requires the existence of a government. But there are also necessary limits to the role of government in the economy. When governments exceed their legitimate role as the maker and enforcer of rules, they can do enormous harm to the economy and can be the source of much injustice.[11] Coercion, aside from that necessary to enforce the laws that protect people from force, fraud, and theft, has no place in the market. As Peter Hill notes,

There is no coerced institutional order that can be appropriately called a market. In contrast to the market, Socialistic forms of organization are an enforced order. What we call a free market society is really just one based upon private property rights with certain individuals deciding to enter into voluntary exchanges. To the extent that each one decides that he or she would be better off engaging in a voluntary transaction with another individual or group of individuals, a market can be said to exist.[12]

One of the most serious errors to be found in much recent Christian writing about economics is the mistaken belief that economic exchange or trading creates no value. Many people believe that while an activity like building a house or painting a work of art creates value, the simple act of exchanging something does not. Once this error is accepted, it is a short skip and a jump to the equally wrong conclusion that economic exchange is a zero-sum game in which one person's gaining something *must* be accompanied by the other person's losing something.[13]

There are several ways in which voluntary exchange (as opposed to forced exchange) produces value. First of all, voluntary exchange produces value by moving some good or service from someone who values it less to someone who values it more. One reason why voluntary exchanges (market exchanges) take place is because people place different values on different things. If everyone ranked everything in exactly the same way, there would be little or no reason to trade. If you pay $5000 for a used Chevrolet, you and the person who receives your money demonstrate the differing values you place on the car and the money. The prior owner of the car values your money more than the car; you value the car more than the money or other things for which you could have traded the money. After the voluntary exchange, both of you are better off in the sense that you have exchanged something you value less for something you value more. It is a mistake to equate wealth with material things like cars, houses, and lands. Things become wealth when they become the possession of someone who places a value on them. Had the fictional parents of Tarzan left behind an original edition of Shakespeare's writings when they were killed, the set of books would hardly have constituted wealth for the Ape-man. But they would become wealth when acquired by someone who valued them.

Economic exchange also creates value because it enables people to specialize in ways that make the best use of their abilities and knowledge. Some people are better electricians than carpenters. It is to the mutual advantage of the electrician and the carpenter to specialize in what they do best and exchange their service for that of the other. Such specialization often works to the advantage of nations which are able to produce some things better than others.

Voluntary exchange also makes possible increases in the quantity and efficiency of production. If free exchange were not possible, individual persons or households would be forced to spend their time and effort producing all of the things they might want. Under such conditions, production would obviously take place on a very small scale. But because free exchange encourages a division of labor where each person can specialize in what he does best, production can take place on a much larger scale. Both labor and machines end up being used much more efficiently. The resulting increase both in the kinds of goods and the quantity of those goods gives people a greater range of choices and thus enhances their freedom.

The view of the market presented in this chapter follows the lead of the Austrian School of economics as typified by such thinkers as Ludwig von Mises and Friedrich Hayek. It rejects views frequently associated with what is often called "mainstream economics" which attaches great importance to such notions as perfect knowledge, perfect competition, and equilibrium.

The word *equilibrium* refers to "a state in which conflicting forces are in perfect balance. When there is a balance—an equilibrium—the tendency for change is absent. Before a market equilibrium can be attained, the decisions of consumers and producers must be brought into harmony with one another."[14] The picture of opposing forces canceling each other out and thus producing a state of equilibrium was probably borrowed from physics. This extremely abstract notion which is never exemplified in the real world plays a surprisingly important role in "mainstream economics." It leads many economists to criticize markets in which imperfect knowledge is accompanied by "imperfect competition."

Israel Kirzner is an example of those members of the Austrian School who criticize textbook models of perfect competition that call for a "tendency for price to gravitate toward the equilibrium level at which quantity demanded equals quantity supplied."[15] Economists like Kirzner reject the *static* view of the market that accompanies the emphasis on equilibrium and perfect knowledge. Kirzner offers instead a *dynamic* model of the market. For Kirzner, the market is constantly in a state of *process*. Disequilibrium in the market "occurs precisely because market participants do not know what the market-clearing price is."[16] As Stephen Littlechild explains,

> "Mainstream" economics is centered upon the notion of competitive equilibrium at a point in time characterized by perfect knowledge and coordinated plans on the part of the participants in the market. [Austrian economists] supplement (or even replace) this notion with that of a process taking place over time which is characterized not only by *lack* of knowledge and consequent *lack* of coordination, but also by *learning* and *increasing* coordination.[17]

According to the Austrian view, the market should *not* be judged in terms of the degree to which it approaches some abstract level of perfect competition or some abstract state of equilibrium. Uncertainty and lack of knowledge are inherent features of a market process in which individuals are constantly making economic choices that reflect the changing subjective valuations they make with regard to their options. What qualifies as "perfect competition" for representatives of "mainstream economics" does not and cannot exist in a market where subjective value, limited knowledge, and uncertainty are inescapable. Hence, it is a mistake to follow the lead of such economists and to conclude that their inability to find "perfect competition" constitutes some kind of defect of the market system. The defect exists not in the market but in the model of those economists who insist on looking for perfect competition. In truth, the market is a process of creative destruction in which competing forces attempt and often succeed in wiping out the opposition.

6
Capitalism I

Most of the recent treatments of capitalism by Christian scholars tend to focus on a rather narrow range of subjects including money and wealth, the poor, and the clash between capitalism and socialism. This chapter and the one that follows will attempt to set the record straight with regard to capitalism. In a later chapter, I will attempt to do the same for socialism.

Even the most casual reading of recent Christian writings on the subject makes one thing clear: most of the Christian scholars writing about economics these days show little regard for capitalism. Such writings often exhibit adulation for socialism and contempt for capitalism. Consider, for example, the following claims by a Latin American Protestant, José Míguez Bonino:

> [T]he basic ethos of capitalism is definitely anti-Christian: it is the maximizing of economic gain, the raising of man's grasping impulse, the idolising of the strong, the subordination of man to the economic production. . . . In terms of their basic ethos, Christians must criticise capitalism radically, in its fundamental intention. . . .[1]

One thing seems clear from these sentences: anyone desiring to carry on a rational discussion with Bonino about capitalism is going to have a difficult time. His misunderstanding of capitalism is exceeded only by his fanaticism. Regrettably, Bonino's confused zealotry is typical of the approach towards capitalism taken by a growing number of Christians.

For Christians like this, capitalism is supposed to be un-Christian or anti-Christian because it allegedly gives a predominant place to greed and other un-Christian values. It is alleged to increase poverty and the misery of the poor while, at the same time, it makes a few people rich at the expense of the many. Socialism, on the other hand, is portrayed as the economic system of people who really care for the less fortunate members of society. Socialism is represented as the economics of compassion. Some writers even go so far as to claim that socialism is an essential part of the Christian gospel.[2]

The confusion of the Christian gospel with the politics and economics of collectivism[3] is apparent in a recent public statement from a group of Canadian bishops (which is not to be confused with recent drafts of a pastoral letter about the economy written by American Catholic bishops). Economist Paul Heyne's comments about the bishops' views are instructive:

> To put it simply, the bishops are rejecting, in the name of Gospel principles, any economic system coordinated by changing relative money prices. For in any such system, people will necessarily be treated impersonally (in some respects), important decisions will be made (within legal and moral constraints) by the criterion of net return on capital, and human wants or needs will (to a large extent) be satisfied only insofar as they express themselves through money bids. The bishops are predisposed to believe that this system *does not work*, they are deeply convinced, on ethical grounds, that it *should not exist*. They will therefore not be easily persuaded that *only* such a system has the capability of feeding, clothing, housing, and otherwise caring for large populations in a manner even remotely close to what almost all Canadians now expect as a matter of right.[4]

A similar bias against capitalism pervades the writings of a growing number of those theologically conservative Protestants known as evangelicals.[5]

A former president of the Evangelical Theological Society has stated that capitalism violates "the basic ethical principles of Christianity."[6] Evangelical Andrew Kirk has declared that capitalism is incompatible with Biblical principles.[7] Kirk thinks that the traditional evangelical definition of the gospel—God's good news of the salvation available to those who believe in the crucified and risen Savior—is too narrow. Following earlier proponents of the social gospel and liberation theology, Kirk claims that there is an essential political and economic dimension to God's kingdom and to the gospel. Not surprisingly, Kirk insists that this essential economic dimension to the gospel turns out to be his peculiar brand of socialism.

If one accepts Kirk's thesis, it follows that anyone who disagrees with Kirk's economic and political views—in short, anyone who supports capitalism—cannot simply be treated as an erring brother or sister who needs instruction in basic economics; he or she must be regarded as a heretic since their error touches the very core of the kingdom message. Kirk's book is only one example of a growing extremism on the part of many evangelicals who have embraced a left-wing economic and political ideology and who seek to identify it as the only proper Christian view.[8]

The Bible has become an important weapon in the hands of those who seek a Christian justification for economic and political positions that dismiss capitalism as anti-Christian. Many writings from the Christian Left illustrate a proof-text approach to the Bible. What these writers normally do is isolate some vague passage (usually from the Old Testament) that pertains to an extinct cultural situation or practice. They then proceed to "deduce" some complex economic or political program from that text. In the process, they exhibit an attachment to a mind-boggling method of Biblical interpretation. They often derive their proof-texts from Biblical chapters that contain many verses they presumably think are no longer applicable. These texts contain instructions, for example, to put people to death for sins that our society does not treat as capital offenses. It is interesting to watch these Christians on the Left pick their way through an Old Testament chapter, ignoring one verse and then basing what amounts to an entire economic system on the very next verse.[9]

What these writers are really doing, of course, is manipulating the Bible for their own secular ends. They simply read their own pet twentieth-century secular theory into a portion of the Word of God that has been torn from its Biblical and cultural context.[10] Attempts to deduce any political or economic doctrine from the Bible should be viewed, initially at least, with skepticism. After all, the Bible is no more a textbook on economics than it is on astronomy or geology. There is no such thing as revealed economics.

My own approach is different. In my view, Christians are required to believe many things, not because they are taught *explicitly* in the Bible, but *simply because they are true!* Every sensible Christian believes many things that are not explicitly taught in Scripture. He holds them because they are true; and because they are true, the propositions will be consistent with what Scripture teaches.

My own approach to the dispute between capitalists and

Socialists rejects the proof-text method and proceeds via three main steps. First, a Christian should acquire a clear and complete picture of the Christian world view. What basic views about God, humankind, morality, and society are taught or implied by Scripture? Then he should put his best effort into discovering the truth about economic and political systems. He should try to clarify what capitalism and socialism really are (not what assorted propagandists say they are); he should try to discover how each system works or whether it can work. He should identify the strengths and weaknesses of each system. He should compare his economic options to the standard of Biblical morality. Which system—capitalism or socialism—should I as a *thinking* Christian choose?

Some Relevant Aspects of the Biblical World View

I have said that the proper way for Christians to approach the question of which economic system they should choose consists of three steps. In step one, we should formulate carefully a well-rounded Christian world view. In step two, we should do the best we can to discover the truth about competing economic and political systems. Step three: after we know what we're talking about, we should compare these systems to the Biblical view of God, man, morality, and society and ask which system is more consistent with the entire Christian world view. In this section of the chapter, I will briefly note four relevant aspects of the Biblical world view.

God as Creator
The Biblical world view teaches that since God is the Creator of all that exists, He ultimately is the rightful owner of all that exists. Whatever possessions a human being may acquire, he holds them temporarily as a steward of God and is ultimately accountable to God for how he uses them.

Human Rights and Liberties
The Biblical world view also contains important claims about human rights and liberties. All human beings have certain natural rights inherent in their created nature and have certain moral obligations to respect the rights of others. The possibility of human freedom is not a gift of government but a gift from God. Freedom has its ground in our created nature.

In the Old Testament, freedom is contrasted with slavery. The opposite of freedom is servitude and constraint, being forced to do the will of another (Exod. 21:2-11; Isa. 61:1; Jer. 34:14-17). So the Old Testament tended to focus on the economic and social dimensions of freedom. But gradually, as one moves into the New Testament, a more spiritual dimension of freedom becomes dominant. Human beings lack freedom, not just because they are slaves to the will of another human being, but because they are slaves to sin (Rom. 7:14; 6:17-20; 2 Cor. 3:17). The Apostle Paul connected true freedom with the believer's new relationship with Jesus Christ (Gal. 5:1). In the words of Jesus, "I tell you the truth, everyone who sins is a slave to sin. . . . if the Son sets you free, you will be free indeed. . . . you will know the truth and the truth will set you free" (John 8:36, 31). Spiritual freedom in the New Testament is deliverance from bondage to sin and is available only to those who come to know God's truth through Christ and enter into the saving relationship with Christ described in the New Testament.

Some interesting parallels between the Biblical account of spiritual freedom and politico-economic freedom should be noted. For one thing, freedom always has God as its ultimate ground. For another, freedom must always exist in relationship to law. The moral law of God identifies definite limits beyond which human freedom under God should not pass. Liberty should never be turned into license.

The Biblical Ethic

The moral system of the Bible is another key element of the Christian world view. While the Ten Commandments do not constitute the entire Biblical ethic, they are a good place to begin. It is important to notice other dimensions of the Biblical ethic that have relevance for our subject as well. For example, Christians on the Left insist that the Biblical ethic condemns individual actions and social structures that oppress people, harm people, and favor some at the expense of others (see Ezekiel 34). I agree. Where I disagree, however, is with the next step taken by Christians on the Left. They claim that capitalism inevitably encourages individual actions and produces social structures that oppress and harm people. On this point, they are wrong. The question as to whether capitalism actually harms people is an empirical and not a normative matter. The Leftists simply have their facts wrong.

Human Sin and Depravity

One final aspect of the Christian world view must be mentioned: the inescapable fact of human sin and depravity. No economic or political system that assumes the essential goodness of human nature or holds out the dream of a perfect earthly society can possibly be consistent with the Biblical world view.

Our Economic Options

I have taken a quick look at some relevant aspects of the Biblical world view. It is now time to examine, in general, our major economic options. The first important thing to note is that there are actually three economic systems to choose from: capitalism, socialism, and somewhere between, the hybrid known as interventionism or the mixed economy. The recognition of interventionism as a distinct option to capitalism is extremely important. For one thing, capitalism is often rejected or criticized because it is confused with interventionism. Herbert Schlossberg is one writer who recognizes the difference between capitalism and interventionism as it is practiced in the United States. To the question, should Christians support capitalism, he replies:

> If by capitalism one means the present system of statist manipulation of resources and people for the benefit of those who run the political system and their adherents [i.e., American interventionism], the answer is no. If it [capitalism] means the free and responsible ownership of resources by all who give value for what they receive, without the application of coercive power, then the answer is yes.[11]

It is important to recognize, as Schlossberg points out, that the economy of the United States is interventionist, not capitalist. Many complaints about the economic policies of the United States are justified. But when the programs and policies that cause problems result from interventionism, it is hardly fair to blame those problems on capitalism. This is especially true in the case of Third-World nations that attack the "capitalism" of the United States and other Western nations in order to justify their own drift towards versions of statism and collectivism. While capitalism may well have problems of its own, it seems unfair to blame it for the problems caused by a different economic system—interventionism.

The need to distinguish between capitalism and interventionism is important for another reason. When interventionist measures lead, as they often do, to problems, interventionist economists never admit that the problems result from their attempts to tamper with the economy. The problems, they complain, result from the fact that there was insufficient governmental intervention in the economy. In this ingenious way, the failures of interventionism are cited as reasons for increased degrees of interventionism.

It is a mistake to regard *capitalism, socialism,* and *interventionism* as words that denote specific positions. It is best to treat them as umbrella-terms that cover a variety of positions along a continuum. One dominant feature of capitalism is economic freedom, the right of people to exchange things voluntarily, free from force, fraud, and theft. Capitalism is more than this, of course, but its concern with free exchange is obvious. Socialism, on the other hand, seeks to replace the freedom of the market with a group of central planners who exercise control over essential market functions. There are degrees of socialism as there are degrees of capitalism in the real world. But basic to any form of socialism is distrust of or contempt for the market process and the desire to replace the freedom of the market with some form of centralized control.

Generally speaking, as one moves along the continuum from socialism to capitalism, one finds the following: the more freedom a "Socialist" system allows, the closer it comes to being a form of interventionism; the more freedom an "interventionist" system allows, the closer it is to capitalism. The real issue in the dispute among these three positions is the degree of economic freedom each allows. The crux is the extent to which human beings will be permitted to exercise their own choices in the economic sphere of life. I will say nothing more in this chapter about economic interventionism. It receives plenty of attention in several later chapters. But because of the more basic incompatibility of capitalism and socialism, my attempt to clarify the nature of capitalism will require some additional comments about socialism.

The Two Means of Exchange

An excellent way of getting at the essential difference between capitalism and socialism is a distinction, drawn most recently by economist Walter Williams, between the two ways in which anything may be exchanged. Williams called them *the peaceful means of exchange* and *the violent means of exchange.*[12]

The peaceful means of exchange may be summed up in the phrase, "If you do something good for me, then I'll do something good for you." When capitalism is understood correctly, it epitomizes the peaceful means of exchange. The reason people enter market exchanges is because they believe the exchange is good for them. They take advantage of an opportunity to obtain something they want more in exchange for something they value less. Capitalism then should be understood as a voluntary system of relationships that utilizes the peaceful means of exchange.

But exchange can also take place by means of force and violence. In this violent means of exchange, the basic rule of thumb is: "Unless you do something good for me, I'll do something bad to you." This turns out to be the controlling principle of socialism. Socialism means far more than centralized control of the economic process. It entails the introduction of coercion into economic exchange in order to facilitate the goals of the elite who function as the central planners. One of the great ironies of Christian socialism is that its proponents in effect demand that the state get out its weapons and force people to fulfill the demands of Christian love. Even if we fail to notice any other contrast between capitalism and socialism, we already have a major difference to relate to the Biblical ethic. One system stresses voluntary and peaceful exchange, while the other depends on coercion and violence.

Some Christian Socialists object to the way I have set this up. They profess contempt for the more coercive forms of state-socialism on exhibit in Communist countries. They would like us to believe that a more humane, noncoercive kind of socialism is possible. They would like us to believe that there is a form of socialism, not yet tried anywhere on earth, where the central ideas are cooperation and community and where coercion and dictatorship are precluded. Either these people are confused or they have a secret that they want kept from the rest of us. It is interesting to note how little information they provide about the workings of this more utopian kind of socialism. They ignore the fact that however humane and voluntary their socialism is supposed to become after it has been put into effect, it will take massive amounts of coercion and theft to get it started. Voluntary socialism is a contradiction in terms. As Edmund Opitz points out, "Such practices as voluntarily pooling goods, sharing the common tasks of a community, working with one's hands . . . do not constitute Socialism."[13] What these Christian Socialists have done is form a utopian ideal of a voluntary community they call socialism. They are unable to explain how their system will work without free markets, and they simply ignore the massive amounts of coercion that will be required to get their system started. Whatever else socialism is, it means a centralized control of the economy made possible by the use of force. Socialism epitomizes the violent means of exchange.

In his book *The Good News of the Kingdom Coming,* Andrew Kirk tries hard to disguise the coercion necessary to bring his own version of Christian socialism into existence. Kirk is totally opposed to economic freedom. He claims that it is inconsistent with the gospel to allow people's holdings to result from the natural outworking of free exchange. The state must determine (presumably with Kirk's advice) when people have accumulated too much. When that point is reached, Kirk wants the state to take any excess and redistribute it among the poor, in the meantime skimming off enough to keep the agents of the state from worrying about their own standard of living. According to Kirk, the Bible teaches that any accumulation of wealth above that absolutely required for the necessities of life must result from violence, fraud, bribes, or theft. No one in Kirk's universe ever prospers honorably.

In Kirk's "just" society, someone (he does not say who) will fix both minimum and maximum pay for every job. In other words, the state will forcibly prevent anyone from working at a particular job at less than the official salary. Fortunately, any pain resulting from this coercion will be eased by the comforting knowledge that unemployment benefits will match this minimum pay. Anyone unhappy about working for the state-sanctioned minimum wage will be able to receive the same compensation for doing nothing. Kirk says nothing about the economic incentives of such a program on workers. He is totally silent about its effect upon working people whose income will be forcibly taken from them by the state and redistributed in the way he describes. Kirk's entire scheme is so bizarre that it is difficult to believe that he has really done much reflecting about his recommendations or their consequences. But he is quite clear about the fact that such policies are required by any "Christian" approach to economics.

All money earned above the maximum wage set by Kirk's state will be "given" to charity. (Socialists come up with such lovely euphemisms to disguise the coercive actions of their state.) Naturally, before any of this money is given to charity, the state will have to take it away. This take-away will be aided, Kirk tells us, by "steeply progressive" tax rates. While Kirk recognizes that many people may resist the statist tyranny he proposes, he studiously avoids telling us what will be done to those who resist.

The massive problems connected with Kirk's so-called Christian socialism go far beyond its restraints upon personal liberty and its enhancement of the powers of the state. It would be difficult to think of a set of economic recommendations more in conflict with basic economic principles. Minimal reflection about the effect such proposals would have upon people's incentives and the long-term damage it would do to any nation's economy is enough to show Kirk's need to get in closer touch with reality.

A Closer Look at Capitalism

I have already explained capitalism as a system of voluntary human relationships in which people exchange on the basis of the peaceful means of exchange. It is time to add more detail to this general picture. For one thing, capitalism is not economic anarchy. It recognizes several necessary conditions for the kinds of voluntary relationships it recommends. One of these is the existence of inherent human rights, such as the right to make decisions, the right to be free, the right to hold property, and the right to exchange what one owns for something else. Capitalism also presupposes a system of morality. Capitalism does not encourage people to do anything they want. There are definite limits, moral and otherwise, to the ways in which people should exchange. Capitalism should be regarded as a system of voluntary relationships within a framework of laws which protect people's rights against force, fraud, theft, and violations of contracts. "Thou shalt not steal" and "Thou shalt not lie" are part of the underlying moral constraints of the system.[14] Economic exchanges can hardly be voluntary if one participant is coerced, deceived, defrauded, or robbed.[15] It is clear that people who condemn the "capitalism" of the Philippines under Ferdinand Marcos have no idea what they are talking about. The corruption deserved condemnation, but the system was not capitalism.

My analysis of capitalism conforms with that found in a number of standard economic texts. For example, Armen Alchian and William Allen define capitalism as "as system of freely exchangeable, private-property rights in goods and services, with the central government protecting and enforcing these rights. Private-property rights, in turn, can be defined as the rights of owners to decide on the use of their goods and resources (including labor and time) as they see fit."[16]

Some writers have criticized the approach I take to capitalism and socialism in a way that evidences a basic misunderstanding of my view. They claim that I am quick to point out the often obvious defects of socialism in the real world. But then, they argue, I cheat by contrasting the imperfect forms of socialism that exist in the real world with a capitalist ideal that obviously does not and cannot exist in reality. Quite frankly, it is difficult to see how anyone who has read my work carefully can think that such a claim is relevant. I began my discussion by pointing out that both *capitalism* and *socialism* are umbrella-terms that refer to a variety of systems. The very notion of a continuum implies that the positions represented at the opposite ends of the scale function as ideals which the systems in the real world merely approach to a greater or lesser degree. The terms *capitalism* and *socialism* can both be used to refer to an ideal capitalist or Socialist system and to the variety of systems that approach, however imperfectly, those ideals in the real world.

In fact, I made this all quite clear in an earlier book when I pointed out that the word *capitalism* is sometimes used "in an abstract sense to refer to an ideal market economy in which people exchange goods and services in an environment free from coercion, fraud, monopoly, and statist interference with the exchange process."[17] I then went on to say that:

> "Capitalism" is also used to describe several systems of exchange in the real world that approximate more or less the freedom of the ideal market. These systems [in the real world] differ, of course, in several significant respects from the abstract perfection of the ideal market. The relationship between the ideal market and real economic exchanges is analogous to that between physiology and pathology. No physician ever expects to find every organ in every body functioning perfectly. His study of physiology provides him with a standard by which he can diagnose pathology. Likewise, the ideal market economy provides standards that can be used to judge the health of economic practices in the real world. Critics of capitalism frequently use the imperfections of existing systems to attack the model. This makes about as much sense as a doctor discarding all his physiology texts because he has never seen a perfectly healthy body.[18]

I certainly do have criticisms of Socialist systems in the real world. They are the economic equivalent of the Black Death. But there are even more fundamental problems with the Socialist ideal. Even if this ideal form of socialism could be actualized in the real world, it could not work.[19] I readily acknowledge all kinds of problems in existing "capitalist" systems. I also acknowledge that no existing economic system matches the capitalist ideal. What I do maintain is that, unlike the Socialist ideal, the kind of capitalism I have described can work. I also maintain that the closer any existing economic system comes to that ideal, the better its economy will operate.

There is no mystery as to why existing economic systems fall short of the capitalist ideal. The reason is implicit in one of the major tenets of the Christian world view noted earlier. Deviations from the market ideal often occur because of defects in human nature. Human beings naturally crave security and guaranteed success, values not found readily in a free market. Genuine competition always carries with it the possibility of failure and loss. Consequently, the understandable human preference for security leads men to avoid competition whenever possible, encourages them to operate outside of the market, and induces them to subvert the market process through behavior that is often questionable and dishonest. As long as the human beings taking part in market exchanges are *fallen,* we can expect to find problems.

One of the sillier objections to capitalism is the claim that it presupposes a utopian view of human nature and consequently conflicts with the Biblical view of sin. My earlier statement about the need for laws to protect people from force, fraud, and theft hardly sounds like capitalism is unaware of the true condition of human nature. In fact, once we grant that consistency with the Biblical doctrine of sin is a legitimate test of economic systems, it is relatively easy to see how well democratic capitalism scores in this regard. One of the more effective ways of mitigating the effects of human sin in society is dispersing and decentralizing power. The combination of a free market economy and limited constitutional government is the most effective means yet devised to impede the concentration of economic and political power in the hands of a small number of people. Every person's ultimate protection against coercion requires control over some private spheres of life where he can be free. Private ownership of property is an important buffer against any exorbitant consolidation of power by government.

The free market is consistent with the Biblical view of human nature in another way. It recognizes the weaknesses of human nature and the limitations of human knowledge. No one can possibly know enough to manage a complex economy. No one should ever be trusted with this power. However, in order for socialism to work, it requires a class of omniscient planners to forecast the future, to set prices, and to control production. In the free market system, decisions are not made by an omniscient bureaucratic elite, but made across the entire economic system by countless economic agents.

At this point, of course, critics of capitalism are quick to raise an objection. Capitalism, they will counter, may make it difficult for economic power to be consolidated in the hands of the state; but it only makes it easier for vast concentrations of wealth and power to be vested in the hands of private individuals and companies. The point here of course is that it is supposed to be capitalism that produces monopolies. But the truth turns out to be something quite different from this widely accepted myth. It is not the free market that produces monopolies; rather it is governmental intervention with the market that creates the conditions that encourage monopoly.[20] The only real monopolies that have ever attained a high degree of immunity from competition achieved that status by governmental fiat, regulation, or support of some other kind. Governments create monopolies by granting one organization the exclusive privilege of doing business or by establishing *de facto* monopolies through regulatory agencies whose alleged purpose is the enforcement of competition but whose real effect is the limitation of competition. More attention needs to be given to the ways in which America's infamous nineteenth-century "robber barons" were aided by special privileges granted by the government.

Conclusion

In this first of two chapters on the subject of capitalism, I have sought to clarify the nature of capitalism. It is impossible to understand capitalism until one first distinguishes it from interventionism, a system with which it is often confused. Capitalism is that economic system in which people are encouraged to make voluntary exchanges within a system of rules that prohibit force, fraud, and theft. In the following chapter, I will continue my discussion of capitalism by considering a number of the more common objections raised against it. My answers to these criticisms will serve to produce an even sharper picture of capitalism. My discussion of capitalism in the next chapter will close with a demonstration of its moral superiority to socialism.

7
Capitalism II

This chapter has two jobs to do. First of all, it will examine the most widely used arguments that attack capitalism on moral grounds.[1] It is arguments like these that appear most frequently in the writings of religious critics of capitalism. Second, I will defend the claim that capitalism is superior to socialism *on moral grounds*. Few people question the economic superiority of capitalism. But, many of its critics maintain, a market system must be restricted or even abolished because it allegedly fails important moral tests.

Before these moral arguments for and against capitalism are presented, it is necessary to eliminate a source of much confusion on this issue. Many times, critics of capitalism demonstrate that they have no idea what capitalism is. The capitalism they attack is a caricature, a straw man. The stereotype of capitalism that is the target of most such attacks often results from an incorrect association of the word *capitalism* with existing national economies that are in fact better described as interventionist. More attention needs to be given to the inappropriateness of regarding the interventionist economic policies of the United States as a paradigm of capitalism.

Many critics of capitalism appear to be controlled more by emotional hang-ups about capitalism than they are by any evidence. Capitalism is blamed for every evil in contemporary society including its greed, materialism, selfishness, the prevalence of fraudulent behavior, the debasement of society's tastes, the pollution of the environment, the alienation and despair within society, and the vast disparities of wealth. Even racism and sexism are treated as effects of capitalism. Many of the objections to a market system result from a simple but clearly fallacious two-step operation. First, some undesirable feature is noted in a society that is allegedly capitalist. Then it is simply asserted that capitalism is the cause of this feature. Logic texts call this the Fallacy of False Cause. Mere coincidence does not prove causal connection. Such critics of capitalism conveniently overlook the fact that many of these same undesirable features exist in interventionist and Socialist systems.

Moral Objections to Capitalism

Exploitation

Capitalism is attacked on the ground that it exploits poor people and poor nations. A crucial but often unstated assumption of this view is the belief that the only way some can become rich is by exploiting others. Poverty is, such critics believe, always the result of exploitation and oppression by someone who profits from the poverty of others.

According to Andrew Kirk, who speaks for many on this point, the reason some nations are poor is because they have been exploited by richer and more powerful nations.[2] To be specific, the West is supposed to be responsible for the persistent poverty of lesser developed nations. In a later chapter, I will examine the evidence and show that the charge is false.

The exploitation model of poverty is simplistic. It is also an excellent example of the ease with which some contemporary Christians insist on reading Marxist ideology into the Bible. It is certainly true that Scripture recognizes that poverty *sometimes* results from oppression and exploitation. But Scripture also teaches that there are times when poverty results from misfortunes that have nothing to do with exploitation. These misfortunes include such things as accidents, injuries, and illness. And of course the Bible also makes it plain that poverty can result from indigence and sloth (Prov. 6:6-11; 13:4; 24:30-34; 28:19). When the problem of poverty is approached with a mind unbiased by ideology, it is easy to see that while some poverty does result from exploitation, some does not. Sometimes people are poor because of bad luck or as a consequence of their own actions and decisions.

Free Exchange Is a Zero-Sum Game

The myth about exploitation lends support to a related claim that often functions as a ground for rejections of capitalism. Capitalism is denounced because of the mistaken belief that market exchanges are examples of what is called a *zero-sum game*.[3] A zero-sum game is one where only one participant can win. If one person (or group) wins, then the other must lose. Baseball and checkers are two examples of zero-sum games. If A wins, then B must lose.

The error here consists in thinking that market exchanges are a zero-sum game. On the contrary, market exchanges illustrate what is called a *positive-sum game*. A positive-sum game is one in which both players may win. We must reject the myth that economic exchanges necessarily benefit only one party at the expense of the other. In voluntary economic exchanges, both parties may leave the exchanges in better economic shape than would otherwise have been the case.[4] Both parties to a voluntary exchange believe that they gain through the trade. If they did not perceive the exchange as beneficial, they would not continue to take part in it.[5]

Selfishness
Capitalism is also despised because it is thought to encourage a number of character traits that are incompatible with Christian values. The three sub-Christian traits most often thought to be encouraged by capitalism are selfishness, greed, and a spirit of competition.

Scripture clearly does condemn *selfishness*. But the catch is that selfishness should never be confused with the quite different characteristic of *self-interest*. When Jesus commanded us to love our neighbor as ourself (Matt. 22:39), He gave implicit approval to self-interest. When a person is motivated by selfishness, he seeks his own welfare with no regard for the welfare of others. But when a person is motivated by self-interest, he can pursue his welfare in ways that do not harm others.

There is nothing sinful in caring about what happens to one's family or oneself. In fact, the New Testament condemns those who lack such concern (1 Tim. 5:8). Since the kinds of voluntary exchanges that characterize the market are mutually beneficial (in other words, are a positive-sum game), selfishness is not an *inherent* feature of capitalism. People who exchange on the basis of market principles engage in activities that benefit themselves and others. The conditions of a free market oblige people to find ways of helping themselves at the same time they help others, whether they do this consciously or not. Self-interest can serve as a powerful engine that pulls society along the road to economic progress. I share the view of economist Alexander Shand that this view of capitalist free markets "is not that they necessarily depend upon self-seeking behaviour but only that they allow the individual to choose some particular line of action."[6] Such a view is clearly compatible with altruistic behavior.

Greed

Capitalism is also criticized for encouraging greed. However, the mechanism of the market actually neutralizes greed as individuals are forced to find ways of serving the needs of those with whom they wish to exchange. There is no question but that market exchanges often bring us into contact with people motivated by greed. But so long as our rights are protected (a basic condition of market exchanges), the possible greed of others cannot harm us. As long as greedy individuals are prohibited from introducing force, fraud, and theft into the exchange process, their greed must be channeled into the discovery of products or services for which people are willing to trade. Every person in a market economy has to be other-directed. The market is one area of life where concern for the other person is required. The market therefore does not pander to greed. It is rather a mechanism that allows natural human desires to be satisfied in a nonviolent way. The alternative to the voluntary means of exchange is coercion.

Competitiveness

The third sub-Christian value that capitalism is supposed to encourage is a spirit of competition. British economist Brian Griffiths does a good job of capturing the mood of people who believe that competition is somehow inconsistent with Christian values. As Griffiths describes these people, they believe that competition "produces aggression, rivalry, conflict, cheating and discrimination which are anathema to the Christian conscience. For the Christian the ideal is not competition but cooperation, which by comparison produces mutual benefits, modesty and harmony."[7] Such a view, Griffiths continues, is often accompanied by the belief that "competitive methods of economic organization are therefore inferior to non-competitive and cooperative ones, with the implication that collectivism in one form or another is superior to a market form of economic organisation."[8]

Such a position is badly off-target. There is nothing wrong or sub-Christian with competition per se. Competition is a necessary consequence of scarcity; it is an unavoidable dimension of human existence in this life. Competition exists whenever the scarcity of something people prize or value results in more people wanting it than can have it. Players in games and contests compete for the sake of winning and for the things that accompany victory. People compete for jobs and promotions. Students compete for grades. Suitors compete for attention and affection. Industries compete for business. Churches compete for converts.

Of course, competition can and often does proceed in ways that conflict with basic Christian values. Competition can lead individuals and organizations to act in ways that are dishonorable or dishonest. But these problems are simply another manifestation of original sin. They do not demonstrate that there is anything wrong with competition itself.

There are two basic ways in which people may resolve conflicts resulting from scarcity. On the one hand, they may seek to deal with scarcity by force or violence. Two nations may go to war; two cowboys in the Old West may have shot it out; one person may attempt to take the prize by force, fraud, or theft. On the other hand, the parties involved might decide to resolve the conflict through some form of nonviolent competition. Hence, competition often has beneficial social consequences by affording people ways of resolving conflicts over some scarce goods in a nonviolent way.

But competition can benefit society and individuals in other ways. For example, the challenge of competition often stirs people to higher levels of excellence than they may have thought possible. Contrary to what one hears from religious critics of capitalism, competition in the economic arena has had enormous social benefits. The allocation of scarce goods by competition in free market exchanges is superior to any other type of economic organization. The competition of the marketplace is not an end in itself; it is a means to the end of providing better goods and services at the lowest possible price. The competition of the marketplace ends up encouraging social cooperation. It benefits the masses and increases the productive capacity of the society. We live as fallen creatures in an imperfect world where scarcity abounds. The alternative to nonviolent competition for these scarce resources is the use of force, violence, and theft.

Morality and the Market System

Many of capitalism's religious critics fail to appreciate that capitalism can be defended not only on grounds of its economic superiority, but also on moral grounds.

Help for the Masses
Critics of capitalism fail to see the extent to which the market process is a force for improving the lot of the masses. History

shows that the poor have benefited greatly from market systems. It is impossible to ease, reduce, or eliminate poverty through a continued division of the economic pie into increasingly smaller pieces. There simply is not enough wealth to go around. What the poor of any nation need is not continually smaller pieces of a pie that keeps getting smaller. They need a bigger pie. Instead of arguing over how the economic pie should be divided, attention should be directed towards the production of a bigger pie.

Peter Hill explains how economic growth in the United States affected this nation's poor:

> [F]rom 1790 to 1980 in the United States, the bottom 20 percent of the income distribution, that is, those ordinarily considered poor, raised their real standard of living 750 percent. This was because of substantial economic growth rather than because of income redistribution programs. Historically, where private property rights have been well defined and enforced, economic growth has occurred and it has redounded to the benefit of those at the bottom of the ladder as well as those at the top. This is not to say that greater equality has resulted, but we must be careful not to ignore very substantial benefits that have accrued to the poor.[9]

Walter Williams notes that "Capitalism has a strong bias toward serving the common man. . . . Parity in the marketplace, nonexistent in the political arena, could be the chief reason free markets are looked upon with disfavor by the elite. Political allocation of resources, regardless of its *stated purpose,* is strongly biased in favor of the elite."[10]

It is still fashionable in some circles to claim that capitalism contributed to the widespread misery of the working class in the nineteenth century. These allegations have been successfully challenged by a number of studies, including a book titled *Capitalism and the Historians,* edited by Friedrich Hayek.[11] The undeniable misery of that century should be seen as a continuation of the wretchedness of previous centuries superimposed on the particular conditions of life in a society becoming increasingly more industrialized. Instead of the poor starving in dirty hovels in the country, they were starving in dirty city slums. As Paul Heyne observes,

> [C]apitalism did not create poverty. The great mass of the world's people always lived in poverty. . . . But capitalism did

change the form of poverty and make it more visible. . . . Poverty would be much less noticeable if our society were less urban and industrialized. It would undoubtedly be much more widespread. But it would not strike us with such jarring impact. Here is the first fact to be kept in mind, then: capitalism and the industrial revolution increased the visibility of poverty. By pulling . . . people out of the country and into the cities, off the small and inefficient plots of land from which they barely eked a subsistence and into the centers of manufacturing and commerce, an industrializing capitalist society created awareness of poverty rather than poverty itself.[12]

Hence, poverty did not begin with capitalism. Capitalism simply made poverty more obvious as the poor flocked to urban areas where work was to be found. It also made poverty more noticeable as more and more of the middle class rose to modest affluence, making the contrast between them and the poor more apparent. The truth is, as Henry Hazlitt explains, that:

Capitalism has enormously raised the level of the masses. It has wiped out whole areas of poverty. It has greatly reduced infant mortality, and made it possible to cure disease and prolong life. It has reduced human suffering. Because of capitalism, millions live today who would otherwise have not even been born. If these facts have no ethical relevance, then it is impossible to say in what ethical relevance consists.[13]

Social Cooperation

Capitalism does more than make it possible for people to make money. It provides the basis for a social structure that encourages the development of important personal and social virtues such as community and cooperation.

One of the major advantages of the market system is that it encourages cooperation rather than competition. This is in rather direct contrast to the usual labeling of a free market, private property system in that such an economy is said to be a competitive one. It is true that competition will exist in a market-based private property system, but competition is prevalent in any society in which scarcity exists. An advantage of the market process is that those who are the best "competitors" are those who best cooperate with, or satisfy others in the society. In order to get ahead in a private property system individuals must engage in voluntary transactions, that is, they must offer a "better deal" than competitors. This encourages cooperative behavior by focusing creative impulses and energy on adding to the satisfaction of others. The person that does this best is the one who succeeds in the market.[14]

Michael Novak finds it ironic that while capitalism is attacked for allegedly encouraging competitive individualism and possessiveness, it actually "seems to favor in its citizens forms of generosity, trust, extroversion, outgoingness, and reliance upon the good faith of others." But while voluntary economic exchanges in a market system are building community and trust, "existing socialist societies seem to narrow the circles of trust, as groups competing for the same allocations run afoul of each other's interests. Collectivism pits man against man. A system which encourages each to seek first his own interests yields liberty and receives in return loyalty and love."[15] Voluntary exchange, therefore, not only benefits all participants in the exchange, it also encourages social cooperation.

Human Dignity
Several economists have drawn attention to the way in which capitalism provides society with an important support for human dignity. Peter Hill points out how:

> Capitalism . . . recognizes the worth of those with little economic and political power and offers them opportunities not readily available under alternative rules. Under a private property, market system, everybody is a "best" producer of some product or service. It is not the case that those with abundant skills or resources can outcompete the unskilled or unproductive across the board. Under the principle of comparative advantage all of us are least-cost producers in some area and thus worthy of attention by others in the society.[16]

Unlike socialism, Brian Griffiths explains, capitalism allows individuals "the freedom to buy and sell, save and invest, choose their preferred form of employment, and develop the skills which they feel appropriate. It allows minorities exactly these same rights too. Socialism does not."[17] Peter Hill carries this same idea even further by noting how capitalism "allows the strong and the weak, the skilled and the unskilled, the powerful and the powerless, to interact for their *mutual* benefit. The strong don't dominate or exploit the weak; rather they find it to their own advantage to seek out those individuals and offer them an exchange that will advantage both."[18] Of course, none of this entails that everyone in a market system will end up with equal power or equal possessions. For that matter, neither does socialism.

Political Freedom

I trust that even Christian critics of economic freedom will concede that political freedom is an important human value. But economic freedom is a necessary condition for personal and political liberty. No one can be free in the political sense if he lacks economic freedom. Economic freedom aids the existence and development of political liberty by helping to check the concentration of too much power in the hands of too few people. As long as a large percentage of the people in a society exercise ownership control, power within that society will be more widely diffused. No one can be free when he is dependent upon others for the basic economic needs of life. If someone commands what a person can or cannot buy and sell, then a significant part of that individual's freedom has been abridged. Human beings who are dependent upon any one power for the basic essentials of life are not free. When that master becomes the state, obedience becomes a prerequisite to employment and to life itself.

As Wilhelm Roepke saw so clearly, "We are not free to combine just any kind of economic order, say, a collectivist one, with any kind of political and spiritual order."[19] Economics is not simply a matter of finding the most expedient way of organizing economic life. There is a necessary connection between economic freedom and political-spiritual freedom. Because collectivism in the economic sphere means the end of political and spiritual freedom, economics is the front line in the battle for freedom. While capitalism is not a sufficient condition for political freedom in the sense that its presence guarantees political freedom, it is difficult to find examples of nations with a significant degree of political freedom that have not made provision for economic freedom.

Private Ownership and Moral Behavior

More attention needs to be given to the important ways in which private ownership can serve as a stimulus to the development of moral behavior. British economist Arthur Shenfield explains:

Every time we treat property with diligence and care, we learn a lesson in morality. . . . The reason for the moral training of private property is that it induces at least some of its owners to treat it as a trust, even if only for their children or children's children; and those who so treat it tend to be best at accumulating it, contrary to popular notions about the conspicuous consumption of the rich, the incidence of luck or of gambling. Contrast our attitudes to private property with our treatment of public property. Every army quartermaster, every state school administrator, every bureaucratic office controller, knows with what carelessness and lack of diligence most of us deal with it. This applies everywhere, but especially in socialist countries where most property is public.[20]

Shenfield is right. People do treat their own personal property differently than they treat public property or the property of others. This fact can be used to teach people some important moral lessons.

Everything Has a Cost

Once people realize that few things in life are free, that most things carry a price tag, and that therefore we will have to work for most of the things we want, we are in a position to learn a vital truth about life. Capitalism helps teach this truth. But, Shenfield warns, under socialism, "Everything still has a cost, but everyone is tempted, even urged, to behave as if there is no cost or as if the cost will be borne by somebody else. This is one of the most corrosive effects of collectivism upon the moral character of people."[21]

Conclusion

Many religious critics of capitalism focus their attacks on what they take to be its moral shortcomings. In truth, the moral objections to capitalism turn out to be a sorry collection of arguments that reflect, more than anything else, serious confusions about the true nature of a market system. When capitalism is put to the moral test, it more than holds its own against its competition. After all, it makes little sense to reject one system on moral grounds when all of the alternatives turn out, in the real world, to have far more serious problems. To quote Arthur Shenfield again, among all of our economic options, only capitalism operates on the basis of respect for free, independent, responsible persons. All other systems in varying degrees treat men as less than this. Socialist systems above all treat men as pawns to be moved about by the authorities, or as children to be given what the rulers decide is good for them, or as serfs or slaves. The rulers begin by boasting about their compassion, which in any case is fraudulent, but after a time they drop this pretense which they find unnecessary for the maintenance of power. In all things they act on the presumption that they know best. Therefore they and their systems are morally stunted. Only the free system, the much assailed capitalism, is morally mature.[22]

The alternative to free exchange is coercion and violence. Capitalism is a mechanism that allows natural human desires to be satisfied in a nonviolent way. Little can be done to prevent human beings from wanting to be rich. But what capitalism does is channel that desire into peaceful means that benefit many besides those who wish to improve their own situation.

The alternative to serving other men's wants is seizing power of them, as it always has been. Hence it is not surprising that wherever the enemies of capitalism have prevailed, the result has been not only the debasement of consumption standards for the masses but also their reduction to serfdom by the new privileged class of Socialist rulers.[23]

Capitalism is quite simply the most moral system, the most effective system, and the most equitable system of economic exchange. When capitalism, the system of free economic exchange, is described fairly, there can be no question that it, rather than socialism or interventionism, comes closer to matching the demands of the Biblical ethic.

8
Socialism

The essence of socialism has already been described in Chapter Six. Socialism is an economic system that replaces the market as the means of providing for consumption, production, and distribution with central planning.[1] Physical capital[2] under socialism is either owned or controlled by the state. Socialism replaces peaceful voluntary exchange with the coercive or violent means of exchange.

As we noticed in Chapter Six, many Christian Socialists object to this analysis. When they talk about socialism, they insist, they have something quite different in mind. One problem with such claims is that if they really did have a different vision of socialism *in their minds,* why don't they ever provide a clear account of how the system would operate *in the world?* Why can't they point to some national economy, past or present, that exemplifies *their* Socialist ideal? Why don't they explain how their variety of socialism differs from limited experiments with "socialism" in small communities, trials that inevitably failed?[3] More attention needs to be given to the possibility that the legitimate longings that many sincere people believe can be satisfied only by socialism may in fact be met best by the capitalism described in Chapters Six and Seven.

I have also discussed the extent to which many church leaders and intellectuals now insist that socialism is the only economic system compatible with Christianity. Such church leaders have one thing going for them. They are in tune with the spirit of our age. As writers like Paul Hollander point out, socialism has definite snob appeal among the intellectual elite. It is chic to be a Socialist. According to Hollander,

> The appeals and values associated with socialism . . . have provided the most powerful incentive for the suspension of critical thinking among large contingents of Western intellec-

tuals. . . . Such intellectuals appear to assume an affirming, supportive stance as soon as a political system (or movement) makes an insistent enough claim to its socialist character. . . . The word "socialism" has retained, despite all historical disappointments associated with regimes calling themselves socialist, a certain magic which rarely fails to disarm or charm these intellectuals and which inspires renewed hope that its most recent incarnation will be *the* authentic one, or at least more authentic than previous ones had been.[4]

Of course, Hollander continues, "There is little evidence that intellectuals, or for that matter nonintellectuals, living in countries considered Socialist are similarly charmed or disarmed by the idea of socialism."[5]

Why Socialism Cannot Work

The miserable performance of Socialist economies is no accident. There is a fundamental reason why Socialist economies do not work, and that is that *they cannot work.* The argument that supports this contention was discovered in 1920 by the Austrian economist Ludwig von Mises.[6] In spite of one or two attempted rebuttals that I will consider shortly, Mises's argument has never been answered successfully.

According to Mises, socialism can never work because it is an economic system that makes economic calculation impossible. And because economic calculation is impossible, socialism turns out to be an economic system that makes rational economic activity impossible. As Giovanni Sartori explains, under socialism it is "theoretically and practically impossible, for the collectivistic planner, to *calculate costs.* His costs and prices are, and can only be, 'arbitrary.' To be sure, arbitrary not in the sense that they are established at whim but in the sense that they are *baseless:* they cannot be derived from any economically significant base or baseline."[7]

One of the great advantages to a market system is the constant supply of information it provides by means of the price-mechanism. That information is not available in a Socialist system. Tom Bethell explains the Socialist's problem this way:

It is one thing for central planners to draw up a plan of production. It is quite another thing to carry it out. . . . How can you (the planner) know what should be produced, before you know what people want? And people cannot know what they want unless they first know the price of things. But prices themselves can only be established when people are permitted to own things and to exchange them among themselves. But people do not have these rights in centrally planned economies.[8]

Without free markets to set prices, Socialists can never attune production to human wants. The impossibility of precise measures of cost accounting under socialism will result in economic disaster.

Mises did not deny that rational action might still be possible under socialism with regard to small and insignificant matters. But under a system that ignores the factors of profit and loss, it would be impossible for production to be consciously economical. Rational economic production would be impossible. In Mises's words, "All economic exchange, therefore, would involve operations the value of which could never be predicted beforehand nor ascertained after they had taken place. Everything would be a leap in the dark. Socialism is the renunciation of rational economy."[9]

The problem of economic calculation under socialism grows increasingly more serious as national economies become more complex. As economist Thomas Sowell explains: "Where conditions are constantly changing in the economy, as in most modern industrial nations, the ability of a price system to make use of the scattered and imperfect knowledge that exists at any given time is one of its primary advantages."[10] But this advantage is lost in Socialist economies.

In a completely centrally controlled economy, it would be necessary for the central planners to actually know what has happened and what its implications are in order to reach the same decision. This is one reason why even countries that believe in central planning on principle do not have 100% central planning in practice. The amount of knowledge required for the thousands of daily adjustments would otherwise be overwhelming. Moreover, some goods—especially in agriculture—vary greatly in quality (freshness, size, taste, etc.). To plan their use centrally without being physically present all over the country to see the actual condition of the strawberries, cabbages, melons, etc., listed on the official statistics would be impossible, especially since what was a good item of produce a few days ago may be approaching spoilage or already rotten today—a fact not discoverable from looking at the statistics in the central planning office, but only by looking at the millions of items themselves, which only the consumers on the spot can do effectively.[11]

Socialism therefore presents us with the picture of a system of planning in which rational planning turns out to be impossible. Without free markets and the vital information supplied by markets, economic activity would become chaotic and result in drastic inefficiencies and distortions. The great paradox of socialism is the fact that Socialists need capitalism in order to survive. Unless Socialists make allowance for some free markets which provide the pricing information that alone makes rational economic activity possible or monitor the pricing information available from nations where free markets are allowed to function, Socialist economies would have even more problems than those for which they are already notorious. In practice, socialism cannot dispense with market exchanges. Consequently, socialism is a gigantic fraud which attacks the market at the same time it is forced to utilize the market process.

A Socialist Response to Mises

During the first two decades of the twentieth century—in other words, prior to the publication of Mises's argument against socialism—the term *socialism* meant *nonmarket socialism*. Socialist theorists in those years clearly regarded socialism and any market process as mutually exclusive. Mises's argument produced a great deal of consternation among Socialist economists in the 1930s. Thanks largely to Mises, nonmarket forms of socialism are seldom touted anymore.

Unfortunately, economists sympathetic to socialism fail to report the debate over Mises's argument fairly. In those rare cases where such economists even pause to mention Mises's thesis, the Socialists add a sentence in which they claim that Mises's position was refuted in the late 1930s by an economist named Oskar Lange. While it is true that Lange *attempted* to answer Mises, it is sheer myth to suppose that his attempt succeeded.

Oskar Lange acknowledged the seriousness of Mises's challenge; he admitted that Mises's argument undercut all nonmarket forms of socialism. But Lange then tried to evade Mises's trap by developing a kind of market socialism. What Lange's so-called market socialism was supposed to do was show how a central planning agency could vary prices by a process of trial and error, the key being the rate at which the factory's inventory would be depleted. The central planners would begin by setting the price for a commodity at a certain level. Based then on whether the inventory increased or decreased, the planners would move the price up or down. Basic to Lange's market socialism is the claim that the central planners in a Socialist economy can have *precisely the same information as entrepreneurs in a free market system.*[12]

Friedrich Hayek denounces such a claim as a "blatant untruth, an assertion so absurd that it is difficult to understand how an intelligent person could ever honestly make it. It asserts a sheer impossibility which only a miracle could realize."[13] Hayek supports his rebuttal by noting:

> The information relevant for and possessed by each entrepreneur will be very different from that possessed by others. To speak of the aggregate of such information dispersed among hundreds of different individuals as being available to the planning authority is pure fiction. What the planning authority would have to know would not be the mere totals but the distinct, peculiar conditions prevailing *in each enterprise* which affect the information about *values* transmitted through market prices but would be completely lost in any statistical information about *quantities* that might reach the authority from time to time.[14]

It is one thing to identify which information a central planning board must have in order to do its job. But it is precisely at this point where the market Socialists encounter their biggest problem. The information that the central board requires is disbursed among hundreds of thousands of people. How then is this necessary information supposed to be transmitted to the central planners? Exactly how do they discover when there is a surplus or a shortage? Moving all of this information to one central point is difficult, expensive, and in many cases impossible.

David Ramsay Steele draws attention to another difficulty with Lange's so-called market socialism:

> In fact, Lange's system is neither a market nor central planning. It is best classified as a *simulated market.* . . . Everyone would pretend that there was a market and act as if there

were a market, but there would be no market in actuality. Such a proposal might have immediately prompted the thought that if the pretense were to achieve the same results as the real thing, it might have to become the real thing.[15]

Henry Hazlitt unmasks the charade that results from Lange's use of simulated markets.

If I am a government commissar selling something I don't really own, and you are another government commissar buying it with money that isn't really yours, then neither of us really cares what the price is. When, as in a Socialist or Communist country, the heads of mines and factories, or stores and collective farms, are mere salaried bureaucrats, and sell their finished products to still other bureaucrats, the so-called prices at which they buy and sell are mere bookkeeping fictions. Such bureaucrats are merely playing an artificial game called "free market." They cannot make a free-market system merely by imitating prices while ignoring private property.[16]

Or as Tom Bethell states the same point: "Prices depend for their formation on the real possibility of personal profit or loss. Try to imagine a serious game of poker played with Monopoly money. All psychological incentive is removed by the knowledge that at the end of the evening, no one playing is really going to lose or gain something."[17]

To summarize this section, socialism has an Achilles heel that was discovered by Ludwig von Mises in 1920. According to Mises, rational economic activity is impossible without certain kinds of information. But that information is supplied only by attending to changing prices in a free market system. Lange's attempt to circumvent Mises's challenge, often cited by later Socialists as the definitive reply to Mises, is more than a failure. It raises enough problems of its own to qualify, in Friedrich Hayek's language, as both a "farce" and a "comic fiction."[18] Socialism is not simply a system with difficult obstacles to overcome; it is a system with obstacles that are impossible to overcome.[19]

Some Additional Problems

Socialism is inferior to capitalism in other ways. Brian Griffiths points to one reason for capitalism's greater efficiency:

The reason that private ownership encourages efficiency and growth is that the rewards from hard work, innovation, risk-taking, restructuring and investment accrue to those who make the decisions. . . . It is impossible to create similar incentives in nationalized industries to those which exist for businessmen with equity interest in small firms.[20]

In other words, a market system provides important incentives that are missing from socialism. Under socialism, Griffiths continues,

Rewards are not related to effort and commercial risk-taking, but to party membership, bureaucratic status, political fiat and corruption. As a consequence, the legitimate commercial entrepreneurial spirit is killed; for perfectly understandable reasons, people devote their resources to hacking a way through the political and bureaucratic jungle of their economies.[21]

In an earlier chapter, I drew attention to the intrinsic link between economic freedom and political freedom. After examining the course of socialism in the Soviet Union and its satellites, in China, Cuba, and now Nicaragua, and in the so-called Third World, sociologist Peter Berger is led to conclude: "Even in the early 1970s it should not have been news that socialism is not good for economic growth and also that it shows a disturbing propensity toward totalitarianism (with its customary accompaniment of terror)."[22] Claims by the leaders of such nations that their adoption of socialism reflects their commitment to justice and equality is not simply empty rhetoric; it is hypocritical deceit. "Put simply," Berger declares, "Socialist equality is shared poverty by serfs, coupled with the monopolization of both privilege and power by a small (increasingly hereditary) aristocracy." While the world has largely accepted the inevitability of this elitist aristocracy in the Soviet Union, the same phenomenon is showing up in every Socialist state. "It seems to be the intrinsic genius of socialism to produce these modern facsimiles of feudalism." Gradually people are beginning to notice the absence of one single example of a Socialist state that has succeeded economically and has not become totalitarian. "We know, or should know, that socialism is a mirage that leads nowhere except to economic stagnation, collective poverty, and various degrees of tyranny."[23]

What must we think of the church intellectuals who tell us that socialism is the only economic system compatible with Christianity? What does such a claim tell us about the economic understanding of people who make such claims? What does it tell us about their moral sensitivity, to say nothing about their sensitivity to the millions who have suffered and the millions more who will continue to suffer from such systems? In Chapter One, I noted Herbert Schlossberg's claim that such Christians are engaged literally in a war against economics. Schlossberg was too kind; they are also involved in a war against humanity.

9

Christianity and Marxism

Many people are only now becoming aware of the strong Marxist presence within American Christendom. In one sense, there is nothing new about this. During the heyday of Josef Stalin, many liberal Christians in America acted as though the kingdom of God was being established in the Soviet Union. Even while Stalin's secret police were murdering millions of people within the Soviet Union, alleged spokesmen for Christ were praising his efforts to bring about a just social order.[1]

Much more recently, of course, a Marxist influence began to appear in the thinking of those thinkers who call themselves liberation theologians. But many American Christians have yet to grasp the growing Marxist influence within pockets of American Christendom that have been theologically conservative. I am referring especially to those American Protestants known as evangelicals. Many readers view politically radical evangelical journals like *Sojourners* as anti-American and anticapitalist. They also find a distinctively pro-Soviet and pro-Marxist stance in such magazines. The magazines exhibit a double standard. Their standards for the United States are strict and severe. Their standards for everyone else, including the Soviets, Cubans, Vietnamese, and Sandinistas, are quite lenient. Over the past several years, *Sojourners* has appeared to blame the United States for most of the major evils in the world including the murder of millions of Cambodians by Communists, the Soviet invasion of Afghanistan, and the Soviets' shooting down of a Korean airliner. In his book *Target America*, author James Tyson discusses the changing content of Communist propaganda on various issues and events of the past few years and documents the extent to which the U.S. media has mirrored that propaganda.[2] Many people who are familiar with the positions of the evangelical radicals will be surprised to find how closely the views of these radicals follow the official party line.

Varieties of Marxist thought have become deeply entrenched on several major evangelical campuses. Some evangelical sociologists criticize their society from a Marxist perspective, while some evangelical economics departments present socialism as the only option for thinking Christians. This pro-Marxist bias is also evident in other departments in these colleges and seminaries.

One book that illustrates the growing Christian fascination with Marxism is José Míguez-Bonino's *Christians and Marxists*.[3] Not only was this book published by an evangelical publishing company, but its contents were first delivered to an evangelical audience in London, England under the auspices of John Stott, noted British evangelical and former rector of All Souls Church in London. In his book, Bonino discusses Communists like Lenin, Mao Tse-tung, and Fidel Castro in the same reverent tones he uses to describe Christian saints and martyrs. Bonino reports how he is moved by "their deep compassion for human suffering and their fierce hatred of oppression and exploitation."[4] Of course, such an observation would have surprised the millions of people who were oppressed, exploited, and murdered at the command of these men.

In one of his more surprising claims, Bonino writes: "Indeed, when we observe the process of building a Socialist society in China . . . we see a significant, even preponderant, importance given to the creation of a new man, a solidary human being who places the common good before his own individual interest."[5] The reader must keep in mind that the China Bonino thinks so highly of is the China of Mao Tse-tung, a China that the Chinese themselves have since denounced. Sociologist Peter Berger provides a healthy antidote to Bonino's ethical short-sightedness when he writes: "*Even if* it were true that Maoism had vanquished hunger among China's poor, this achievement could not morally justify the horrors inflicted by the regime—horrors that entailed the killing of millions of human beings and the imposition of a merciless totalitarian rule on the survivors."[6]

But Bonino is not through praising Marxist dictatorships. He writes:

> The political and economic quality and the human value of Socialist revolutions has consistently increased as we move from the USSR to China and Cuba. The social cost has been reduced, the measure of compulsion and repression, particu-

larly in the last case, has been minimised, the welfare of the people has been given at least as much priority as economic development, the disruptive consequences of a blind drive towards industrialization have been avoided. The Chinese and Cuban revolutions have created a sense of participation and achievement on the part of the people and have stimulated a feeling of dignity and moral determination.[7]

Such words would not be surprising if uttered by paid propagandists of Mao or Castro. But they come from a self-professed evangelical who was speaking to other evangelicals—who believed him! One must wonder why Bonino was so silent about the millions who died under Communist rule in China and in the U.S.S.R. Why did he fail to mention the persecution of the Christian church (and other religions) by these dictators he finds so admirable?

Another sample of contemporary evangelical attitudes towards Marxism is Andrew Kirk's book, *The Good News of the Kingdom Coming*.[8] Kirk's position is another troubling example of the unbalanced sympathy for Marxism that exists in certain evangelical circles. Kirk is associate director of the London Institute for Contemporary Christianity, an off-shoot of the group that gave Bonino the platform for the lectures on which his book is based. Kirk's institute has strong ties both to John Stott and to All Souls Church, an important and influential center of evangelical training in London.

Kirk presents Marxism "as a strong defender of the dignity of human beings." Under Marxism, Kirk thinks, "Every person has a right to develop himself freely and enjoy the fruit of his work." Many readers will wonder where this kind of Marxism is on public display. Marxism, Kirk continues, has "a deep compassion for people. Unlike present political systems—big business, even the Church—it [Marxism] does not seem to have any particular vested interests to defend." Moreover, Kirk tells his Christian readers, Marxism "contains a strong element of hope. . . . Marxism's crowning assertion is that Communist society is the only place where man can find his own real humanity by discovering that of his neighbor."[9]

Something seems desperately wrong here. Some may rush to the defense of evangelicals like Bonino and Kirk by claiming that such quotations misrepresent their views. After all, it might be claimed, there are different kinds of Marxism and perhaps Christian Marxists only mean to speak kindly of nonrepressive forms of

Marxism, forms that may in fact express concerns that theologically conservative Christians can share. While this interesting suggestion may get Kirk off the hook to some extent, it hardly rescues Bonino from his fawning over ruthless Communist dictators. Since it is true that different versions of Marxism exist and, in fact, compete with each other, there is value in distinguishing these varieties of Marxist thought in order to see if it throws any light on the contemporary Christian fascination with Marxism.

The Three Faces of Marxism

When someone identifies himself as a Marxist these days, he may mean any one of a number of things. The basic varieties of Marxism have become so incompatible that advocates of the different versions fight among themselves as to which is the true Marxism. In the order in which they appeared, the three dominant versions of Marxism are: (1) Social-Democratic Marxism, (2) Marxism-Leninism, and (3) Humanistic Marxism.

Social-Democratic Marxism

Because the Social-Democratic interpretation of Marx was the first view to develop, it is sometimes called the classical view of Marx. The major proponents of this interpretation include Friedrich Engels (following Marx's death), the German Karl Kautsky (1854-1938), the Russian George Plekhanov (1856-1918), and the American Daniel De Leon (1852-1914). As its name implies, advocates of the Social-Democratic version of Marxism believe that Marxism is compatible with democracy and political freedom. They believe that the "revolution" Marx and Engels wrote about could be realized through peaceful means—namely, through democratic elections. What is especially important to note with regard to this interpretation is that the "movement towards socialism is a movement towards democracy."[10] As philosopher Sidney Hook explains this version of Marxism: "Political democracy must be used to achieve a complete democracy by extending democratic values and principles into economic and social life. Where democracy does not exist the Socialist movement must introduce it. . . . Where democracy already exists, the working class can achieve power by peaceful parliamentary means."[11]

Marxism-Leninism

The second major interpretation of Marx to develop was the brainchild of Lenin. A major deviation from the Social-Democratic view which was held by the Russian Socialists known as Mensheviks, Lenin's view became the official position of his party, the Bolsheviks. Lenin used his theory to justify the Communist Revolution of October 1917 that overthrew the democratic Mensheviks. There is no place for democracy in Lenin's version of Marxism. For Lenin, the Communist Party knows what is best for the workers, whether they agree with the conclusions of the Party or not. Marxism-Leninism is totalitarian by definition.

Humanistic Marxism

This last version of Marxism will be examined in much greater detail since it is the view most often held by Christian Marxists. The humanistic interpretation of Marx differs from the other forms of Marxism in terms of the importance it attaches to a number of Marx's early unpublished manuscripts.[12] Several things should be noted about these early writings. (1) Marx made no effort to publish them. Since he never displayed much reluctance about publishing many apparently less important writings, some have concluded that Marx did not regard these early scribblings as worthy of publication. (2) Marx wrote these early manuscripts four years before he and Engels published the *Manifesto of the Communist Party* in 1848. In the opinion of many Marxist scholars, Marx wrote these early manuscripts before he himself even became a Marxist! (3) The early manuscripts were not published (in German) until 1932. Publication of English translations would come years later.

The most important doctrine contained in the early manuscripts is Marx's teaching about alienation. The doctrine of alienation is the trademark of the Humanistic version of Marx. It is also a centerpiece of the system that many so-called Christian Marxists have developed as a result of their reconstruction of Marx's thought.

Marx is thought to have identified four different but related forms of worker alienation. First, capitalism causes the worker to become alienated from that which he produces. Because the capitalist system creates false needs and provides false satisfactions, workers are manipulated into wanting things and then seduced into buying them. The worker becomes dominated and controlled by the things he is forced to make.[13]

Second, the worker is estranged from the labor process itself. Of course, it takes little effort to note how many men and women hate their jobs. This alienation is not restricted to those who must labor at menial, repetitive, boring, dirty, or degrading tasks. Even professional golfers and philosophers have been known to hold an occasional loathing for their jobs. It is easy to see, therefore, how people who become aware of this second form of alienation can believe that something fairly profound can be mined in Marx's early writings.

Third, the worker under capitalism becomes alienated from other men and women, a fact easily observed by noting the widespread competitiveness, hostility, and animosity among human beings. Proponents of the Humanistic version of Marx want us to believe that all manifestations of these traits in the modern world can be blamed on capitalism.

In the fourth kind of alienation, the worker not only becomes alienated from what he produces, from his work, and from other workers—he finally becomes alienated from himself.

Since human alienation in any of these four forms is serious business, Christians should be concerned about it. What is much less clear is the extent to which Marx should be given credit for discovering the problem or for recommending a solution. For one thing, the theory of alienation is neither unique to Marx nor original with him. It can be found in a number of thinkers before Marx, and it was developed independently by several writers after Marx. Moreover, human alienation is hardly unique to capitalist societies. It is difficult to believe that a garbage collector in Moscow is any happier with his job than a garbage collector in Boston, Cleveland, or Beverly Hills. Alienation and dehumanization are serious problems, but it simply is not true that they result exclusively from conditions existing in capitalist societies and vanish once those societies have become Socialist.[14] Human alienation is no more an exclusive effect of capitalism than baldness.

Strangely missing from most Christian discussions of alienation is a recognition of a fifth variety of human alienation, a type ignored by Marx. Scripture teaches that every member of the human race is *alienated from God*. In fact, the Bible clearly implies that all of the forms of human alienation that concern contemporary Marxists result in some way from man's more fundamental alienation from his Creator. Recognition of this Biblical truth could introduce an important new dimension into discussions of alienation.

The development of the Humanistic version of Marx obviously had to await the publication of Marx's early writings, an event that took place in 1932. In the setting of the early 1930s, the early manuscripts revealed a Marx quite different from the official Marx of Stalinism. For people weary of or frightened by the ruthless tyranny of Stalin, it was possible to appeal to the authority of Marx in defense of individual human dignity and freedom.

The appearance of anti-Stalinist attitudes and the gradual rejection of Marxism-Leninism among a number of Communists in Eastern Europe after World War II added to the appeal of the Humanistic interpretation. As Sidney Hook explains,

> Aware that they could only get a hearing or exercise influence if they spoke in the name of Marxism, [such non-Leninists] seized upon several formulations in these early manuscripts of Marx in which he glorifies the nature of man as a freedom-loving creature—a nature that has been distorted, cramped, and twisted by the capitalist mode of production. They were then able to protest in the name of Marxist humanism against the stifling dictatorship of Stalin and his lieutenants in their own countries, and even against the apotheosis of Lenin.[15]

In other words, the Stalinist contempt for human rights gave added incentive to some Marxists to find a new Marx whose name and authority could be used to bring about a restoration of humanitarian concerns in the brutal conditions that prevailed under Stalin.

A number of people in Western Europe took these appeals to the early Marx seriously and began to claim that the Humanistic Marx was the true Marx all along. In their view, "the conception of man and alienation in the early writings of Marx is the main theme of Marx's view of socialism, the aim of which is 'the spiritual emancipation of man.' "[16] So what began in Eastern Europe as an attempt to find an acceptable basis for humanism within a Marxist context became in the West a new way of glorifying Marx for those seeking his authority for their own causes. Daniel Bell finds it remarkable that "a whole school of neo-Marxists . . . has gone back to the early doctrines of alienation in order to find the basis for a new, humanistic interpretation of Marx."[17]

Outside of the Soviet Union, its satellites, and such former allies as China, the most popular version of Marxism today is the Humanistic interpretation. On this view, Sidney Hook explains,

> Marxism is not primarily a system of sociology or economics, but a philosophy of human liberation. It seeks to overcome human alienation, to emancipate man from repressive social

institutions, especially economic institutions that frustrate his true nature, and to bring him into harmony with himself, his fellow men, and the world around him so that he can both overcome his estrangements and express his true essence through creative freedom.[18]

In this way, a Marxist message is propagated that is an alternative to the totalitarian terror of Bolshevik Leninism.

The Christian Use of Marxism

Once the Humanistic version of Marx gained an intellectual toe-hold, some advocates of the view began to explore the possibility of a rapprochement between this new variety of Marxism and Christianity. Humanistic Marxism became the basis for a growing dialogue between Marxists and Christians. As things became even more confused, many Christians already committed to socialism jumped on the bandwagon and carried things even further. Some became so enthusiastic that they thought they saw signs that the "true Marx" was even a crypto-Christian. The Marxist-Leninist interpretation was discarded by many of these people as a perversion of the true Marx. The even older Social-Democratic view got lost in the shuffle.

By now, Christian thinkers representing a wide range of theological commitments have accepted uncritically the new interpretation of Marx. No doubt, the wish to find a new Marx whose authority could be used to advance their own concerns has played a major role in all this. Until recently, the Marx that appears in the thought of most liberation theologians has been the Humanist Marx. Many liberation theologians have claimed that the Marxism-Leninism represented by Soviet-style communism is a heresy, unsupported by a careful study of the full corpus of Marx's writings.

A good example of the Marxist revisionism practiced by some liberation theologians is Jose Miranda's book *Marx Against the Marxists*.[19] Miranda offers scores of passages from Marx's writings which he thinks contradict the official Marxist-Leninist reading of Marx. Miranda believes that the Marxist orthodxy that prevails in Soviet-controlled nations is a falsification of Marx's true message. Miranda's Marx is neither a materialist nor an atheistic economic determinist. He is instead a man with high moral ideals whose commitment to humanitarian goals was so sincere and so uncompromising that Miranda feels no hesitation in regarding Marx as a

Christian. In fact, Miranda's book carries the bizarre subtitle, "The Christian Humanism of Karl Marx." Miranda's strained efforts to show that Marx was really a Christian is an indication of the extent to which liberation theologians will go in their attempt to make Marxist revolutionary activity respectable in the eyes of the Christian church.

Challenges to the Humanistic Interpretation of Marx

The Humanistic interpretation of Marx is rejected by advocates of the classical Social-Democratic version of Marx. Until recently, Marxist-Leninists opposed Humanistic Marxism even more forcefully than advocates of classical Marxism. When the Humanistic interpretation first appeared in the early 1930s, old-style Leninists and Stalinists were taken off guard. Early proponents of the view who had the misfortune of being where Stalin could get his hands on them were either forced to recant publicly or they simply disappeared. Marxist-Leninists were especially uncomfortable with attempts to integrate Marx into a new Christian struggle for what was called "social justice." But as we will see, the Marxist-Leninist attitude has changed as they have found ways to use the Christian view of the Humanistic Marx for their own purposes.

A central issue in the dispute among the three interpretations of Marx is the place Marx's early writings and the views expressed in them should have in any "correct" understanding of Marx's system. Advocates of Humanistic Marxism regard the early manuscripts and the doctrine of alienation as the heart and soul of true Marxism. Advocates of the Social-Democratic and Marxist-Leninist views have tended to dismiss both the early writings and their teaching about alienation. In the official Marxist-Leninist interpretation, Marxism must be identified with Marx's writings *after* 1847. The early writings should either be interpreted in light of the later writings or else discarded.

According to the Humanist interpretation, the later writings should be interpreted in light of the early writings. Representatives of the Humanist Marx attempt to find the humanistic concerns of the early Marx in his later writings. Erich Fromm expresses this view: "[I]t is impossible to understand Marx's concept of socialism and his criticism of capitalism as developed except on the basis of his concept of man which he developed in his early writings."[20] According to the Humanistic view, Marx's position remained basically the same from his early 1844 writings through his later publications. The key that unlocks the meaning of the entire system lies hidden in the early unpublished manuscripts. In the view of the Humanistic Marxists, the teachings for which Marx became most famous (the labor theory of value, dialectical materialism, the class struggle) are largely ignored. The new Marx is a philosopher whose primary concern is to draw attention to human estrangement caused by an oppressive society.

While some interpret Marx's later writings on the basis of his early unpublished works and some think the later writings provide Marx's most important message, others believe that there are two different systems that are quite incompatible. The humanism of the early Marx is not germane to the concerns of the later Marx, they say.

The rest of this section will survey some of the challenges that have been raised to the Humanistic interpretation of Marx. Given the widespread and largely uncritical acceptance of the Humanistic version, it may be helpful to recognize that a case against that interpretation has been made.

Sidney Hook observes: "The most fantastic interpretations have been placed on these [early] groping efforts of Marx towards intellectual maturity."[21] One of the more jarring consequences of the Humanistic interpretation is the implication that no one really understood Marx until 1932, the year his early manuscripts were first published. Even though Marx devoted twenty years of hard labor to his book *Capital* and even though it was a work for which he sacrificed almost everything in his life including his health and family, the Humanistic version of Marx turns *Capital,* in the words of Robert Tucker, into "an intellectual museum piece . . . whereas the sixteen-page manuscript of 1844 on the future of aesthetics, which he probably wrote in a day and never even saw fit to publish, contains much that is still significant."[22]

Sidney Hook is not alone in observing that there are too many differences in focus and emphasis between the early and later Marx:

> The old Marx is interested in the mechanics or organics of capitalism as an economic system, in politics as the theatre of clashing economic interests, and in the theory and practice of revolution. He is so impatient of the rhetoric of piety and morality that he sometimes gives the impression of a thinker who had no moral theory whatsoever, and whose doctrines logically do not allow for considered moral judgment. The

new Marx, barely out of his intellectual swaddling clothes, sounds like *nothing but* a moralist. . . .[23]

Critics of Humanistic Marxism go on to argue that the notion of alienation practically disappears from Marx's later writings. Attempts to locate something like the early doctrine of alienation in passages where the mature Marx mentions psychological phenomena are persuasive only to those already committed to the Humanistic interpretation. Such passages as *Capital*, I, 1, 4 are sometimes cited by advocates of Humanistic Marxism to show that even though the later Marx did not use the same language one finds in the unpublished writings (such as the term "alienation"), he continued to refer to the concept in different language. But such claims depend on a superficial reading of Marx that ignores important differences in the different stages of his thought. There are obvious inconsistencies between the early doctrine of alienation and the later passages that are supposed to express the same view in different language. In the early Marx, alienation was the *cause* and private property was the *effect*. But in the later Marx, the psychological phenomena that are interpreted as reappearances of the doctrine of alienation in new language are explicitly treated as *effects* of private ownership of the means of production. In other words, the later Marx did a complete 180-degree turn and treated private property as the cause of what is supposed to be the equivalent of alienation in the mature writings. The two positions are inconsistent.

But there is an even more serious difficulty with the Humanistic interpretation. Marx actually repudiated the notion of alienation. Daniel Bell regards efforts to discover a radical analysis of society in the early Marx as an attempt to create a new myth that will support attempts to use Marx's name and authority in support of new causes. While Bell agrees that these views may be found in the early Marx, they cannot be found in the *historical* Marx. "The historical Marx had, in effect, repudiated the idea of alienation."[24] Even in *The Communist Manifesto*, Sidney Hook argues, "Marx explicitly disavows the theory of alienation as 'metaphysical rubbish,' as a linguistic Germanic mystification of social phenomena described by French social critics."[25]

If scholars like Sidney Hook and Daniel Bell are correct, and the mature Marx really did abandon his earlier immature opinions on alienation, then the entire position known as Christian Marxism rests on a questionable interpretation of questionable writings that are the basis of a questionable theory that, in all likelihood, Marx himself repudiated. The Christian use of Marxism, it appears, is a system built upon quicksand.

The Marxist Use Of Christianity

As noted earlier, most so-called Christian Marxists have rejected Marxism-Leninism and grounded their synthesis of Marxism and Christianity on the Humanistic interpretation of Marx. However, a major change is in the winds. In some places, Christian Marxism is now being used to push nations in the direction of Marxist-Leninist totalitarianism. Liberation theology is being taken over by Marxist-Leninists and being used to support Soviet-bloc political ends.

For decades, Marxist-Leninists opposed the Humanistic version of Marx and its evolving dialogue with sympathetic Christians. With the advent of liberation theology, however, and its growing influence in the so-called Third World, Fidel Castro has taught his Soviet counterparts how they can use Christian Marxism.[26]

Peasants and workers with strong religious convictions have often been the strongest opponents of communism. This has certainly been the case in two of the most heavily Roman Catholic nations in the world, Poland and Nicaragua. But thanks largely to Castro, hard-line Marxist-Leninists now see a way of defusing religious opposition to communism in countries like Nicaragua. The initial resistance that many workers and peasants have to communism, an opposition grounded on their religious convictions, can be weakened by teaching them that Marx's values were really Christian values. What can make the situation even more promising is if workers and peasants are taught the Christian version of Marx by their own priests or pastors. After much of the initial opposition to Marxism is worn down, efforts can be made to win the new Marxist converts to the more radical views of Marxism-Leninism. In this way, liberation theology can be used as an anesthetic while the patient's Christianity is removed. Liberation theology becomes the Trojan Horse by which Marxism-Leninism gains access to nations that would otherwise have rejected it on religious grounds.

According to many close observers of the scene, including former supporters of the Sandinistas, this is precisely what is happening in Nicaragua. As one former ally of the Sandinistas puts it:

> Of course, this awareness of the importance of Christians for
> the revolution did not involve a change in Marxist philosophy,

nor did it signal an openness or new tolerance toward religion. It simply meant a new consciousness of the need to use Christians and, as a corollary, a tactical decision not to present an openly antireligious face. . . . [R]evolutionary Christians [in Nicaragua] have encouraged other Christians to support the Sandinista government. They have done this by reinterpreting Christian beliefs in ways that lead to an endorsement of the main Marxist-Leninist tenets regarding man and society. They have advanced the view that true Christianity is, in fact, Marxism.[27]

Liberation theology therefore aids Marxism-Leninism by helping to remove or weaken religious opposition that is usually the biggest obstacle to a Communist takeover in traditionally Catholic nations like Nicaragua. Of course, once Marxist-Leninist totalitarianism does gain control over a nation, all pretense of support for religious freedom and tolerance soon ends.

As observers of the Nicaragua situation point out, the cooperation between Christians and Marxists in that country has resulted in many Christians abandoning their religious faith and becoming converts to atheistic Marxism.[28] It is interesting to note that in his book *Christians and Marxists,* self-styled evangelical José Míguez-Bonino shows little interest in inviting Marxists to become Christians. One searches in vain through his "dialogues" with Marxists for any declaration of the gospel.

According to Humberto Belli, revolutionary Christians in Nicaragua

> have lent credibility to the Sandinista contention that they [the Sandinistas] are not Marxist-Leninists but a novel regime where Christianity and revolution can walk together. They have served as a visible front to attack the Christian churches and to undermine their authority and teachings, thus minimizing for the Sandinistas the potentially high cost of a more direct confrontation . . . [and they have hidden] from the view of Christians abroad, the fact that there is religious persecution in Nicaragua today.[29]

While liberation theology in Nicaragua originally inspired Christians to oppose a right-wing dictatorship, it has become a tool that is now being used to justify support for a left-wing dictatorship. In Nicaragua, at least, the Marxist-Leninists have found a Trojan Horse that let them inside the gates of power.

Conclusion

This chapter has examined three interpretations of Marx. Attempts to interpret Marxism as a force that could bring about Socialistic democracies that would respect human rights were countered by the totalitarian brand of Marxism developed by Lenin and adapted by Stalin and Mao Tse-tung. A Humanistic version of Marx was welcomed as an antidote to Soviet-style, Stalinist repression. But the Humanistic interpretation of Marx was clearly in trouble as an explanation of the mature Marx's true convictions and intentions.

Humanistic Marxism developed first outside the bounds of organized religion as the basis of a new critique of so-called capitalist societies and as an alternative to Soviet-style Marxism-Leninism. For more than thirty years, there has been an evolving form of Christian Marxism which, until recently, sided with the Humanistic version of Marx. But as recent events have shown, Marxists-Leninists who have no intention of changing their totalitarianism have found ways of using this Christian Marxism for their decidedly non-Christian and nonhumanitarian ends. To this point, it appears, few Christian Marxists seem to comprehend or care about the extent to which they are being used.

10

True and False Liberation Theology

Most of the economic errors that are the concern of this book come to a head in the writings of representatives of the movement known as liberation theology. In its most narrow sense, liberation theology is a movement among Latin American Catholics and Protestants that seeks radical changes in the political and economic institutions of that region along Marxist lines. There also exist other versions of liberation theology which relate to feminist (the liberation of women) and racial concerns (black liberation). Various individuals seeking a Christian use of Marx or a Marxist use of Christianity in Asia and Africa have recently begun to use the liberation banner for their cause. It is interesting to note that Christians in Eastern Europe (for example, Polish Catholics) who seek freedom from Communist repression never use the phrase *liberation theology* to describe their movements.

Liberation theologians do more than promote a synthesis of Marxism and Christianity; they often attempt to ground the radical political and economic changes they seek on their interpretation of the Bible. They insist that the Biblical ethic condemns individual actions and social structures that oppress and harm people and that favor some at the expense of others. One does not have to be sympathetic to liberation theology to agree with this last claim.

The fundamental objective of most liberation theologians is Christian action on behalf of poor and oppressed peoples. Only recently—as discussed in the last chapter—has it become apparent that in some situations, liberation theology is being used as a tool by committed Marxists-Leninists to justify the establishment of left-wing dictatorships.

Liberation theology comes in a variety of packages. But regardless of how extreme its commitment to Marxism may be (or which variety of Marxism it promotes), and regardless of how extreme its commitment to the use of violence may be in the pursuit of its revolutionary ends, liberation theology seeks to replace the economic and political structures alleged to cause poverty and oppression. Ignoring for the moment the question of how much violence (if any) Christians should be prepared to use in support of allegedly just causes, liberation theologians insist that the church should be at the very center of the revolutionary activity they promote.

For liberation thinkers, the "radical political transformation of the present order is a central component of the living out of Christian faith."[1] As Humberto Belli, a former Marxist explains,

> Revolutionary political action becomes, in theologies of liberation, the way to make Christian love for the poor truly effective. Failure to engage in the revolutionary struggle would be failure to respond to the poor's yearning for liberation and would place Christians in the camp of the oppressors. Since it is in the poor that Jesus dwells in a hidden but real way, for Christians not to commit themselves to the revolution would be to turn their backs on Christ.[2]

Commitment to the revolution, then, is an essential part of what it means to be a Christian—according to liberation theologians.

It is important to understand that Christian opponents of liberation theology do not dispute the Christian's obligation to care for the poor and to seek means to alleviate poverty and oppression. What is in dispute is the agenda by which liberationists insist this duty must be fulfilled. In the case of the most extreme representatives of this ideology, the so-called "revolutionary Christians" in Nicaragua, support for the Sandinista revolution is not simply permissible; it is a *duty*. "There is *no other way* to be a Christian in Nicaragua than by supporting the Sandinista revolution."[3]

The professed liberationist goal of helping the poor and oppressed is a legitimate Christian objective. But a growing number of people are beginning to wonder about other elements of liberation thought. Tough questions are being asked about the commitment of liberation thinkers to essential Christian beliefs, about their understanding of economics, about their commitment to democracy, and about their opposition to violence and totalitarianism. Since the movement calls itself liberation *theology*, it is proper to inquire into the soundness of its theology. Since it calls itself *liberation* theology, it is legitimate to inquire about the soundness of its economics and political theory. Is its theology sound? Is its economics sound in the sense that it really does pursue means that will deliver people from poverty? And is its understanding of political power sound in the sense that it will deliver people from tyranny?

An important distinction must be drawn between two kinds of liberation theology: true liberation theology and false liberation theology. Traditional Catholics and Protestants have five important criteria at their disposal that they can use to test the legitimacy of liberation systems. The first three tests are theological: is the liberation theology being proposed theologically sound? The last two tests relate to its alleged emphasis on liberty: will it really deliver people from poverty (economic liberation) and will it deliver people from tyranny (political liberation)?

Three Theological Tests

Test Number One

A true liberation theology will be faithful to the essential theological concerns of the historic Christian faith. Christianity has always had those within its fold who wished to use Christian language, symbols, and institutions while seeking to change the very nature of the faith. Unfortunately, many so-called liberation theologians fit this description.[4] Any liberation theology that omits or distorts essential elements of the Christian gospel is a false liberation theology. As the Apostle Paul once declared, "If we or an angel from heaven should preach a gospel other than the one we preached to you, let him be eternally condemned" (Gal. 1:8, NIV).

Since many liberation thinkers are so one-sided in their commitment to a political agenda, it is often difficult to say what their view of the Christian gospel is. However, a careful study of their writings reveals a defective understanding of the gospel in many representatives of the movement. To a great extent, their bad theology is a consequence of the way many of them handle the Biblical revelation. Liberation thinkers allow their understanding of the Bible to be determined by the way they see society. They begin with the historical situation and interpret the Bible in the light of that situation. This fact, coupled with the clear suggestion that many of them have doubts about the normative character of the Biblical revelation, may explain the ease with which some of them are brought to the brink of heresy. Some liberationists have blurred the distinction between the church (the company of redeemed believers) and the world. Some have suggested that the poor are saved simply because they are poor. Others imply that God cares more about the poor than He cares about the rich.

It is heresy to state that God's love for people varies in proportion to their wealth. It is absurd to suggest that all the poor are good and all the rich are evil. Jose Miranda is wrong when he dogmatizes that knowing God means nothing more than seeking justice for the poor.[5] Much liberation theology alters the meaning of such central Christian notions as salvation and redemption. As Michael Novak warns, liberation theology is conceptually inconsistent with Christian theology. It is, Novak states, "a kind of gnostic heresy."[6] To the degree, then, that any liberation theology omits or distorts essential elements of the historic Christian faith, it is a false liberation theology.

Test Number Two

A true liberation theology will proclaim the truth of the gospel. Christians are not only obliged to believe the truth that God has revealed in Christ and in His Word; they are commanded to share that truth through evangelism. "Go ye into all the world and preach the gospel," they are told.

What kind of evangelism do liberation theologians practice? What gospel do they preach? To what message and cause do they seek converts? While it is important to feed the hungry, this duty does not replace the church's obligation to feed the spiritually hungry with the bread of life. According to people with firsthand knowledge of the situation, the major emphasis of revolutionary Christians in Nicaragua is not conversion to Christ but conversion to the cause of the Sandinista revolution. Consequently, one of these observers writes, "[I]t is not accidental that while in Nicaragua there is no available evidence of the conversion of Marxists to Christ due to the preachings of the revolutionary Christians, there is ample evidence of the opposite phenomenon. Christians have become atheists through a process that began with their conversion to liberation theology."[7] Attempts to find samples of liberation writings that attempt to evangelize unbelieving Marxists and non-Marxists to the Christian faith always come up empty-handed. So-called Christian Marxists, it seems, are more interested in converting Christians to Marxism than they are in converting Marxists to Christianity. This failure with regard to Test Number Two brands all such efforts as false liberation theology.

Test Number Three

A true liberation theology will give priority to its gospel message. Jesus commanded His followers to seek the kingdom of God *first* (Matt. 6:33). Even if a self-professed liberation theologian accepts the truth of the New Testament gospel and fulfills his obligation to share that message through evangelism, his failure to give that gospel priority over his secular interests and ideology will mark his system as a false liberation theology. The gospel message must not be subordinated to a political agenda. But one of the more serious problems with liberation theology is its tendency to produce a reorientation (a conversion, if you will) within its followers where the historically essential concerns of the Christian faith are replaced by or subordinated to a revolutionary political agenda.

Christians need to learn that there may be liberation theologies

> which are not liberating at all. The case of Nicaragua shows that what has been advanced by many revolutionary Christians as the most advanced form of liberation theology has been nothing else than a justification for Marxism-Leninism clothed in a religious garment—a revolution that is not for Christ, nor even for the poor but for communism . . . in the name of Christ.[8]

As Humberto Belli goes on to explain, the revolutionary Christians in Nicaragua "have been instruments of a subtle ideological campaign to substitute for the Christian gospel the Marxist creed, and for the unconditional loyalty due to Christianity the loyalty to a political organization, totally secular and even atheistic."[9]

Since so many liberation thinkers are Roman Catholic, it is helpful to remember that the message of Pope John Paul II to the Third General Conference of Latin American Bishops held in Puebla, Mexico (1979) contained a clear warning to liberation theologians. The pope spoke of people who

> depict Jesus as a political activist, as a fighter against Roman domination and the authorities, and even as someone involved in the class struggle. This conception of Christ as a political figure, a revolutionary, as the subversive from Nazareth, does not tally with the Church's [teaching]. . . . Jesus unequivocally rejects recourse to violence. He opens his message of conversion to all. . . . His mission . . . has to do with complete and

integral salvation through a love that brings transformation, peace, pardon, and reconciliation.[10]

Clearly, the pope agrees that the gospel must not be made subordinate to secular ends.

An Economic Test

Liberation theologians have a lot to say about poverty. In fact, that from which their theology seeks to liberate people is poverty. Unfortunately, liberation theology cannot offer a proper remedy for poverty because it fails to understand the disease. Liberationists accept the myth that poverty results exclusively from one person or nation exploiting another. Michael Novak explains:

> What most hinders liberation theology is a Latin tradition, many generations old, of blaming outsiders, while exempting oneself from responsibility for one's own future. The current form of this tradition is to aspire to the benefits of capitalism while refusing to recognize the moral validity of its requisite habits and institutions: of invention, forethought, saving, investing, punctuality, workmanship, and the like.[11]

What liberation thinkers seem to do best is blame others for the problems of Latin America. But as Michael Novak has shown, their claims that Latin American nations are dependent upon the United States are greatly exaggerated.[12] First-World nations are not responsible for Third-World poverty which antedates capitalism and which, in fact, used to be far worse than it presently is. As Novak has shown, Latin America has for decades had the resources required to begin easing its poverty and destitution.[13]

Liberationists attack capitalism on the ground that it exploits the poor. On their view, the only way some people can become rich is by exploiting others. In other words, the attack against capitalism depends on the assumption that voluntary economic exchanges are a zero-sum game. And so liberation thinkers conclude, the reason some nations are poor is because they have been exploited by richer and more powerful nations. While it is true that some nations have exploited others (witness the recent history of the Soviet Union), this fact does not support the conclusion that colonialism or dependence is either a necessary or sufficient condition of Third-World poverty. In fact, some of the most developed areas in the world today (Malaysia, Singapore, and Hong Kong) are former colonies (Hong Kong is still a British colony), while some of the poorest nations in the world (such as Afghanistan and Ethiopia) were never colonies.

It is false to claim that the West is the major cause of worldwide poverty. As William Scully explains: "Actually, much of the developing world that has had contact with the West owes its economic development to such contact, which provided access to Western markets, Western enterprise, capital, and ideas. Today's poverty in [areas like Latin America] is much more the result of domestic mismanagement and unsound domestic policies than of Western interference and domination."[14] The West did not become rich at the expense of the poor.

Liberation theology therefore fails to understand the real causes of poverty. Since it misunderstands the nature of the disease, it cannot hope to provide a cure. It is deficient both in its diagnosis and in its prescription. In recommending a cure, liberationists are never able to think beyond the old Marxist line of redistribution. Advocates of economic redistribution frequently mention the miracle when Jesus fed the five thousand. They refer to Jesus' obvious compassion and pity for the hungry and how He proceeded to feed them. However, the redistributionists always drop their analogy at just this point and move on to other subjects. I suggest they need to stay with the analogy a bit longer.

It is certainly important to note that Jesus took pity on hungry people and fed them. But we should follow the story to its conclusion and observe that Jesus performed a miracle by actually *producing* wealth—in this case, the food. If Jesus' compassionate feeding of the hungry is to be taken as an analogy of how Christians today are to have an interest in the needs of the poor, His miracle of producing wealth (the bread and fish) should also lead us to ask by what means we should seek not just to distribute wealth, but also to produce it. But it is precisely at this vitally important point—how wealth will be produced—that the silence of liberation thinkers is so eloquent. Before wealth can be distributed, it must first be produced.

The creation of wealth does not happen by accident. On the contrary, it results from human action and social cooperation. When proper attention is given to the necessary role that the creation of wealth must play in relieving poverty, it is clear that capitalism offers the poor their only real hope of economic deliverance. Socialism can only increase the misery of the masses while encouraging the growth of tyranny. The only way in which the poor of any nation can be delivered from poverty is through an economic system that first of all produces enough wealth so that all are capable of sharing. Economic systems that decrease or discourage the production of wealth can never succeed in eliminating poverty; they can only make it worse.

It is interesting to note how liberation theologians never mention formerly poor nations like Taiwan, Singapore, and Hong Kong that have achieved the highest rates of economic growth in the world. Perhaps they ignore such countries because the nations have succeeded by consciously rejecting Socialist models and have followed a free-market approach.

No workable economy is feasible that does not take account of the operations of the market. Any economy that violates the principles of a market economy is doomed to failure, and even worse, is bound to create conditions in which human liberation becomes less attainable. What the impoverished nations of the world need is a *new* liberation theology, by which I mean one that recognizes the failure of socialism and works to reestablish free-market principles.

The Final Test

I have said that liberation theology should be tested by its fidelity to the Christian message and mission. It should also be tested in relation to its refusal to subordinate the Christian gospel to any secular ideology. I have also said that liberation theology should be tested by the soundness of its economics: how well it can deliver on its promise to liberate people from poverty. Finally, we should ask liberation theology about its ability to liberate people from tyranny.

Father James Schall of Georgetown University wonders if liberation theology is not leading an entire continent "to commit itself to a system in which the presumed elimination of poverty will rather result in the elimination of freedom, with only a minimal attack on poverty."[15] Michael Novak warns that in opting for the road to Utopia, liberation theologians "seem to imitate the Grand Inquisitor, who out of pity for the people promised bread, not liberty."[16] Not only do the people need bread, they also long for liberty. But socialism can provide neither bread nor freedom.

Liberation theology's lack of interest in political freedom is apparent in its almost total silence about totalitarianism in Eastern Europe. After all, people in Eastern Europe are also oppressed and poor. Should not liberation theologians who profess to be opposed to poverty and oppression say something on behalf of poor and oppressed Eastern Europeans? Why, for example, are they so silent about suffering Christians in Poland? People who claim to be concerned about justice and freedom should condemn bondage wherever it exists, including the Marxist states of the world. Ironically, there is a modest revolution beginning in Eastern Europe; but it is a revolution *against* Marxism.

Richard John Neuhaus observes that warnings about totalitarianism are all too necessary. Liberal democracy has many self-professed enemies.

> In both the long and short term, the more ominous adversaries of liberal democracy are those forces that are totalitarian *in* principle. The only global movement of this kind today is Marxist-Leninism. . . . After World War II, and despite loose talk that equates any repressive regime with "fascism," only Marxist-Leninism is left as a theoretically comprehensive and, to many, morally compelling global adversary of liberal democracy.[17]

Susan Sontag shocked many fellow liberals in 1982 when she suggested that acts of repression in such Marxist states as Poland were not the exception but the rule with respect to Marxism-Leninism. While the Left regularly warns about the threat of fascism, Sontag argued that this warning should finally be expanded to include communism. In her moving words:

> We had identified the enemy as fascism. We heard the demonic language of fascism. We believed in, or at least applied a double standard to, the angelic language of communism. . . . The émigrés from communist countries we didn't listen to, who found it far easier to get published in the *Reader's Digest* than in *The Nation* or the *New Statesman,* were telling the truth. Now we hear them. Why didn't we hear them before? . . . The result was that many of us, and I include myself, did not understand the nature of the Communist tyranny. . . . What the recent Polish events illustrate is a truth that we should have understood a very long time ago: that communism *is* fascism. . . . Not only is fascism the probable destiny of all Communist societies, but communism is in itself a variant of fascism. Fascism with a human face.[18]

Liberation theology's lack of commitment to political freedom is especially apparent in Nicaragua. As Humberto Belli observes:

> Thus a perhaps unforeseen danger of liberation theology, shown by the Nicaragua case, is that it aggravates the totalitarian drift of the Marxist revolution with which it cooperates. It supplies Marxists with a religious justification for their political messianism and its accompanying repression. . . . Thus, in the laboratory of Nicaragua, it can be seen that liberation theology has led Christians full circle, from opposition to a right-wing dictatorship to support for a left-wing dictatorship.[19]

This same writer warns:

> Western Christians concerned for the problems of the Third World must outgrow their tendency to naively welcome revolutions which use high-sounding rhetoric to disguise totalitarian convictions. Christianity can be manipulated in behalf of non-Christian causes. A romanticized view of Third-World revolutionaries fighting shocking injustices avoids confronting the fact that, regardless of their apparent idealism, Marxist revolutions harbor the seeds of even more cruel oppressions than the ones they are striving to dethrone. Such forces are unyieldingly hostile to Christianity.[20]

Theologian Carl Henry adds his own dismay about theologians who talk about liberation and freedom and who have so little to say about Marxist tyranny: "While the church of Christ may well be disconcerted that it took Christianity almost nineteen centuries to eradicate slavery, the whole world should be terrified . . . that it took communism only a single generation to bring it back."[21] A self-proclaimed liberation theology that lacks a strong commitment to political freedom and that fails to distance itself from political tyranny, including that practiced by Marxist states, is unworthy of the name.

Conclusion

When liberation theology is tested in light of the five criteria I have identified, it fares poorly. Since the concerns I have noted must be met if any liberation theology is to exemplify *true* liberation theology, it is necessary to conclude that most of the versions presently being promoted are examples of false liberation theology. In order for a system to qualify as an example of true liberation theology, it must be faithful to the Biblical content of the gospel, to Biblical evangelism, and must not subordinate the concerns of God's kingdom to secular ideologies. A true liberation theology will also recognize that deliverance from poverty requires a rejection of Socialist measures that ignore the creation of wealth. And a true liberation theology will never support a totalitarianism of the Right or of the Left.

11

Interventionism

Many people are attracted by the possibility of an economic system that would fall somewhere between capitalism and socialism, that would—they think—combine the "best features" of each. One of the dominant myths of twentieth-century America is that defects inherent within capitalism caused the Great Depression and that the only thing that brought the nation out of the Depression was its rejection of laissez-faire capitalism in favor of economic interventionism. The truth turns out to be quite different. As the following two chapters will demonstrate, it was economic interventionism that brought on the Depression, and it was interventionism that prevented economic recovery. Interventionism does not take the best features of capitalism and merge them into a superior system at all.

Interventionism results from the belief that governmental intervention in economic matters can successfully achieve desired results while still falling short of the total controls that characterize a Socialist system. A mixed economy is supposed to be a workable third alternative to the freedom of a market system and the total state control of a Socialist system. The state, interventionists believe, interferes with the market process in order to attain some desirable social goal or to avoid some social evil.

This is what a mixed economy is *supposed* to be. In reality, it turns out to be a system in which government interferes with the normal operation of the market system in order to alter the terms of trade in ways that benefit some at the expense of others. Interventionism is a result of one group inviting government to enter the market process and change the rates at which exchanges take place. Advocates of interventionism never explain that this is what interventionism really is. Instead, they talk in lofty moral terms about the importance of certain social goals and how those goals can only be attained if government intervenes in ways that will counterbalance the selfishness of some in order to bring about the good for all.

The Fundamental Weakness of Interventionism

The fundamental defect of interventionism was uncovered by Ludwig von Mises, whose devastating critique of socialism was noted in an earlier chapter. According to Mises, no third alternative to a free market and socialism is possible in practice. The partial governmental controls that are supposed to distinguish interventionism from the more total controls of a Socialist system inevitably fail. Interference with market processes will not only fail to attain the interventionist's goals, it will produce conditions worse than those he sought to alter through his controls. This is not to say that things may not appear better in the short run. But in the long run, the unforeseen consequences will be worse.

One reason interventionist controls fail is because whenever government intervenes in the market, private owners and entrepreneurs react in ways that thwart spontaneously the objectives of the state.[1] Moreover, when government intervenes in the economy, for example by restraining price rises, it shuts off important signals that entrepreneurs might otherwise use in making economic decisions. As I explained in an earlier chapter, one of the most important features of an unhampered market economy is its informational function. Economic interventionism interferes with the informational function of the market, causes it to send misleading signals, and thus produces significant economic harm.

Mises's objections to economic interventionism can be summed up in three words. Interventionist acts are useless, superfluous, and harmful. Writing with the specific example of price controls in mind, Mises argued that this kind of interventionism "is superfluous because built-in forces are at work that limit the arbitrariness of the exchanging parties. It is useless because the government objective of lower prices cannot be achieved by controls. And it is harmful because it deters production and consumption from those uses that, from the consumer's viewpoint, are most important."[2] According to Mises:

> The effect of intervention is the very opposite of what it was meant to achieve. If government is to avoid the undesirable consequences it cannot stop with just market interference. Step by step it must continue until it finally seizes control over

production from entrepreneurs and capitalists. . . . Government cannot be satisfied with a single intervention, but is driven on to nationalize the means of production. This ultimate effect refutes the notion that there is a middle form of organization, the "regulated" economy, between the private property order and the public property order.[3]

Because every instance of governmental intervention with the economy will fail and produce consequences opposite to what was expected, the state has only two choices. Either the government can return to a free market economy and allow the damage resulting from its intervention to ease gradually; or else the state can keep adding more and more controls until all economic freedom ends. In the first case, the interventionist admits his errors and moves in the direction of a free market system. In the second case, he compounds his errors by pushing the economy towards the more total controls of socialism. There can be no consistent, successful middle ground between the market and socialism.

But interventionists are seldom bothered by little things like reason and evidence. Whenever confronted by the failures of their partial controls, they have a predictable response. The failures of the mixed economy are judged to show that previous controls did not go far enough; what is necessary is more interference with the market, not less. In other words, it is always the market process and never interventionism that receives the blame for failure. Through this remarkable sleight of hand, past failures are never regarded as grounds for abandoning interventionism. Rather, the mistakes of the past are used as justification for even more total controls in the future. In this way, interventionism tends to move increasingly closer to the more total controls of socialism.

Governmental Intervention with Prices

One of the most frequently occuring kinds of interventionism is governmental action with regard to market prices. Price control occurs when the government makes it illegal to sell a good or service above a certain level. But governments can interfere with price in another way—namely, price supports. In this second case, government sets minimum prices for commodities like agricultural products.

Price Control

We are all familiar with various ways in which government interferes with market prices. As recently as the early 1970s, President Nixon imposed wage and price controls. The controls were justified on the grounds that they were needed to help slow the rate of inflation. Nixon knew full well that the real cause of the inflation was other governmental interventionism. But because an election was coming and inflation was perceived as a problem, it was politically expedient for Nixon to act. Since I will consider earlier examples of this kind of interventionism in the following chapters on the Great Depression, I will limit myself in this section to a consideration of rent controls.[4]

Rent controls make it illegal for property owners to charge a price above a certain level. Rent controls are justified on the grounds that they help poor people by making acceptable housing available at an affordable price. Rent controls have the effect of keeping rental prices at a level below what they would otherwise be if they were allowed to fluctuate in response to market forces.

As surely as night follows day, certain consequences will follow the imposition of price controls. Price controls—or in our case rent controls—will always result in unanticipated shortages. Rent controls will always lead to a shortage of rental housing. The reasons have been given in the earlier chapters of this book. While the government can make it illegal for a landlord to rent his property above a certain price level, it cannot (in a relatively free society) prevent the landlord from doing other things with his property in an effort to counter the effect of the rent control.

Some landlords may divide their property into smaller units in ways that will produce a greater income. Others may convert their property into condominiums, which has the effect of removing that property from the rental market. Or they may choose to sell their property to people who will use it for purposes other than housing. While current landlords may have no choice but to offer their property at the price required by the state, people who might otherwise have made their property available for rent at some future time will consider other options. Since the rent controls have a negative effect on the rate of return to old rental property, investment money may be channeled away from the construction of new rental property. Rent controls will reduce the amount of rental housing that is available in both the present and the future.

But rent controls will also affect the quality of rental housing.

As we noted earlier in the book, everything has a cost. If the government forces landlords to maintain what they charge for rent at the same price and if the landlord's other costs increase, something will have to give. In such cases, what is often sacrificed is the quality of the rental housing. Needed repairs and improvements are delayed, and the quality of the housing begins to deteriorate. Sooner or later, the quality of the housing will reflect its price.

Price controls do more than cause shortages; they also produce black markets. As a shortage of rental units develops, landlords and frustrated prospective renters will both seek ways to circumvent the controls. This may take various forms such as secret payments or an agreement to rent furniture at prices high enough to compensate for the low rent. With price eliminated as a factor in the distribution of rental housing, landlords will come to depend on other ways of deciding who rents increasingly scarce property. Governmental intervention with the market makes it easier for those people who wish to discriminate. Without price controls, it might have cost a racist landlord profit if he offered his property to a white family while some black family was willing to pay a higher rent. But with the aid of the government's mandated rent control, there is no longer any danger that discrimination will cost the landlord money.[5]

No city in the United States is more closely associatied with rent controls than New York City. Not surprisingly, New York City is a perfect example of the inevitable results of rent controls. Former rental properties have been converted to condominiums or other uses. Landlords and tenants make under-the-table deals to increase the price to the landlord without officially breaking the law. The quality of rental housing has deteriorated, and a serious shortage exists.

In the short run, governmental intervention in the form of rent controls might result in lower-priced housing for some people. But in the long run, there will be less quantity and poorer quality. Without rent controls, a temporary increase in rents would have led to an increased number of rental units being offered. This increase in supply would then result in two things: a market-induced decrease of price and an improvement in quality as market conditions forced landlords to be competitive.

Price Support

During the 1930s, the federal government got heavily into price support programs for agricultural products. The original intent was to help farmers by raising prices for such crops as wheat, tobacco, cotton, rice, and feed grains. Taking wheat as our example, the government established a minimum price for wheat that was higher than the market price. It also promised to buy any wheat not sold at the support price. Since this measure promised farmers more money than they would have otherwise made had the price for their wheat been determined by market conditions, farmers understandably began to grow more wheat. Since the government had given farmers an incentive to grow more wheat, they grew more wheat. Obviously, this led to a huge surplus of wheat.

Then the government had a new problem on its hands—the huge supplies of wheat it owned. The government not only had to buy the extra wheat it had promised to purchase, it then had to pay storage costs. Large amounts of wheat spoiled. There was also a great deal of public criticism because of widespread fraud. In an effort to correct the damage resulting from its original intervention, the government tried to ease its problems through additional intervention. It restricted the number of acres on which farmers could plant wheat. But this was no obstacle for creative farmers. Sometimes they found ways of increasing their yield per acre; or sometimes they diverted their more productive land to wheat and used less productive acreage for other purposes. The wheat surplus did not go away.

Even after a great deal of fine-tuning (or favorable changes in market conditions) managed to bring supply and demand closer together, other negative effects continued to exist. For one thing, all of the government's tinkering with the wheat market increased the costs of producing a certain quantity of wheat. Before the governmental restrictions on acreage, a farmer could have increased his wheat production by simply increasing the amount of land seeded in wheat. But after the governmental acreage restrictions, farmers were forced to increase yields by spending more money on fertilizer and better machinery.

All this time, of course, there was another mechanism that would have brought the supply of wheat closer to the demand—the mechanism of the market. But the politicians thought intervention with the market would be more efficient.

Farmers of many commodities have come to depend on government programs. But in the long run, farming is no more profitable after the imposition of price supports and acreage allotments than before. In the short run, higher profits were realized by some of the farmers who were in a position to take advantage of the governmental programs. But in the long run, things evened out—as they always do. For one thing, the government's actions raised dramatically the price of farm land. This increased the costs of later entrants to the farm market. The people who benefitted from governmental price support programs and acreage allotment programs were those who received allotments at the time the programs were established. Once inevitable competition for scarce allotments led to higher prices for land, the profit received by current owners in comparison to the market price of their land is no greater than if the price support programs had never been enacted.

The history of America's cotton production since 1955 provides another good example of how counterproductive and harmful intervention with agriculture can be. In 1955, the United States produced half of the world's cotton (some eighteen million bales). But by 1969, only eleven million bales were harvested in the U.S. This dramatic decline resulted from growing competition from foreign cotton growers and the development of synthetic fabrics. But what gave added strength to foreign intrusion into the market were interventionist measures in the American cotton market. As a 1969 article in *Time* explains:

> Ironically, both synthetic makers and foreign growers were given access to cotton's domain as an unforeseen result of U.S. Government policy. The troubles began with rigid, Depression-born price supports, which eventually reached a peak of 32¢ a pound in 1955. They were aimed at propping the grower's income, but in the process they raised the price of U.S. cotton above the going world rate. The government's solution to that problem was to subsidize exports, beginning in 1956. That move, in turn, created a crisis for domestic millers, who complained that they had to pay more for U.S. cotton than competing foreign mills. Washington's answer was to add a third subsidy, this time for the millers.[6]

Step by step, federal intervention with the cotton market did precisely what Mises had predicted. This first interventionist act produced negative unforeseen consequences. To ease this problem, the government tried more interventionism. By now, the harmful effects were hitting other segments of the economy. But true to form, the interventionists did not admit their errors; they continued to intervene in additional ways.

Time proceeded to note eventual changes in the cumbersome three-tiered support program; but the damage was already done. Foreign growers had already become established. As *Time* concluded, the cotton industry was "harmed more than helped by the complicated schemes spun by federal bureaucrats. . . ."

Governmental Intervention with Wages

Minimum wage laws stipulate that all workers covered by the legislation must be paid no less than the stated hourly wage rate. Such laws are justified on the ground that they will provide significant economic help for the working poor. But many economists believe the actual effect of minimum wage laws is just the opposite.[7]

There are several things that legislators have not yet found a way to do. They can force employers to pay wages higher than the market would have required. But the government cannot force employees to increase their productivity. Nor can it (at least in democratic societies like the U.S.) force employers to continue to employ the same number of workers they used prior to passage of the minimum wage law. Since such a law increases the employer's costs, it forces him to make adjustments in the way he uses labor. In all likelihood, he will attempt to recover some of the additional costs of his higher wages by increasing prices. But he will also be forced to get more productivity for his labor dollar. This means that less productive workers or those with less marketable skills will be fired or not hired. While the minimum wage law will benefit some workers (those who remain employed and now earn the higher wage rate), it will do so at the expense of others—namely, those who would have had a job at the lower market wage, but who now have no job at all. The negative effect is more serious for those workers who have less marketable skills.

Economist Walter Williams asks, "Who bears the burden of the minimum wage?" His answer is, the most marginal workers. "These are workers who employers perceive as being less productive or more costly to employ than other workers."[8] This is bad news for young workers whose skills are understandably less developed. "These workers are not only made unemployable by the minimum wage, but their opportunities to upgrade their skills through on-the-job-training are also severely limited."[9] Economists James Gwartney and Richard Stroup point out:

Many inexperienced workers face a dilemma. They cannot find a job without experience (or skills), but they cannot obtain experience without a job. This is particularly true for youthful workers. Employment experience obtained at an early age, even on seemingly menial tasks, can help one acquire work habits . . . skills, and attitudes that will enhance one's value to employers in the future. Since minimum wage legislation prohibits the payment of even a temporarily low wage, it substantially limits the employer's ability to offer employment to inexperienced workers.[10]

On the job opportunities are greatly restricted; entry-level jobs decrease; and dead-end jobs tend to dominate the market for unskilled workers. This is the legacy of minimum wage laws. Walter Williams notes the importance of even menial jobs that allow workers to develop habits, skills, and attitudes that will open better employment opportunities in the future.

It is important to note that most people acquire work skills by working at "subnormal wages" which amounts to the same thing as paying to learn. For example, inexperienced doctors (interns), during their training, work at wages which are a tiny fraction of that of trained doctors. College students forego considerable amounts of money in the form of tuition and foregone income so that they may develop marketable skills. It is ironic, if not tragic, that low-skilled youths from poor families are denied an opportunity to get a start in life. This is exactly what happens when a high minimum wage forbids low-skilled workers to pay for job training in the form of a lower beginning wage.[11]

One way to rectify this—since the repeal of minimum wage is unlikely—is the adoption of a significantly lower minimum wage for younger workers.

Black economists like Thomas Sowell and Walter Williams have examined the inordinately high unemployment rates for black teenagers. Today, the unemployment rate for black youths averages two to three times that of white youths. In some large urban areas, unemployment of black youths is higher than 50 percent. This information is even more shocking when contrasted with the situation just a few decades ago. During the late 1940s and early 1950s, unemployment rates among black teenagers were no greater and in fact were sometimes less than unemployment rates among white teens.[12] Walter Williams shows how the percentage of black unemployment increased with each increase in the minimum wage.[13] According to Williams and Sowell, this huge increase in black teenage unemployment was not caused by racial discrimination. In Williams's words, "Teenagers in general, and black teenagers in particular, are the victims of government-backed collusion. The minimum wage law of the Fair Employment Standards Act is the tool."[14]

A number of economists, including Sowell and Williams, have drawn attention to how minimum wage laws encourage racial discrimination. As Walter Williams explains:

> Suppose an employer has a dislike for blacks relative to whites. For simplicity, we assume that the workers who are to be employed do not differ except by race. If there is a law, such as a minimum wage law, that requires that employers pay the same wage, no matter who is hired, then the employer can discriminate at *zero cost*. However, if there were no minimum wage and blacks were willing to work for a lower wage, the cost to the employer to choose whites over blacks would be positive. The cost is the difference between the wages. The market would penalize such an employer because there would be firms that would hire blacks and through lower production costs tend to drive discriminating firms out of business. This line of reasoning follows from the Law of Demand. The argument is given additional weight when we recognize that even during relatively racially hostile times black unemployment was less and labor force participation rates higher than in "racially enlightened" times. That is, to the extent that a black was willing to, and was permitted to, work for a lower wage than a white there was a positive cost to the employer to indulge his racial preference.[15]

The well-known support of large labor unions for minimum wage laws should not be regarded necessarily as a reflection of the union's goodwill towards unskilled, often minority, workers. Imagine an employer who can get a particular product or service either by employing one highly skilled union worker at $400 a week or three unskilled workers at $150 a week apiece. The employer, under these conditions, would hire the one skilled worker and in this way minimize his costs. But suppose the worker's union demands an increase in his pay to the point where he would receive $500 a week. The skilled worker knows that such a demand would have the likely result of the employer switching to the three less skilled workers whose total pay would come to $450. So the skilled worker argues that it is unjust to hire low-skilled workers for less than $175 a week. If he gets the state to pass such a law, his activity on behalf of the minimum wage law has benefited not the poor and less skilled workers; it has helped him.

Organized labor's apparent interest in raising the minimum wage of unskilled workers is an interesting maneuver. The real objective seems to be the creation of a situation that organized and highly skilled workers can use to increase their own advantaged position. Minimum wage laws decrease the competition higher-skilled workers face from lower-skilled workers.[16]

Minimum wage laws then are another example of how governmental intervention produces consequences quite different from those that were intended. Such laws increase unemployment, restrict access to important entry-level jobs for low-skilled workers, and in spite of the best of intentions on the part of the lawmakers, encourage racism. The government handicaps the very people it professes interest in helping. It does this either by raising the costs of actions that would be truly beneficial or by lowering the costs for actions that will prove ultimately harmful. High black unemployment is a result of well-intended actions by an interventionist government.

Conclusion

As British economist Arthur Shenfield explains, the interventionist story "is a grim one of error, illusion, and failure. The root is the inability to understand the signals of the free economy and their system of coordination. To the planner, the free economy is chaos. By attempting to plan the whole economy, he forbids the very planning which is possible and necessary, namely the planning by individuals of their affairs."[17]

In the short run, interventionism may result in a few people being better off. But in the long run, it always results in the majority of people being worse off. And even those short-run benefits fail an important moral test because they benefit one interest-group at the expense of other individuals. Even in the short run, interventionism results in someone's ox being gored. The awesome power of the state is used to alter the terms of trade in favor of one group at the expense of others.

Interventionism cannot be justified in the short run because it fails the moral test. And interventionism cannot be justified in the long run because it fails the economic test.

12

The Great Depression I

The Great Depression is often cited as the primary example of the failure of free market economics. According to the official interventionist interpretation of the Depression, both the economic collapse that began in 1929 and the nation's eventual recovery prove that the American government must never again allow its economy to operate in a noninterventionist way. The common view is that the 1920s in America was a period of unbridled free enterprise. The Depression is proof that free market economics no longer works. In order to restore stability to the nation's economy and bring the nation out of the depths of the Depression, the government had to step in and do what businessmen could not or would not do to correct the weaknesses of the free market system. The decade of the 1930s proves the importance of governmental control over the economy and justifies continuing interventionist measures.

It would be difficult to imagine an explanation that is more in conflict with the evidence. This commonly accepted view of the Depression is grounded on four myths.

Myth Number One: *A free market economy is notoriously unstable and leads inevitably to economic cycles in which periods of prosperity are followed by recessions and depressions. These irregularities in a nation's economy can be either eliminated or made less severe by proper government intervention.*

Myth Number Two: *Prior to the economic collapse of 1929, America's economy was an example of unbridled capitalism. The severity of the Depression reflected the extreme degree of America's experiment with free enterprise.*

Myth Number Three: *President Herbert Hoover was an ardent advocate of free market economics. His unfortunate attempts to defend the principles of that economic viewpoint after 1929 had the effect of making the Depression far worse than it would have been.*

Myth Number Four: *President Franklin Roosevelt led the nation out of the Depression by rejecting Hoover's noninterventionist measures. Roosevelt became America's economic savior by introducing massive governmental intervention into the economy, thereby proving for subsequent generations the necessity for economic interventionism.*

Because of the importance of the subject and the seriousness of the errors contained in these four myths, two chapters will be devoted to the Great Depression. This chapter will examine critically the first two myths. In the process, it will discuss the economic and political factors prior to 1930 that did in fact cause the Depression. The discussion in the following chapter will be structured around the last two myths. It will detail the precise actions taken by Hoover and Roosevelt and explain their economic consequences. While the present chapter will examine conditions that led up to the Depression during the decade of the 1920s, the following chapter will discuss the actual course of the Depression during the decade of the 1930s.

The First Myth:
The Cause of Business Cycles

The recurrence of business cycles is one of the most frequently cited reasons for the need of governmental intervention with the economy. The often unstated and always unproven assumption behind this claim is that business cycles and, more specifically, economic depressions are caused by free-market economics. This assumption is clearly false.

Business cycles in general and depressions in particular are caused not by free markets, but by governmental intervention with a nation's economy, specifically with its money supply. As nations expand credit and the money supply, a pattern becomes apparent. First, there is a governmentally-induced period of economic expansion as easy credit and a larger money supply mislead businessmen into making bad investments. As we saw earlier, unhampered markets keep sending signals to astute investors and entrepreneurs. The rise or decline in prices along with the cost of borrowing money (interest rates) can tell a wise investor whether a particular opportunity is a good risk at that particular time. But governmental intervention in the form of monetary and credit expansion affects the reliability of normal market signals. Interest rates may be artificially (and temporarily) reduced while inflation causes many prices to rise.

But the rise in prices eventually affects the prices of capital goods required for business expansion. This increase in business costs finally affects the profitability of many businesses, leading them to find ways to cut costs. In the later stages of the boom, interest rates begin to rise, which also increases the cost of doing business and often affects loans incurred when money was much cheaper.

As economist Murray Rothbard explains, the governmentally-induced expansion of the economy

> distorts the structure of investment and production, causing excessive investment in unsound projects in the capital goods industries. This distortion is reflected in the well-known fact that, in every boom period, capital goods prices rise further than the prices of consumer goods. The recession period of the business cycle then becomes inevitable, for the recession is the necessary corrective process by which the market liquidates the unsound investments of the boom and redirects resources from the capital goods to the consumer goods industries. The longer the inflationary distortions continue, the more severe the recession-adjustment must become.[1]

Because such governmental intervention with the economy sends the wrong signals to businessmen and investors, their subsequent investment in the wrong things at the wrong time makes a day of reckoning inevitable. While that day can be postponed by even more expansion of credit, it cannot be postponed forever. When the quantity and degree of bad investments in any economy passes a certain point, the economy can no longer absorb them. Ventures must be terminated; businesses must be closed; bills must be left unpaid; workers must be laid off; unemployment will increase; savings will be depleted.

A recession or depression therefore is a necessary step in an economy's return to normal after the misinformation and distortions caused by monetary inflation during the boom have produced a large amount of malinvestment. The recession or depression that follows periods of governmentally-induced boom is a necessary time of readjustment. Prices must be readjusted to new consumer preferences. Interest rates must be readjusted to reflect the new demand for savings along with the actual supply of savings. Bad investments must be reduced or written off. The costs of doing business must be lowered through such means as greater managerial efficiency or reduced labor costs. These lower costs may be reached through greater productivity; often they result from a business employing fewer workers. There must be a general cutting back across the board until businesses can once more be profitable, until investments can earn a proper return, and until the economy can once more function efficiently. What people call a recession or depression, therefore, is actually an adjustment of the economy to the wasteful and mistaken errors made during the boom. The process of adjustment is a return to a more sane set of economic arrangements which means, among other things, that many of the bad investments are liquidated.

The theory of business cycles outlined above is confirmed by a study of the major downturns of the American economy. The depression of 1819, for example, was caused by currency inflation by the Second Bank of the United States. The economic slump of 1837 was caused by unsound paper currency issued by state banks. Following a decade of monetary and credit expansion, the nation's economy went through another period of adjustment and retrenchment in 1857. In this case, state governments had expanded money and credit that produced obligations that had to be picked up by the banking systems of the respective states. In 1873, a depression occurred in which the economy adjusted to inflation resulting from governmental actions in connection with the Civil War. Between 1893 and 1895, a serious panic and depression followed years in which the federal government inflated the economy with paper notes and depreciating silver. In 1921, the nation experienced a brief but marked economic decline brought on by expansion of currency and credit to finance World War I.

During each of these earlier economic cycles, there were factors other than governmental expansion of money and credit. But in each case, the central factor proves to have been governmental intervention with the supply of money and the availability of credit. As one source goes on to explain:

> This is not to say that business fluctuations would not take place otherwise, for businessmen will often guess wrong, make mistakes, and will invest too deeply in the wrong place at the wrong time. Even in a free economy dislocations will occur and adjustments will be necessary. But the effect will be local and short-lived. With the inexorable push of deliberate government policy, the entire economy usually finds itself

swept along on a nationwide wave of speculation that builds higher and higher—and then collapses.[2]

The common thread that runs through these periods of economic decline is governmental manipulation of the money supply. The obvious culprit in these economic downturns is not the free market but the government. What then should one think of economists and politicians who appeal to such periods of economic decline as justification for increased amounts of the very types of economic interventionism that produced the depressions?

But what about the Great Depression? As everyone knows—or thinks they know—the decade prior to the economic collapse of 1929 was a period of unbridled economic freedom. It was, so the official doctrine goes, the extent of America's experiment with free enterprise in the 1920s that led to the greatest depression in our history. But this belief is also a myth that must now be unmasked.

The Second Myth: The Unbridled Capitalism of the Twenties

As we have seen, interventionists believe that whenever any nation's economy is based upon free markets, economic cycles are inevitable. According to the official interventionist dogma, the seriousness of the Great Depression was in direct proportion to America's reliance upon a noninterventionist economy during the decade of the twenties. The unparalleled economic freedom of the twenties did more than make the Great Depression inevitable; it also made it the worst depression in the nation's history.

Even a brief survey of the evidence, however, will reveal how mistaken the common wisdom about the twenties is. The decade that preceded the Crash of 1929 was anything but a period of unbridled capitalism. It was actually a time of continued governmental intervention with the money supply. The foundations for the Depression can indeed be found throughout the preceding decade. But the causes of the Depression were a string of governmental actions that resulted in an expansion of credit and the money supply that was similar to the interventionism that led to earlier economic downturns.

A good place to begin one's search for the causes of the Great Depression is the establishment of the Federal Reserve System in 1913. The Federal Reserve was given the power to increase the nation's money supply in response to what it regarded as justifiable circumstances. Economist Murray Rothbard explains what the creation of the Federal Reserve System has meant for the nation's economy:

> Since the inception of the Federal Reserve System in 1913, the supply of money and bank credit in America has been totally in the control of the federal government, a control that has been further strengthened by the U.S. repudiating the domestic gold standard in 1933, as well as the gold standard behind the dollar in foreign transactions in 1968 and finally in 1971. With the gold standard abandoned, there is no necessity for the Federal Reserve System or its controlled banks to redeem dollars in gold, and so the Fed may expand the supply of paper and bank dollars to its heart's content.[3]

For most of the sixteen years following the creation of the Federal Reserve System in 1913, the nation's money supply was subjected to an almost steady increase. Between 1914-1917, this took the form of massive amounts of credit extended to nations like England and France for their purchase of war material. Following America's own entry into the war, the money supply was expanded even more as a way of paying for our own war effort. When the war was finally over, the now greatly expanded money supply resulted in inflation.

The higher postwar prices led in turn to an increase in cheaper imports. But this hurt American businesses, which led businessmen, farmers, and labor unions to pressure Congress to do something about foreign competition. This pressure led to two unfortunate tariff acts; tariffs are clearly antithetical to capitalism. The Emergency Tariff Act of 1921 increased duties on such commodities as wool, sugar, and wheat. Another tariff act passed in 1922 imposed the highest duties to that time in the history of the nation. It also gave the President the power to change tariffs as he thought necessary. These high tariffs produced a serious instability in agriculture, other export industries, and the rest of the American economy.

All of this intervention with the economy had the effect of reducing foreign trade. Prospective foreign customers could not buy American products until they accumulated credits; but such credits could be accumulated only after they first sold their products to us, something the increased tariffs made much more difficult. In an effort to offset some of this harm, the government adopted cheap money policies. To make it easier for foreign buyers to purchase American goods (while still making it difficult for them to sell their goods in the U.S.), bankers floated enormous loans and bond issues in this country. Between the end of World War I and 1929, American lenders provided more than $9 billion in foreign loans. This was done primarily to shore up America's sagging export markets, which had been hurt as a result of earlier interventionist measures (the tariffs) to reduce imports. While the cheap money policy of the twenties produced temporary increases in exports, it was accompanied by a huge burden of internal and international debt.

The Federal Reserve System continued to follow an easy money policy during the second half of the twenties. Between July 1924 and 1929, the money supply increased more than 20 percent. Farm and urban mortagages increased more than $10 billion between 1921 and 1929. Because much of the new money created by the system was channeled into speculation in real estate and the stock market, rapid price rises occurred in the stock market and in real estate.

The extent to which the results of governmental intervention in the economy are apparent will depend to a great degree on other characteristics of the economy. The inflation of the currency was disguised to some extent by a relatively stable level of prices. Significant technological advances and greater economies in the production of certain goods tended to hold down inflation when under normal conditions the expansion of the money supply would have been accompanied by a much higher rate of inflation. Two exceptions to this were rising prices in Florida land and stocks, both fueled by speculation. Sooner or later, all of the malinvestments that the easy money policies of the twenties had encouraged would have to be corrected. Early in 1929, the Federal Reserve began to make those corrections.

If the general groundwork for the Great Depression was the government's expansion of credit and the money supply during the 1920s, the immediate cause was the attempt by the Federal Reserve System to slow down the money machine. Concerned by the extent of speculation its easy money policies were fueling, the Federal Reserve began to deflate the currency. It raised the discount rate, which in turn made it necessary for many banks to call in loans. There was a sharp drop in the money supply.

As important as the Stock Market Crash of October 1929

was, it did not mark the beginning of the Great Depression. The economy actually began to recede during the summer of 1929. Economic troubles had been brewing long before the crash. What the collapse of the stock market did was make those troubles visible and mark the end of an incredible period of speculation that had to end sometime.

The crash was caused to a great extent by the sudden contraction of the money supply and by investors' awareness of the inevitable results of the now expected increase of tariff rates in what became known as the Smoot-Hawley Tariff Act. The government was sending signals that told smart investors trouble was coming. The stock market actually reached its high in mid-September and then sank slowly for the next five weeks while the public continued to buy heavily. Starting on October 24, 1929, thousands of people rushed to sell their stocks. Eventually the word went out to sell at any price. The stock market crashed in a wave of panic. When the panic hit, many people acted without the slightest idea of what had started the avalanche.

Even though the Smoot-Hawley Tariff Act was not passed until June of 1930 (thus leading some economists to treat it primarily as an event that deepened and prolonged the Depression), the research of Jude Wanniski makes the now infamous bill a significant culprit in the advent of the economic crisis. Some discussions of Smoot-Hawley make it appear that the bill was an emergency measure rushed through Congress to help American industry and farmers as they struggled with declining markets and revenue following the October crash. But in fact, this kind of tariff bill had been widely discussed and debated in Congress throughout much of 1929. In the view of Jude Wanniski, Wall Street had begun to realize, by the Fall of 1929, that passage of the tariff bill was certain. It also realized that President Hoover would not veto the damaging bill. Hence, the damage from Smoot-Hawley was not confined to the period of time following its passage. It also had a major effect on events prior to its passage, including the crash of the stock market.[4]

On the day of the Stock Market Crash in October 1929, no one predicted that anything like the Great Depression was beginning. It was commonly believed that what was starting would be an economic recession like many that had preceded it. People continued to believe that things would soon get better. After all, they had always improved in the past.

It is important to remember that what is called the Great

Depression lasted eleven years. Things did not get better as people expected. The economy continued to decline for four more years. Unemployment reached epic proportions. During the long eleven years of the Depression, there were numerous ups and downs, most of which can be explained in terms of governmental actions that frequently made things worse. The end never came until the nation's need to meet the challenges of a new world war helped end the economic nightmare.

13

The Great Depression II

The stock market crash is often exaggerated with regard to its supposed effects on the Great Depression. While the crash was clearly very bad for the many unwise investors and speculators who had been wiped out, America was still far from anything resembling what we now think of as the Great Depression. That was still to come; and like previous depressions, it would result from further governmental mismanagement. The collapse of the stock market provided clear evidence that badly mistaken policies had been followed. The time for necessary readjustments had finally come.

Even with the crash of the stock market, the economy was strong enough so that the nation should have entered a normal period of readjustment.[1] Even during 1930, unemployment averaged less than 8 percent of the work force. Barring mistakes on the part of the government, 1931 should have been the start of a recovery. Obviously it was not, and the reason can be found in the mistaken, often foolish policies of the federal government.

The economic decline that began at the end of 1929 could and should have been of short duration, if only Hoover and the Congress had acted in an economically responsible way. Unfortunately, they did not. Hoover and his administration were in no mood to admit their mistakes. Had they taken their medicine, paid their dues, and suffered through the severe but limited depression that would have followed, the economy soon would have made the proper adjustments. Instead, the Hoover administration piled error on top of error. Their mistakes plus the blunders of Congress plus the economic malfeasance of the Roosevelt administration turned what would have been an economic downturn like every other one in the previous history of the country into an economic nightmare that lasted eleven years.

At the start of the previous chapter, attention was drawn to

four myths about the Great Depression that have become ingrained
in American thinking about the period. The first two myths were
discussed in the last chapter. The stage is now set for an examination of myths three and four, a study that will take us through the
decade of the 1930s.

The Third Myth: Hoover's Commitment to
Free Market Economics Deepened the Depression

As we have seen, interventionists want to lay all of the blame for
the Great Depression at the feet of the free market. With such a
convenient scapegoat available, they can then use the Depression to
justify the interventionist measures they wish to impose upon the
economy in the future. Their rewriting of history requires, however, that they turn Herbert Hoover into a flaming advocate of free
market economics whose stubborn refusal to adopt interventionist
measures made the Depression worse until Franklin Roosevelt's
courageous adoption of wise interventionist policies finally turned
things around. Nothing could be farther from the truth.

In late 1929, the nation's economy was in need of a number of
major readjustments. But these required readjustments all took the
form of *decreasing* or *terminating* various interventionist measures
of the twenties that had produced the Depression. What Hoover
and his administration did, however, was reject the adjustments
that should have been made and opt instead for a course of *more*
governmental control over the economy. According to economist
Tom Rose,

> [W]hen bad times finally came, the culprit [the federal govern-
> ment] attempted to play hero by even grosser interventions
> into the economy. The dislocations produced by earlier gov-
> ernment mismanagement were used as excuses for futher fed-
> eral interventions and controls by the national government,
> which controls have continued and grown more stringent up
> to the present time.[2]

Herbert Hoover was not a champion of a free market economics whose conservative principles helped first to produce the
Depression and then caused it to worsen. In truth, Herbert Hoover
was a proven interventionist whose interventionist policies helped
bring about the start of the Depression and whose succeeding
interventionist actions helped to make it worse.[3] During the presi-

dential campaign of 1932, even Franklin Roosevelt accused Hoover of leading the country down the road to socialism. Of course, once in power, Roosevelt's own interventionism made Hoover look like an amateur.

Following the 1929 Crash, the Hoover Administration and Congress committed four major blunders that were to deepen and prolong the Depression. What must be noted about each of these actions is that they were typically *interventionist* measures.

(1) The Hoover Administration reduced the money supply even more. It is important to remember that initial contractions of the money supply earlier in 1929 had helped to produce the stock market crash. In spite of this, the government continued its reversal of the expansionist policies of the twenties. During 1930, the Federal Reserve System reduced the money supply by 4.2 percent. This relatively slow decline was speeded up in the following two years. The money supply was further reduced by 7.1 percent in 1931 and an additional 12.3 percent in 1932. This reduction in the money supply coupled with the already serious effects of the stock market crash helped to produce the severe recession in the middle of Hoover's term as President. Continued Federal Reserve money mismanagement permitted over five thousand banks to go under, which led to a multiple contraction of the money supply. Between 1929 and 1932, the actions of the Federal Reserve System reduced the money supply by some 30 percent. This fueled economic uncertainty, reduced demand for goods and services, and led to deflation.

Both the decline in the money supply and the widespread economic uncertainty that followed produced an enormous downward pressure on wages and prices. The reduction in the money supply affected the purchasing power of the money still in circulation and affected long-term contracts such as mortgages. People had made long-term financial commitments in the boom climate of the twenties only to find that falling wages and prices made it impossible for them to meet those obligations in the thirties. Widespread bankruptcies led to many bank failures, which added to the fear and uncertainty that people felt. This in turn led people to reduce even more their activity in economic exchanges, especially those involving long-term contracts. Under the circumstances, people could hardly be blamed for refusing to enter into long-term economic commitments. But this was still one more blow to the nation's economy. Economic growth and development results when people exchange in circumstances where all parties have something to gain. The benefits from the economic exchanges that people avoided were lost forever. In all of these ways, the government's reduction of the money supply helped to worsen the economic downturn.

(2) Hoover did everything he could to keep wages and prices high during 1930. For one thing, his administration took action designed to keep the prices of wheat, cotton, and other agricultural products up. The unfortunate result of these farm policies was to encourage larger crops and greater farm surpluses for which no markets could be found. This had the effect of depressing farm prices even more.

Also in 1930, Hoover attempted to persuade business leaders to keep wages and prices high. In place of cutting wages and prices—the normal practice in a time of recession—Hoover urged businessmen to increase their spending on wages and capital outlay in the belief that this would preserve the purchasing power of consumers. The Hoover Administration pursued a policy of deficit spending and public works projects. Local and state governments were asked to borrow money to support their own public works projects.

(3) The Hoover Administration instituted large tariff increases that had a disastrous effect on international exchange. With tariffs already higher than they should have been and a huge burden of international debt hanging over the world's economy, Hoover went along with the Congress's passage of a huge increase in tariffs.

Already high tariffs made it almost impossible for foreign goods to reach our markets. Hoover's acceptance of a new round of even higher tariffs was the major blunder that turned the recession of 1930 into the Great Depression. The Smoot-Hawley Tariff Act of June 1930 was the most protectionist law in the history of the nation. America's borders were effectively closed to foreign goods. The government's intentions with regard to the new tariff act no doubt seemed good at the time. It wanted to raise farmers' low incomes that resulted from the low prices they were getting for their products. But in economics, good intentions often produce disastrous consequences.

Other nations responded to the increase in our tariffs by raising their own. Protectionism became a standard economic policy among our nation's normal trading partners. This had the effect of cutting off international markets and narrowing lines of trade. The new protectionist policies created enormous problems for countries that owed money and needed to pay off their debts with goods. Since so much of this mountain of debt was unsound to begin with, creditors could not collect. In the two years that followed passage of Smoot-Hawley, American exports declined by almost two-thirds. The politicians had ignored a fundamental principle of international exchange: exports pay for imports. If people in other nations cannot sell their goods to us, they cannot earn the money they need to buy our products. Closing the door to imports will result eventually in closing the door to exports.

While farm prices dropped precipitously throughout 1930, the sharpest decline followed passage of the Smoot-Hawley Act in June. While American exports had totaled $5.5 billion in 1929, they had by 1932 fallen to just $1.7 billion. All of this led to a collapse of American farming. Hundreds of thousands of American farmers lost their farms. America's recession was being turned into a world-depression.

(4) The government proceeded to raise taxes, an incredible move under the circumstances. In fairness to Hoover, it should be noted that much of the blame for the tax increase belonged to the Congress. After the midterm elections of 1930, there was a Democratic majority in the House of Representatives.

The tax increase of 1932 was the largest increase in federal taxes in the history of the nation. The income tax was doubled. Estate taxes were raised, corporation tax rates were increased, exemptions were lowered, and postal rates were raised. There was also a 2¢ tax on checks, a 3 percent automobile tax, a tax on telephones and telegraph messages, and a 1¢ a gallon gasoline tax. Faced by declining revenues, state and local governments followed Washington's lead and imposed new taxes of their own. The total tax burden of the nation almost doubled in the period after 1932. If the politicians had been seeking a way to bring the nation's economy to its knees, they could not have found a better strategy. The huge tax increases guaranteed that the Depression would not end soon. Real Gross National Product fell by 14.8 percent in 1932, the year the tax increase went into effect. An unemployment rate that had averaged 3.2 percent in 1929 and 7.8 percent in 1930 jumped to almost 25 percent in 1932.

What were the results of the economic interventionism practiced by the Hoover Administration and Congress between the crash of 1929 and the end of Hoover's term? By the end of his term, unemployment had reached 25 percent of the work force or more than twelve million workers. The Depression had spread beyond the borders of the United States and had become a worldwide depression. Nations like Germany and Austria stopped making foreign payments and froze American credits. England ended gold payments in September 1931. Foreign bond values fell drastically, which led to a collapse of the bond market in America. This proved to be an additional blow at American banks, in this case, a blow at their own investments.

The collapse of so many American farmers put their major creditors—the rural banks—in jeopardy. Many of them were forced to close. Between August 1931 and February 1932, approximately two thousand banks closed, still owing depositors more than $1.5 billion. Banks that didn't close were often forced to take extreme measures. New loans were often refused, and old loans were pressured to make payment. This banking panic led to even greater pressures on the market as many banks dumped many of their own holdings.

Bank runs and other banking difficulties did not occur to any great degree until the Fall of 1930. But once a number of Midwest and Southern banks failed, confidence in banks was undermined and many people rushed to withdraw their funds. In mid-1929, America had almost twenty-five thousand commercial banks. By the time of Roosevelt's inauguration in 1933, this number had fallen to about eighteen thousand. Hence, almost seven thousand American banks closed their doors or were forced to merge with others, between mid-1929 and early 1933. Another three thousand were eliminated by the end of 1933.

Murray Rothbard provides an evaluation of Hoover's efforts to deal with the Depression:

> [I]f we define "New Deal" as an anti-depression program marked by extensive governmental economic planning and intervention—including bolstering of wage rates and prices, expansion of credit, propping up of weak firms, and increased government spending . . . Herbert Clark Hoover must be considered the founder of the New Deal in America. . . . To scoff at Hoover's tragic failure to cure the Depression as a typical example of laissez-faire is drastically to misread the historical record. The Hoover rout must be set down as a failure of government planning and not of the free market.[4]

There is no way to exaggerate the tragic desperation of the nation at the end of Hoover's Presidency. But Hoover and his administration refused to admit that the disaster was a result of their interventionist policies; they continued to blame businessmen and speculators. But the truth is that Hoover's economic interventionism had only made things worse—far worse.

The Fourth Myth: Roosevelt's Interventionism Succeeded in Bringing the Depression to an End

The basic error in this fourth myth does not concern Roosevelt's interventionism. If anyone was an economic interventionist, Franklin Roosevelt was. The mythical component in our fourth claim concerns the mistaken belief that the ultimate end of the Depression was a result of any of Roosevelt's economic policies. The evidence makes it clear that late into the 1930s, Roosevelt's interventionist measures were only making things worse! The best way to make this clear is to track Roosevelt's efforts and their results from his inauguration in 1933 to the end of the decade.

During his first one hundred days in office, Roosevelt and his administration refused to remove the barriers to prosperity raised during the Hoover years. Instead, he erected dozens of new barriers. Roosevelt's first significant action with regard to the economy was to undercut the quality of the dollar by seizing people's private gold holdings. This action was an important symbol of Roosevelt's intentions. As one source explains:

> When there exist no restrictions on the ownership and use of gold, people are ultimately free to accept or reject paper money depending on their assessment of the integrity of those who have issued it. Private ownership of gold represented a potential road block to New Deal economic controls. Accordingly, the administration quickly set about to acquire physical possession and legal title to all gold in the nation.[5]

In 1933 and early 1934, private holders of gold were forced to turn over their gold to the government. They were paid a price well *below* the *market* price, but *equal to* the *official* price of gold. By this act of confiscation, the federal government gained legal and physical control of the nation's gold, which it replaced with certificates. The action of the government was legalized theft. Later, in 1934, the government raised the *official* price of gold to $35 an ounce, which was above the market price. This devaluation produced a de facto profit for the government of $2.8 billion.

A dollar thus became worth whatever the government said it was worth. According to later reports of Secretary of the Treasury

Henry Morgenthau, Roosevelt one day decided to raise the price of gold by 21¢. When asked about his reason for this precise amount, Roosevelt explained that 7 is a lucky number and 21 is 3 times 7.[6] Morgenthau confided to his diary that if the nation had been aware of the arbitrary grounds on which the price of gold was determined, all confidence in the dollar would have been shattered.

Then Roosevelt's advisors proposed the National Recovery Act (NRA), instituted in 1933 as a way of increasing the purchasing power of American workers. The Act established minimum wages, prices, and rates for specific industries. Its purpose was to raise prices at the same time that it increased purchasing power. The government did this by forcing employers to increase their payrolls by means of shorter work weeks and a minimum wage. It also banned jobs for youth. This government-mandated increase in business costs acted as a further brake on economic recovery. Unemployment increased still more, to almost thirteen million. The minimum wage provisions of the law caused enormous suffering in the South, where approximately a half million blacks were forced out of work.[7] In 1935, the Supreme Court declared that the NRA was unconstitutional. But the policies of the NRA had given the economy another severe jolt which had the effect of postponing any recovery.

Roosevelt's results with American agriculture were just as bad. Congress passed the Farm Relief and Inflation Act, also known as the Agricultural Adjustment Act (AAA). It was supposed to increase the income of farmers by reducing the number of acres under cultivation and by destroying crops already in the field. Farmers were paid not to plant. The program spread rapidly from its original coverage of cotton to all basic cereals and meat and then to all cash crops. This expensive program was supposed to be paid for by a so-called "processing tax." The new tax that the AAA placed on the agricultural industry provided money that was used to destroy crops and livestock. Healthy animals were slaughtered, and fields of cotton, wheat, and corn were plowed under. Farmers were paid not to plant crops. Like all interventionist acts, the government thought it was aiding one group of people in the market. But of course this "aid" would have to come at the expense of the many others who were forced to pay for it. Even if the program had helped the farmers—which it did not—it would have done so at enormous cost to the millions who had to pay higher prices or had less to eat.[8]

When the Roosevelt interventionists saw that things were not going as they had planned, they decided that the ensuing disaster was not the result of their efforts. It was a result rather of their measures not going far enough. What the nation needed was more priming of the economy by the federal government. Roosevelt's budget message in January 1934 promised a $7 billion deficit in a total budget of $10 billion. This attempt to prime the economic pump failed to revive the economy. A slight recovery in the first half of 1934 was followed by a decline to an even lower economic level by September of 1934.

Roosevelt's administration raised taxes in 1933, in 1934, and again in 1935. Federal estate taxes became the highest in the world. By now, it was clear that the increased taxation was aimed not at the production of more revenue but at the redistribution of income.

When the Supreme Court judged that both the NRA (in 1935) and the AAA (in 1936) were unconstitutional, two awesome burdens were removed from the American economy. The end of NRA helped to increase productivity and reduce labor costs. The end of AAA lowered taxes on agriculture and ended the destruction of crops and livestock. Unemployment began to come down in the mid-1930s. But the planners in the Roosevelt Administration had not yet learned anything from their past mistakes. Anxious to earn the support of organized labor for Roosevelt's reelection bid in 1936, Roosevelt and the Democratic majority in Congress gave them the Wagner Act of July 1936, a prize that Big Labor never forgot.

The Wagner Act or the National Labor Relations Act was a response to the Supreme Court's decisions with regard to NRA and AAA. The Act totally revolutionized labor relations in the country. No longer could labor disputes be settled in the courts; they were now under the jurisdiction of the National Labor Relations Board, a new federal agency which served as judge, jury, and prosecutor. Following Roosevelt's reelection in 1936, the big unions began to consolidate the massive new powers granted them under the Wagner Act. Millions of workers were forced to join unions. While wages were forced up, worker productivity declined. Strikes idled many plants. The ensuing jump in labor costs produced another decline in economic activity. Unemployment once again passed the ten million mark. At the end of 1937, the American economy collapsed once more. The Roosevelt Administration had accomplished something never before achieved in history. It actually managed to produce a depression within a depression. Nothing illustrates the harm generated by Roosevelt's New Deal measures better than the unemployment figures for each year of the Depression.[9]

Year	Number of Unemployed	Percentage of Labor Force
1929	429,000	0.9
1930	3,809,000	7.8
1931	8,113,000	16.3
1932	12,478,000	24.9
1933	12,744,000	25.1
1934	10,400,00	20.2
1935	9,522,000	18.4
1936	7,599,000	14.5
1937	6,372,000	12.0
1938	10,099,000	18.8
1939	9,080,000	16.7

These numbers show that while Roosevelt inherited an unemployment problem, he certainly did not fix it. Unemployment in 1933 was higher than the year before. During three years of Roosevelt's Presidency, unemployment topped ten million. In only two of the seven years between 1933 and 1939 did unemployment drop below eight million. These are the unemployment figures during the heyday of Roosevelt's New Deal. In 1938, unemployment jumped more than it did during the first year of the Depression, reaching 18.8 percent of the labor force. Viewed as an economic experiment to put people back to work, the New Deal was a fraud and a farce. The massive unemployment that still characterized the nation's economy after years of New Deal intervention with the economy was ended only by the nation's need to draft more than ten million men into the military.

The Depression did not result from some defect inherent within capitalism. It did not result from this nation's love affair with unbridled free enterprise during the twenties. The first two claims concerning the Depression that were examined in the previous chapter are clearly untrue.

The genesis of the Great Depression lay in the inflationary monetary policies of government in the 1920s. It was prolonged and exacerbated by a litany of political follies: tariffs, taxes, controls on production and competition, destruction of crops and cattle, and coercive union legislation, to recall just a few. It was not the free market which produced twelve years of agony; rather, it was political bungling on a scale as grand as there ever was.[10]

According to Benjamin Anderson, the nation's failure "to get out of the depression in the years 1933 to 1939 [was] due to the great multiplicity of New Deal 'remedies,' all tending to impair the freedom and efficiency of the markets, to frighten venture capital, and to create frictions and uncertainties, and impediments to individual and corporate initiative."[11] Murray Rothbard ends his long study of the Depression by stating: "The guilt for the Great Depression must, at long last, be lifted from the shoulders of the free market economy, and placed where it properly belongs: at the doors of politicians, bureaucrats, and the mass of 'enlightened' economists."[12]

Our study of economic events during the 1930s has revealed more than the mythical character of Hoover's alleged commitment to free market economics and the supposed success of Roosevelt's interventionism. It has unmasked the extent to which the enormous suffering of the thirties was a consequence of bad economics—to be more specific, interventionist policies that were proposed and enacted with good intentions.

14

Social Security

The American Social Security system is worth studying both from an economic and a moral standpoint. Economically, it makes sense to ask if Social Security taxes, an obligation that is fast becoming the largest part of most working people's tax burden, are used in the most economically efficient way. More is at stake economically than the simple ability of the system to pay all of the benefits promised to present and future retirees—an extremely unlikely prospect in spite of repeated attempts to fix the system by reducing benefits and raising taxes. Another important economic question concerns whether recipients could have been much better off with a different kind of system. Had a different approach to Social Security been adopted, would the nation's economy be in better shape today? Could the impending future crisis of Social Security and the devastating effect it will have on the economy and the lives of millions of individuals have been avoided? Therefore, Social Security is worth studying economically.

But Social Security is also interesting from a moral perspective. The major moral question about Social Security arises from a central feature of the program that few people seem to understand. An example may help. Most of us are familiar with pyramid schemes such as the chain-letter plans that people hatch every so often. Some businesses have prospered by using a variation of the pyramid plan. First, a few people get an idea for a line of products they can sell. They then entice a second level of people to join the organization. In order to qualify, they must not only pay a hefty fee to those on the first level, they must agree to turn over a percentage of their profits to their "managers" on the first level. But the people on the second level then have the right to recruit additional workers at a third level, who in turn must pay their fees and commit a percentage of their profits to their "managers" on the second level, who in turn pass their percentage still lower. Obviously, in such a scheme the people who get in the earliest are the ones who stand to profit. The hope that drives all pyramid schemes is that the number of late-joiners will continue to grow, thus providing an ever increasing basis of support for the early joiners. But it is a matter of mathematical certainty that eventually the system will run out of the late-joiners it needs to keep operating. Eventually, of course, all pyramid schemes collapse for this reason.

The Social Security system is neither a savings nor an insurance program. Many people mistakenly believe that their Social Security taxes become part of a huge reserve fund, and that when they retire they draw "their" money from "their" fund. In fact, Social Security is a pay-as-you-go operation. The money received from Social Security taxes is paid out almost as soon as it is paid into the system to meet its current obligations. As the workers of today are taxed, the money they pay into the system is almost immediately redistributed to current recipients. As things stand now, payroll taxes are used to provide the benefits of people already retired. There is no individual trust fund or account for individual workers. There is barely enough in the reserves of the system to keep it afloat.

The Social Security system therefore is an elaborate pyramid scheme in which late-joiners are forcibly taxed to meet the cost of benefits assigned to earlier joiners. The generations of younger workers are required to accept on faith the principle that still future generations of workers will absorb all future costs and will pay the taxes that will cover their benefits. Unfortunately, there is one enormous problem with this assumption: the number of future *recipients* keeps growing at the same time that the number of future *workers* whose taxes are needed to pay for future benefits is declining. In 1950, each person receiving benefits from Social Security was supported by sixteen workers who paid Social Security taxes. But by 1970, just twenty years later, each recipient was supported by only four workers. In the mid-1980s, the ratio of workers to recipients is only three to one.

While the situation is supposed to stabilize during the 1990s (although this depends on a number of major assumptions about such things as the health of the economy), serious trouble is likely to arise around the year 2010 when the huge baby-boom population born right after World War II begins to retire. When that happens, the ratio of workers to recipients will be about two to one. In order for this relatively small number of workers to support the enormous future obligations of the system, it is estimated that within seventy years Social Security taxes will have to take as much as 40 percent of a worker's income. That means that a worker earning, say, $30,000 a year will have to pay out $12,000 just in Social Security taxes. From what is left, he or she will then have to pay all of the other federal, state, and local taxes. As always happens with any pyramid scheme, its fraudulent character will become evident sooner or later.

The Social Security system is interesting ethically because of the rivalry it is creating between generations, a problem that will become increasingly apparent in the decades to come. There is good reason to believe that the Social Security system will cause social divisiveness in the future between the large number of retirees who expect to receive their promised benefits and the relatively small number of workers who will have to pay increasingly higher taxes required to keep those promises.[1]

And then, speaking of ethics, there is the collection of politicians who over the years have helped to create this Frankenstein's monster. Careful students of American politics have little difficulty naming past and present members of Congress who used Social Security to frighten older voters into voting for them when the alternatives suggested by their opponents were precisely the changes the system needed. Many politicians have been less interested in the welfare of the workers who are compelled to pay the taxes or the welfare of beneficiaries of the system than in using the system to enhance their own personal advantage or that of their party in the next election.

In practice, Social Security has become a political sacred cow that even honorable politicians are afraid to touch for fear that demagogic opponents will misrepresent their efforts and frighten uninformed, frequently older voters. Dishonorable politicians make it extremely difficult to get people to understand the truth about the system and what is needed to put the system in order. Politicians have often gained immediate goodwill from the electorate by voting for increased benefits while delaying the tax increases needed to pay for those benefits. When those tax increases take effect slowly and silently years later, voters tend to overlook the political decisions made years before that are responsible for their smaller paychecks. By the time some of those tax increases take effect, some of the politicians have left public life, having seen to it that their own retirement benefits do not depend on Social Security.

But why, it might be asked, is it that whenever some poll is taken of Social Security recipients, the system receives such high marks? If the system is so questionable economically and morally, why is there not more criticism of it from the retired people who receive its benefits? To some extent, the answers to this question should be obvious. Present beneficiaries of the system have little reason to complain. Ask any group of people are the early-joiners in a pyramid scheme what they think of it and they will give it high marks. Many beneficiaries of the system have received or will receive far more than they ever contributed in the form of payroll taxes. It is interesting that no one has yet taken a poll of what a group of workers under, say, the age of forty think about the system after they have been given a complete picture of how their payroll taxes will continue to increase and what is likely to be the under-funded status of the system when they are ready to retire. No one in the government is telling younger workers that they will never begin to receive in benefits what they paid out in Social Security taxes.

Nor is anyone in government telling present retirees how much better off they and their heirs would be if the system had been operated as a true insurance program with a trust fund for each individual contributor that would earn compound interest. Suppose Social Security had been set up as something other than a pay-as-you-go system. Suppose instead that each person's contributions (taxes) had been deposited to his or her private account. Suppose further that this account had been allowed to earn compound interest at market rates. A significantly smaller tax could have resulted in a much larger pool of retirement money. A system designed in this way would have had several other significant advantages. For example, consider what happens under the present system if a person who has paid Social Security taxes for forty-five years dies without a surviving spouse shortly before or shortly after retiring. His or her heirs receive nothing from the thousands of dollars paid into the system except the tiny death benefit.

But in a privatized system where each individual has his or her own retirement account that is earning compound interest, any remaining balance from the principal and interest would be available to the heirs of the person's estate. Furthermore, if the amounts presently going into the Social Security system were channeled instead into private pensions, huge amounts of money would be available for loans to businesses and individuals. Because present Social Security taxes do not end up as a usable pool of money drawing interest until the individual is ready to use it, the reduced pool of loanable money contributes to higher interest rates, which in turn creates a drag on investment and the formation of capital.

The present system also has a negative effect on savings. First, the payroll tax means that workers have less disposable income to save.[2] Secondly, for the millions of people who don't know better and who mistakenly believe that future Social Security checks will pay for their retirement, there is less incentive to save for postretirement years.

There is probably more misinformation about the Social Security system than about any program of comparable size and influence. The false information that the public has about the program plays a major role in hindering efforts to improve the system. The most recent example of misinformation appears in the form of claims that legislation passed in 1983 has finally put Social Security on a firm financial basis. Those changes, we are asked to believe, have made the system financially sound for the next seventy-five years. While the statement is patently false, the degree to which it misses the mark depends upon which set of assumptions one makes about such things as the future performance of the American economy and the longevity of present and future beneficiaries.

According to the most optimistic set of assumptions about the nation's economy, which are in fact far more optimistic than past economic performance warrants, the system will remain in good financial shape until about the year 2010 or 2015 when the baby-boom population born after World War II begins to retire. According to a more realistic set of assumptions (which includes the possibility of economic downturns, higher unemployment, and inflation), the Social Security system trust funds will be totally exhausted before the year 2000, more than a decade before the baby-boom generation swells the ranks of the retired. Whether the shortfalls in the trust fund come in 2035 or in 2015, they will be so enormous as to be incomprehensible. According to Peter Ferrara, while we are being told that the system is financially sound for the next seventy-five years, the government's own most optimistic scenario leads to figures that show

> Social Security running a cumulative deficit 50 percent greater than the total amount raised by new revenues or by cuts in benefits under the 1983 legislation passed to save Social Security from bankruptcy. These projections indicate, in other words, that Social Security still faces a long-term financing

crisis that will impede the system's ability to honor its obligations to today's young workers.[3]

Ferrara's words must not be allowed to slip by unnoticed.
What he is saying is this: even if we take the government's most
optimistic set of assumptions about the future, and even if we
calculate all of the money the system is supposed to take in over
that period (taking into account all of the future tax increases that
were built into the 1983 legislation), the total shortfall for the
system will still exceed income by 50 percent. Ferrara estimates
that in order for the system to pay all of the benefits that today's
younger workers are being promised, the payroll tax would have to
be increased from the present 14.1 percent to 23 percent.[4] But once
again, this future crisis is based on assumptions so optimistic that
they border on being utopian.

If we adopt a more realistic set of assumptions, not even the
word *crisis* is appropriate to describe the problems that will con-
front the nation. Under a more realistic set of projections, Ferrara
warns,

> annual surpluses [will] never develop and the trust funds for
> the entire program will be completely exhausted in 1998. This
> means that the program would be unable to pay its promised
> benefits.
>
> By 2035, when young workers entering the work force
> today will be retiring, Social Security expenditure obligations
> under these projections would be 2.3 times as large as rev-
> enue. Paying all these promised benefits in that year would
> require a total Social Security payroll tax rate of about 37
> percent. . . . The cumulative deficit for Social Security over
> the 75-year projection period, under these [more realistic]
> assumptions, would be more than 4.5 times as large as the
> financial gap closed by the 1983 legislation.[5]

Adding to the woes of the Social Security system is the huge
increase in the number of people over age sixty-five that will occur
in the next fifty years. While there are presently about twenty-nine
million Americans over the age of sixty-five, this number is estimated to clumb to around eighty million by the year 2035. Social
Security benefits in 2035 are expected to be five trillion dollars a
year, twenty-five times the current total.

The threat of massive future increases in the Social Security tax should not divert attention from the huge increases that have been enacted over the past thirty years. In 1956, the taxable wage base for Social Security was $4,200. The combined employee/employer tax rate that year was 4.0 percent, making the maximum combined tax only $168. In 1986, for the first time the maximum combined employee/employer tax will exceed $6,000. The maximum 1986 payroll tax for self-employed persons will be $5,166. This huge increase from a 1956 maximum tax of $168 to a combined 1986 maximum tax exceeding $6,000 is a result of steady increases in the tax rate and the taxable wage base. Additional increases in the payroll tax are already scheduled to take effect in 1988 and 1990.

Many people tend to ignore the employer's share of the Social Security tax. This is another example of how misled we can be by economic ignorance. The employer's share of the payroll tax is one of his costs of doing business. Like all such costs, it is passed on to his customers. Hence, every customer (which includes the worker who pays his own Social Security taxes and the retired person who receives Social Security benefits) pays a higher cost for goods and services. Without the additional payroll tax, employers would be able to pay higher wages or provide more fringe benefits to employees. The employer's matching contribution to Social Security is not a free gift to the worker's retirement program. In one way or another, every worker pays for the employer's share of the tax through higher prices for goods and services, or lower wages and benefits. But the politicians were smart. Dividing the total tax in this way helps to disguise the total cost of the program.

None of the criticisms made in this chapter are intended to challenge the concept of Social Security. The United States needed a program that would help provide for its elderly citizens. Nor do these criticisms reflect opposition to policies that force younger workers to set aside a portion of their present income to cover their financial needs after retirement. There is certainly no thought of denying present or future retirees the full benefits they were promised. Morally, the federal government is obligated to keep its promises.

But important questions need to be asked. Was there a better way to set up a program of Social Security? Could important improvements have been made twenty years ago that would have effectively eliminated the future problems that still exist? Is there still time to adopt measures—however much more painful they will be under the present circumstances—that could ease the pressure on future generations? Are there changes that can still be made that are morally acceptable and that will enable the system to meet its future obligations in a way that is economically more efficient?

The rest of this chapter will review a number of suggestions currently being made. These suggestions, it is claimed, will help the Social Security system to keep its current promises, ease the future crisis facing the system, and help younger workers gain a more secure financial base for their retirement years. But regardless of what changes are contemplated and actually effected, absolutely nothing should be done to diminish the benefits of those already retired. The government should make it clear that it has every intention of keeping its promises.

(1) In its present form, Social Security performs two functions: welfare and insurance. Peter Ferrara suggests a division of these two functions into different programs. While a separate program to help the poor is developed, the insurance function should be turned over to the private sector. As much of the program as possible should be privatized, should be moved out of the federal budget. But the elderly should be given assurances that their benefits will not be cut. This can be done by giving retired people a U.S. government bond guaranteeing their promised benefits. Such bonds would have the same legal status as Treasury bonds. Any attempt to refuse payment would be unconstitutional.

(2) Once this is done, incentives should then be provided to encourage people to save for their own futures. One way to do this is through an expansion of IRAs. As Ferrara explains:

> The maximum annual contribution limit should be set equal to one-half the maximum annual combined Social Security tax. Nonworking spouses should be allowed to contribute the same amount as working spouses. IRA benefits should be made tax exempt, providing an immediate incentive for increased savings at virtually no cost now.[6]

Even though Ferrara would allow workers to receive a full tax credit for their contributions to these new "Super IRAs," such credits would produce a proportional reduction in future retirement benefits under Social Security. But because these reduced Social Security benefits would be less than the accumulated funds in these expanded IRA accounts, the workers would be much better off after retirement.

With this reform Social Security would be substantially strengthened financially, since payroll taxes financing Social Security would be maintained in full [save for repeal of legislated increases after 1986], while the tax credit for Super IRA contributions would be taken against income taxes, not payroll taxes. Moreover, over the long run Social Security expenditures would be reduced, as workers relied increasingly on their Super IRAs rather than Social Security. If this change were adopted now, and expanded over time, Social Security taxes could be cut in the 1990s. By the time the baby-boom generation retired, Social Security expenditures could be reduced sufficiently to enable the benefit obligations made to the baby-boomers to be financed in full. Moreover, as the option was continually expanded, Social Security expenditures would be reduced commensurately, and payroll taxes could be cut steadily.[7]

(3) The massive increases in the payroll tax set to take effect in 1988 and 1990 should be repealed because of the enormous harm they will do to the economy.

(4) Many economists also discuss the importance of lowering the expectations of current workers about future benefits. People are now living longer and experiencing better health. For this reason, retiring at age sixty-five should not be the issue in the 1990s that it was, say, in 1940 or 1950. Modest gradual increases in the eligibility age would not diminish the normal benefit period that future recipients would have relative to the number of years during which earlier generations of retirees received benefits. A gradual elevation of the eligibility age from sixty-five to sixty-eight would hardly penalize new retirees whose life-expectancy continues to increase. Such an action would increase the number of workers paying Social Security taxes at the same time that it would reduce the number of people receiving benefits. The objections to such a change reflect the expectations of people long accustomed to thinking that retirement at age sixty-five is their birthright. That is why the public relations and psychological dimension of this task must be handled effectively.

The present but destined to be short-lived solvency of the Social Security system has been bought at the price of repeated increases in the taxes that workers and employers are forced to pay. Additional increases are already scheduled to take effect. The program has become a bad bargain for those who must still look forward to many years of forced contributions. Efforts to ease the impending financial crisis of the system by means of even higher taxes will make things even worse for younger workers. For these younger workers, it could be a serious mistake to put all or most of their retirement eggs in the Social Security basket. Basic reforms are needed. But it is not necessary for such reform to deprive older citizens of benefits that they have been promised and have based their retirement hopes upon.

However, as Peter Ferrara observes, young people today "recognize that Social Security is not suited to the modern economy and today's workers. Individuals want expanded opportunity and control for the future. They will not long tolerate the periodic rounds of tax increases and benefit cuts and the 'let them eat cake' mentality of the current Washington establishment."[8] Continued refusal by Congress to face the truth about the coming crisis and to act in a way that is both economically and morally responsible will only increase the injury that the system will do to today's younger workers.[9]

15
Money, Mammon, and Wealth

Many Christians exhibit a schizophrenic attitude towards money and wealth. On the one hand, its necessity in enabling people to meet their own basic needs—to say nothing about dispensing charity towards others—obliges us first to earn it and then use it in economic exchange. But on the other hand, many Christians have difficulty reconciling their inescapable involvement with money with Biblical passages that seem to contain dire warnings about money, mammon, and wealth. Since it is easier for a camel to pass through the eye of a needle than for a rich man to enter heaven, they think there must be something dirty and sub-Christian about money. Adding to the dilemma that many Christians face with regard to money is an understandable feeling of guilt. After all, this world is not supposed to be their home; they are supposed to lay up their treasures in heaven. The world is full of millions of poor and starving people. And yet these Christians have so much in the way of material goods.

Now, of course, there is one obvious way of dealing with all of this. Christians who have more than they need could fulfill what they take to be their Christian duty and give their money away in ways that will help people in need. This requires trust in the integrity and competence of the individuals and agencies who distribute that money. Other Christians who regard their abundance as a trust under God choose to invest excess money in ways that may help others. Too little attention is given to the fact that a Christian who invests in a business is helping others by providing jobs and also providing goods and services that people value. If that business should prove successful, new wealth can be created that can benefit an increasing number of people. This is especially true when such investments are made in ways that create jobs and produce useful goods in poor countries.

But a growing number of Christians appear to have little use for the kinds of voluntary measures described in the previous paragraph. Their approach to dealing with those who manage to accumulate more than is required to meet the basic necessities of life involves the use of force. Instead of educating Christians in the importance of Christian stewardship and then encouraging them to use their money voluntarily in ways that accord with Biblical teachings, the new class of Christian collectivists insists that the state use its coercive powers and take whatever it regards as properly excessive and use it in whatever way seems best to the elitists who happen to control the state at that particular time. Since these views are discussed in other chapters, nothing more need be said about them here.

What is relevant for this chapter is the growing conviction—usually found in those Christians of the Left who have such confidence in the wisdom of the state—that money and wealth are somehow evil or at least sub-Christian. One place where this attitude towards money is apparent is Jacques Ellul's book *Money and Power*.[1] First published in Europe a number of years ago, Ellul's book has recently been translated into English. Its U.S. publication by InterVarsity Press was accompanied by an endorsement in *Christianity Today*, the major journalistic voice for mainstream Protestant evangelicalism.

There is something self-defeating about a book that condemns money as evil. One way to see this problem is to ask if Ellul's publisher has been giving his book away for free. Even if we assume that Ellul might have written his book without any promise of royalties (money), even if the translator had done her work without promise of an honorarium (money), InterVarsity Press would never have gone to the expense (money again) of publishing the book without some expectation of receiving enough money in return to cover more than their costs, something that nonradical Christians call profit. Booksellers would not stock the book without some confidence that customers would be willing to exchange their evil money for the book.

Ellul's book meshes with a strange mood that has spread throughout segments of evangelicalism. This mood has led many to act as though piety can cover a multitude of intellectual sins. If we are sincere enough and care enough and are pious enough, these people seem to suggest, we can simply ignore the economic and political realities of life.

One reason Ellul detests money is because it "creates what

could be broadly called a buying-selling relationship. Everything in this world is paid for one way or another."[2] Some readers might conclude that Ellul has gotten lost in the thickets of his own metaphors. "The world," he continues, sees buying and selling "as normal. Without constant exchange, we could not continue to live."[3] So says the world, according to Ellul. But so also says Ellul's publisher, the bookstores that sell his book, and so too says Ellul himself as he engages in his daily activities. One would like to believe that Ellul has a deeper message here, one that lies beneath the absurdly utopian message that his words convey when taken at face value. But no amount of digging seems to turn up that deeper message. There are certainly all kinds of evil to which improper uses of money can lead. In the fallen world in which we live, an inordinate devotion to money often leads people to treat others in a dehumanizing way. But Ellul is so captivated by his oversimplified approach to the world that he fails to see that buying and selling can be done in ways that do not dehumanize people.

Ellul then turns to a new point. He states that "all subordination of humankind to money is intolerable."[4] When this claim is understood in its normal sense, it is certainly true. For example, slavery—a clear instance where people are subordinated to money—is intolerable. So too is any exploitative relationship where some people dominate others for financial reasons. But Ellul is not satisfied with such obvious illustrations of his thesis. He takes a great leap and concludes that *any* situation in which a worker exchanges his time and effort for a wage is necessarily a subordination of humankind to money. According to Ellul, people are being exploited and dehumanized even when they choose voluntarily to exchange their time and labor for wages. It seems clear that Ellul's point depends on the unstated assumption that such economic exchanges are a zero-sum game, an assumption that we have already found reason to challenge. While exploitation may be a feature of some economic exchanges, it is not inherent in all economic exchange. On the contrary, voluntary economic exchange is a positive-sum game in which both parties win.

Ellul goes on to maintain that the subordination of humans to money occurs "in each selling transaction, which inevitably sets up a destructive, competitive relationship even when the sale is of an ordinary object."[5] The reader must pause to reflect about what Ellul is claiming in this sentence. He is saying that even the sales of the most ordinary, innocent objects set up a destructive and competitive relationship that Christians should denounce. Ironically,

Ellul seems unaware of how this judgment applies to every transaction in which someone purchased his book. Ellul turns every religious bookseller into a participant in a destructive, evil relationship. His judgment also applies to the transaction in which his publisher exchanged its royalties for Ellul's book. Every time a child buys candy or an adult pays for electricity, he is a participant in an evil and destructive relationship. "In every case," Ellul continues, "one person is trying to establish superiority over another."[6] Ellul implies that parents should warn children who request quarters to buy candy bars that they are about to enter into an exploitative relationship. And heaven help the storeowner who dares to sell that child the candy. "The idea that selling can be a service is false; in truth the only thing expressed by the transaction is a will to power, a wish to subordinate life to money."[7]

Ellul has still other things to say about money, and they will be noted in due course. Lest one think that he is alone in his attitude towards money, Andrew Kirk's own misadventures in the area of economics would not be complete if he had neglected to share his convictions about the subject before us. While Kirk shies away from stating that money is evil, he leaves no doubt about the fact that the Bible teaches that wealth is evil. He writes: "There can be no doubt, if we approach the Bible with honesty, that private accumulation is usually deemed to be the result not of harmless transactions in the market place, but of either violence, fraud, bribes or expropriations. . . ."[8] In Kirk's universe, apparently, no one ever prospers honorably. The simple fact that someone possesses more than the bare necessities of life is proof enough for Kirk that the person is defective morally. Kirk supports this indictment of *all* the people whom he judges as having more than they should by appealing to a number of proof-texts from the Bible. A quick examination of Kirk's proof-texts, which include Micah 2:2, Hosea 12:8, and Jeremiah 5:28, will reveal the shallow nature of his Biblical exegesis. The verses he cites as proof that all rich people have acquired their holdings dishonestly actually say something quite different. Actually, Kirk appeals to texts that condemn the dishonest pursuit of wealth and uses them in support of a totally different claim—namely, that the Bible condemns all wealth.

Before noting any more examples of what contemporary Christian writers have to say about money and wealth, it may be helpful to pause and ask some rather basic and elementary questions about money. I will offer a brief account of the nature of money. I will then examine the New Testament in order to see, among other things, what Jesus actually taught about money, mammon, and wealth. It turns out to be something quite different from the claims made by writers like Ellul and Kirk.

What Is Money?

Money is first and foremost a medium of exchange. As human society became increasingly more complex, it became inconvenient for humans to barter one commodity or service for another or to exchange a certain quantity of labor for a certain quantity of some commodity. No one invented money; it simply developed. People who wanted to exchange something found that it was sometimes difficult to find someone who had exactly what they wanted and who at the same time wanted exactly what they had to exchange. In order to make exchanges easier, the circle of exchanges widened from two parties to three or more. A had what B wanted; B had what C wanted; C had what A wanted. In this way, indirect exchanges began to develop. Over a period of time, specialized goods that were more difficult to trade were exchanged for goods that were more easily marketed. As a consequence, the more marketable goods became even more marketable because demand for them increased. Eventually, the most marketable or saleable of these goods acquired the function of money, a medium of exchange. Many goods have served as money. In the cultures with which we are most familiar, money tended to take the form of precise weights of such metals as gold and silver.

In this sense of a medium of exchange, money is both a social and an economic convenience. It makes complicated economic exchanges more convenient and more efficient than if each person had to barter commodities and services directly with other people. Money is an important social institution. A complex society simply could not function without some kind of common medium of exchange. Money also allows people to specialize in what they do best and thus increase their efficiency in ways that benefit both themselves and others. People no longer have to produce everything that they need in the way of food, clothes, and housing. They can concentrate on what they do best, exchange that good or service for money, and then exchange that money for whatever else they want. As people specialize in this way, their productivity is increased.

In addition to its use as a medium of exchange, money has acquired several subsidiary functions. For example, it is useful as a measure of value. Money is used as a standard by which we measure the value of various things. When a farmer goes to buy a new truck or tractor, he does not have to think in terms of the number of cattle he will have to exchange in order to acquire the tractor. He can think solely in terms of the monetary cost. Obviously, it is easier and more efficient to handle such transactions in terms of a common denominator than to engage in a continuing series of calculations in which one estimates the interrelated exchange values for a large number of items. Money eliminates the need for such complex procedures by serving as the one commodity with reference to which the price of anything can be compared.

Money is also useful as a measure of deferred payment. When selling something, it is not necessary that the seller demand full payment in the present. He may opt instead for a deferred payment in order to receive interest. Money is also useful as a store of wealth. It is an easy form by which people can save and store that part of their wealth that they choose not to consume in the present.

Given the important social functions of money, it is difficult to understand what Christians like Ellul really have in mind when they denounce money. The conviction of some Christians that money is evil appears to be grounded on several serious economic errors. Such Christians seem to have little comprehension of what voluntary economic exchange is and how it is a positive-sum game in which both parties can win in the sense of leaving the trade in better position than they were before the trade. They also seem unaware of the necessary social functions money performs as a medium of exchange, as a measure of value, and as a store of wealth. Much of Ellul's confusion in this area seems to result from his failure to draw a clear distinction between *money* (anything that may be used as a means of exchange) and *mammon* (which is money personified and deified).

Money and Mammon

Christians like Ellul are right in warning that money can often assume a sinister power over human lives. But whenever this happens, money (something ethically neutral) has become mammon. Ellul refers to the texts where Jesus spoke about mammon (Matt. 6:24; Luke 16:31). Most people interpret Jesus' words in these texts as teaching that money has the potential of becoming a power that can assume control over people. Ellul rejects this interpretation as insufficiently radical. In his words: "Money is not a power because man uses it, because it is the means of wealth or because accumulating money make things possible. It [money] is a power *before* all that, and those exterior signs are only the manifestations of this power which has, or claims to have, a reality of its own."[9]

Ellul appears to believe that mammon is a personal, spiritual force or power in opposition to or in conflict with God. Money is a power that "acts by itself, is capable of moving other things, is autonomous (or claims to be), is a law unto itself, and presents itself as an active agent."[10] One would like to think that Ellul is simply spiritualizing here, as some preachers are prone to do when their rhetoric gets the best of them. Unfortunately, that does not seem to be the case. Ellul really seems to think that money is a personal, spiritual force or power existing in opposition to the true God. Like many of the other things he says about money, many of his readers will find it difficult to believe that Ellul means what he says. Has he possibly allowed his metaphors to get the better of him?

A more sensible way of explaining Jesus' teaching about mammon is this. Because human beings are sinners, they are capable of turning anything into an idol. Such idols can and often do assume sinister control over the people who treat them as gods. Even though money is a social institution that can be the source of much good, it—like anything else in God's creation—can be turned into an idol. It is when this happens that money becomes mammon. On the view being suggested here, what should concern the believer is not money (something necessary for economic exchange) but improper attitudes towards money.

Ellul's possible confusion between money and mammon may explain some other strange things he says. For example, he insists that Christians sin if they save money for their future. Given Ellul's confusion, such a claim seems to make sense. If money is evil and if every economic transaction in the present is evil, then it is clearly just as wrong for Christians to put money aside for their future. But Ellul's incredible claim that saving for the future is an act of unbelief is another example of his misreading of Scripture and his shallow grasp of economics. His position is reminiscent of those Christian anti-intellectuals who used to advise Christians not to worry about getting an education since Christ might return at any moment; or of misguided pietists who tell Christians not to worry about good nutrition or health habits since God has promised to take care of them. It never occurs to such pietists that one way in which God takes care of them is through their practice of proper nutrition. God clearly expects Christians to provide for themselves and their families. In fact, those who do not are said to be worse than unbelievers (1 Tim. 5:8). Fortunately, most Christians will ignore Ellul and recognize that one way in which God may take care of them is through their own saving for the future. Some who might heed Ellul's advice will no doubt end up on public welfare, which they will then interpret as God's way of caring for them through the use of other people's money.

What Does the Bible Teach about Wealth?

Claims that the Bible condemns wealth or that God hates all the rich are clearly incompatible with the teachings of Jesus, who saw nothing inherently evil in money, wealth, or private ownership. While Jesus certainly condemned materialism and the compulsive quest for wealth, He never condemned wealth per se. Jesus did not teach that being rich means necessarily being evil.[11] Jesus did not see anything sinful in the ownership of houses, clothes, and other economic goods. He had wealthy friends and followers (Luke 14:1); he stayed in the homes of wealthy people; he ate at their tables (Luke 11:37).

A number of Jesus' parables provide insights into his views on wealth. In Luke 16:9 and the accompanying parable, Jesus taught that His followers should use their resources with the same dedication and keen judgment as the unjust steward. In the parable of the rich farmer (Luke 12:16-21), Jesus did not condemn the farmer for making money but rather for his single-minded concern with his own wealth and happiness. The man was a fool because he was a self-centered materialist who had forgotten God; he was not a fool because he had been a successful businessman. The parable of Lazarus and the rich man (Luke 16:19-31) does not teach that a person's eternal destiny is determined by the amount of possessions he acquires in this life. It is clear that the rich man went to hell because of a godless and self-centered life, a fact made evident by the way he used his wealth and by his indifference to the poor. The parable also implies that Lazarus was a believer. Any interpretation of the parable that suggests the poor man entered heaven simply because he was poor would contradict everything the New Testament teaches about regeneration.

Jesus' teaching stresses human obligations that cannot be fulfilled unless one first has certain financial resources. For example, passages that oblige believers to use their resources for God's purposes presuppose the legitimacy of private ownership.[12] Jesus taught that children have an obligation to care for their parents (Matt. 15:3-9) and that His followers ought to be generous in their support of worthy causes (Matt. 6:2-4). It is rather difficult to fulfill such obligations unless one has certain financial resources.

Jesus often spoke about wealth without condemning it (Matt. 13:44-46; 21:33-46). When He did call on people to renounce their possessions, His statements reflected special conditions; in one instance, for example, he made this demand in a situation where people had made their possessions into a god (Luke 18:22-24). Instead of condemning wealth, then, Jesus' teaching offered an important perspective on how people living in materialistic surroundings should view the material world. What Jesus condemned was not wealth per se but the improper acquisition and use of wealth. Every Christian, rich or poor, needs to recognize that whatever he or she possesses is theirs temporarily as a steward under God. Wealth that is accumulated dishonestly or that becomes a controlling principle in one's life falls under God's judgment. Wealth resulting from honest labor and wise investment, wealth that is handled by people who recognize their role as stewards under God does not.

Those who draw attention only to passages in which Jesus indicted prosperous people are presenting only part of His teaching. Jesus also praised those who through wise management and careful stewardship created wealth. We must avoid the temptation of selecting a few passages from the Gospels and attempting to show that Jesus' views conformed to our preferred opinions and lifestyle. Jesus' teaching about money, wealth, and poverty is extremely diverse.

Some Biblical Principles about Money and Wealth

While the Bible contains no systematic teaching on economics, it does have some important things to say about economic matters. This section of the chapter will note some of the more significant Biblical principles dealing with money and wealth.

The Creation of Wealth
As noted earlier in this chapter, Scripture does not treat either money or wealth as inherently evil. On the contrary, Christians have a mandate to create wealth. Brian Griffiths explains that God placed us in his world to "cultivate it, improve it and harness its resources for our own use. Man has been created to have dominion

in this world. The urge to control, direct and manage the resources of this world is part and parcel of man's nature and vocation. Idleness is at root alien to human personality."[13] God did not intend that humans simply scrape by. "God intended us to enjoy his world. . . . No Christian should feel a sense of guilt from living in a decent house, driving a solid car, wearing a proper suit of clothes or eating a good meal. If we take seriously the fact that this world is God's world, then the business of creating wealth has a Christian foundation."[14]

Since the world is God's creation and since God placed us in such a close relationship to the material world, the creation and use of wealth is a perfectly proper activity. As Griffiths observes,

> Life itself demands that we be continually involved in the process of wealth-creation. The basic necessities for living are not provided like manna; the land has to be cultivated, the sea has to be harvested, minerals have to be extracted, the city has to be supplied with services. God created us with the capacity and the desire to do all these things. Life itself, therefore, demands that we use what God has given us to provide the necessities.[15]

Other chapters of this book discuss the nature of and necessary conditions for the creation of wealth. They also touch on the economic importance of wealth-creation, especially for the poor. It is important to recognize, therefore, that one economic principle in Scripture is the human mandate to create wealth.

The Warning About Money

While there is nothing inherently evil about money or wealth, and while the creation of wealth is a legitimate Christian concern, nevertheless the Bible contains a clear warning that money can and often does have a negative effect on people's character and spiritual relationships. Money can be hazardous to a person's spiritual health. While neither the parable of the rich farmer (Luke 12) nor Lazarus (Luke 16) condemn wealth per se, they illustrate the extent to which the pursuit of wealth can damage a human soul. In Matthew 13:22, wealth was one of the things that choked the growing seed. The rich young ruler could not bring himself to renounce his wealth in order to follow Jesus (Luke 18:18-23). The love of money is the root of all kinds of evil (1 Tim. 6:10).

Brian Griffiths, whose defense of wealth-creation has been noted, also recognizes the peril of wealth.

> The mere fact of owning wealth tends to produce a spirit of arrogance and self-reliance. Success tends to breed a philosophy of possessiveness: things become mine, my money, my property, my company, my work force. Wealth gives people a false sense of security; it deadens the life of the spirit; it makes people unresponsive to the good news of the gospel.[16]

Without question, then, the pursuit of money can become an obstacle that can make it difficult or even impossible for some to enter the Kingdom of God (Mark 10:25). Concern with wealth can encourage the development of such character traits as arrogance, selfishness, self-satisfaction, materialism, and a total indifference to the plight of the needy. Money has the potential of becoming a god that competes for our devotion and commitment.

The Doctrine of Stewardship

Human beings are only stewards of their possessions. Since God is the Creator of all that exists, He ultimately is the rightful owner of all that exists (Psa. 24:1; Job 41:11). Whatever possessions a human being may acquire, he holds them temporarily as a steward of God and is ultimately accountable to God for how he uses them as well as for how he acquires them. Christians have a duty to use their resources in ways that best serve the objectives of God's Kingdom (Matt. 25:24-30; Luke 19:11-27).

The doctrine of stewardship is consistent with the human right to private property. In fact, the Biblical norm is not collective or state ownership but private ownership. Many who notice that God ordered the land of Israel to be divided among Jewish families somehow miss the point that this clearly made property rights within Israel private and not public. While the Old Testament views God as the ultimate owner of all that exists, it also teaches that God passed delegated ownership rights on to families.

Unfortunately, the doctrine of Christian stewardship is often misused by Christian Leftists in an attempt to justify the aggrandizement of the state, a necessary step in the implemention of their political ideology. In such a view, the enhancement of social justice requires the transfer of increasing degrees of authority, power, and money to the government which alone has the compassion and the means to take care of the poor. In this way, Christian stewardship is perverted into a doctrine that obliges Christians to surrender their judgment, will, and resources to the state which, in the view of the Religious Left, becomes God's surrogate on earth.

The Obligation to Share

The followers of Jesus are responsible for those they can help (Matt. 25:31-46). Jesus' disciples were to demonstrate a constant willingness to share their possessions with others (Luke 6:29, 30). However, the New Testament says nothing about this sharing being coerced by the state. Once Christians acknowledge their obligation to care about the poor and to take action on behalf of the poor, the next question concerns the best means to do this. I take it that acceptable means in this matter will result in actions and programs that work, not just in the short run, but in the long run. There are certainly times when the poor do require help in the form of cash and noncash benefits in the present, in the short run. But a system of "aid" that encourages people to become dependent on the dole, that robs the poor of any incentive to seek ways of helping themselves, that leads the poor into a poverty trap, is hardly a model of genuine compassion or of wise public policy. Exception must be taken to those Christians who insist that the only approved means of easing poverty is a welfare state, especially when such measures are now known to be so counterproductive.[17]

The Call for Justice

Christians have an obligation to seek justice both on a personal level and on the level of the structure of society. The God of the Bible is a God of justice (Deut. 10:17, 18). God's people are to rectify instances of economic injustice (Jer. 22:13-17; Lev. 19:13; Malachi 3:5; Jas. 5:4). The Bible clearly condemns those who abuse economic power.

The Christian Left, however, twists the Biblical call for justice in an attempt to use it as a justification for political and economic views that have no basis in Scripture. One way they do is by reading twentieth-century meanings into words like "justice." The basic idea in the Old Testament notion of justice is righteousness. Christian radicals ignore this and attempt to read contemporary notions of distributive justice into Biblical pronouncements about justice. When the Bible says that Noah was a just man, it does not mean that he would have voted the straight Democratic ticket; it means simply that he was a righteous man.

Old Testament prophets like Amos and Isaiah attacked prevailing forms of injustice including dishonesty, fraud, theft, bribery, and exploitation of the weak, poor, and powerless.[18] All such actions reflect a lack of personal righteousness. The prophets also denounce injustice on the level of social structure—for example, an unjust legal system. In Scripture, both individuals and nations can be guilty of sin. But missing from these Biblical calls for justice is any equivalent of the modern welfare state in which government forcibly takes the possessions of some in order to give it to others. According to Brian Griffiths, the Old Testament prophets

> never suggest that the remedy [for such injustice] is therefore an economic redistribution conducted in some sort of spiritual vacuum. They invariably pinpoint the root cause of the trouble as spiritual: the nation has departed from God and economic injustice is one result. The priority therefore is not socio-economic reform but spiritual repentance. In this they showed great insight. Massive redistribution of wealth and complex laws to coerce the rich to divest their properties would be of no avail whatever if there were not a simultaneous commitment on the part of those involved to change their values and behaviour. It was this that the prophets saw as the basis for a just society.[19]

The position of the Religious Left with respect to justice also illustrates an interesting logical fallacy. Their argument usually begins with a major premise such as "God condemns injustice." They derive this major premise from the Bible. Their minor premise is then something like "Capitalism is unjust." Obviously, support for the minor premise must come from evidence based on observation of the world. The conclusion they proceed to draw from their premises is something like "God condemns capitalism." What the Religious Left wants its audience to believe is that the conclusion that God hates capitalism is taught by or follows from Scripture.

Two things must be said about this line of reasoning. First of all, the claim that capitalism is unjust is an empirical claim; its truth or falsity will depend on the evidence. One major argument of this book is that the claim is false. If the minor premise is false, then the argument is unsound. But there is something seriously wrong with any attempt to persuade people that the claim that God condemns capitalism is taught by the Bible. It is true that the Bible teaches that God condemns injustice. But the Bible does not teach the minor premise, "Capitalism is unjust." Therefore, the Bible does not teach the conclusion that "God condemns capitalism."

Summary

The Biblical principles we have noted make it clear that Christians are to beware of the enticements of money and wealth. They should beware of allowing their necessary relationship with money to become so important that they fall victim to acquisitiveness, materialism, selfishness, or idolatry. Christians should remember that whatever they have, they possess it temporarily as a steward of God. They should share with those less fortunate than themselves; they should practice economic justice, encourage economic justice on the part of others, and seek to correct instances of economic injustice. But none of this implies that Christians are to shun money and wealth as necessary evils. In spite of the dangers that accompany money and wealth, Christians are called to create wealth and then make certain that they use it in ways that are consistent with their other Christian obligations.

The Radical View of Jesus

The Religious Left is not content simply to advance a defective understanding of money and attempt to justify that view on a misinterpretation of Scripture. Nor are they content to misuse Scripture, including the teaching of Jesus, in an effort to support their radical political and economic views. They go even further and attempt to turn Jesus into a social reformer committed to the very social causes they represent. This is apparent, for example, in the way they distort the meaning of Luke 4:16-19.

According to Luke's account, Jesus entered into a synagogue and read from Isaiah 61:1, 2—"The Spirit of the Lord is on me, because he has anointed me to preach good news to the poor. He has sent me to proclaim freedom for the prisoners and recovery of sight for the blind, to release the oppressed, to proclaim the year of the Lord's favor."

Many Christians on the Left use this text to reinterpret Jesus' earthly mission in exclusively economic and political terms. In such a view, Jesus came primarily to deliver those who were poor and oppressed in a material sense. But in the traditional Christian understanding of this text, the poverty in view in Luke 4 is *spiritual* poverty. Every member of the human race is poor in the sense of being spiritually bankrupt. None of us have any righteousness of our own. All of us are too blind spiritually to see the nature of our problem or the way of deliverance. All of us are oppressed by the chains of sin. Jesus came to deliver us from the power and penalty of sin. He came to give us spiritual sight and to end our spiritual poverty by making available the righteousness that God demands and that only God can provide.

Although Brian Griffiths understands Luke 4:16-19 somewhat differently than I, he agrees that the text should not be interpreted in political and economic terms. Rather, he writes,

> They are best understood in terms of what Jesus actually did during the three-year period of his ministry which directly followed his making them [the claims in Luke 4]. He went about and did preach the good news to the poor, he miraculously healed the blind, he liberated those who had been imprisoned by evil spirits, he healed a great many people. There is no evidence whatever to suggest that his own interpretation of these words, judged by what he actually did during his own ministry, involved a call to political action.[20]

Jesus did not come into this world as a social reformer.

> Despite poverty around him and the oppression and injustice of the colonial situation in which he found himself, he [Jesus] rejected a secular interpretation of salvation. When tempted, he refused to turn stones into bread. In a similar vein he refused to establish a government which would throw off the shackles of Roman domination. His primary task was to establish a kingdom but it was a kingdom whose dimensions were spiritual and not secular.[21]

Jesus' basic message dealt with such things as human sin and independence from God, the human need for deliverance from sin, and the establishment of His Father's Kingdom. It was not a blueprint for changing society economically or politically.

Conclusion

This chapter began by noting the attempts of some Christian thinkers to argue that the Bible views money and/or wealth as evil. Such claims involve a serious misreading of the Bible. They also evidence a failure to distinguish between money and mammon. Money is an important social institution. A proper reading of Scripture makes it clear that the Bible condemns neither money nor wealth. A careful search of Scripture reveals a number of important Biblical principles that are compatible with an economically responsible view of money. Attempts to enlist Jesus on the side of any political or economic position dishonor Him and misrepresent the teaching of Scripture.

16
Poverty in America

For most Christian discussions of economics these days, the bottom line (real or imagined) is the subject of these next two chapters—the poor. One thing must be clearly understood at the start: Christians have an inescapable obligation to the poor. It is clear from Scripture that God has a special concern for the poor; it follows therefore that God's people had better share that concern. Professing Christians who are unmoved by scenes of starving children in Africa, homeless people sleeping in cardboard boxes, people living in squalor and filth, and children suffering for lack of medical care have a serious spiritual problem.

Unfortunately, discussions about poverty from those on the Christian Left (and from others who do not know better) often confuse compassion for the poor with the quite separate matter of how that compassion should be manifested in positive action to help the poor. In other words, the Christian Left often confuses the *end* of helping the poor and the proper *means* by which that end may be pursued. In truth, the Christian Left often goes even further and suggests that any who reject their specific recommendations demonstrate their lack of concern and compassion for the poor. Their major premise goes like this: if you don't accept the political and economic programs I recommend, then you clearly don't care for the poor. Since the simplistic judgmental arrogance of this line of thinking is obvious, I will ignore it and focus instead on the present Christian dispute over the proper *means* to help the poor.

Some Overlooked Information about Poverty

Noneconomic Dimensions of Poverty
It is a mistake to think of poverty exclusively or even primarily in terms of economics. Obviously people are poor when their re-

sources (usually measured in terms of money) are insufficient to meet basic needs. But to limit one's reflection about poverty to this obvious fact is about as enlightening as saying that the reason a certain number of people are buried in a particular cemetery is because their hearts stopped beating.

One of the more important books dealing with the noneconomic dimensions of poverty is Edward C. Banfield's *The Unheavenly City Revisited.*[1] Banfield invites us to consider whether there are personal factors that predispose some people to a life of poverty. He thinks there are.

Banfield provides a sociologico-psychological analysis of factors that result in people ending up in different social classes: upper class, middle class, and lower class.* A key factor, Banfield finds, in such differences is what he calls a person's "time horizon."[2] Upper-class people tend to be much more future-oriented than lower-class people. They think about the future, they plan for the future, they make present sacrifices for the sake of future gains. Lower-class people, according to Banfield, lack the ability to think beyond the present. They are reluctant to sacrifice anything in their present for some greater gain in the future. They often appear unable to think about the long-range effects of their actions; they tend to live moment to moment. If the lower class person

> has any awareness of a future, it is of something fixed, fated, beyond his control: things happen *to* him, he does not *make* them happen. Impulse governs his behavior, either because he cannot discipline himself to sacrifice a present for a future satisfaction or because he has no sense of the future. He is therefore radically improvident: whatever he cannot use immediately he considers valueless. His bodily needs . . . and his taste for "action" take precedence over everything else—and certainly over any work routine. He works only as he must to stay alive, and drifts from one unskilled job to another, taking no interest in his work.[3]

Informed Christian thinking about poverty should reflect upon and interact with Banfield's theory. One reason many (I do not say all) people are poor is because of a time horizon that results

---

* It is important to note that Banfield does not equate the class of poor people with the group of lower class people, even though there is obviously some overlap.

in their being unable to think beyond the present. While Banfield is correct, his theory only opens the door to a group of new questions: is a present-oriented time horizon genetic? Is it induced primarily or even exclusively by environment? Can people with defective time horizons be helped? Can their children be helped? How does one get present-oriented people to gain the necessary orientation towards the future that is a necessary condition for any lasting relief from poverty?

Banfield's theory is mentioned not to judge members of any social class but to suggest that the problem of poverty for people who exhibit a defective time horizon cannot be dealt with until we address the question of how such people can become more future-oriented.

In the chapter that follows this one, I will examine a number of other examples of the noneconomic dimension to poverty, factors that help explain poverty in nations other than the United States. These factors are sometimes characteristics of the culture. The moral and religious beliefs of a people can provide an environment that is more or less conducive to economic growth. Poverty is affected by such things as literacy, education, and the health of people. Another noneconomic factor affecting the degree of poverty in a nation is that country's political stability.

Because there is more to poverty than the poor not having enough money, adequate approaches to poverty must give proper attention to the ways in which noneconomic factors function as causes of poverty.

Some Unrecognized Factors Affecting Income Distribution

Many important factors that account for people's ranking with regard to income distribution often go unnoticed. For example, the amount of income a person receives during any given year of his life will vary considerably depending upon the person's age, experience, and skills. Retired people, students, unskilled workers or laborers without much experience, and young workers all tend to have lower incomes for reasons that are quite understandable. Skilled or experienced workers in their prime will obviously have significantly higher incomes.

Economists recognize how most people's earnings over their lifetime exhibit a similar pattern. Most people start out earning comparatively little during the years when they are young, inexperienced, and lack important skills. People also end up receiving relatively little income after they retire. In the years between starting out and retirement—assuming that their life-cycle is normal and unaffected by such things as illness and injury—their income pattern will show a gradual but steady increase. This cyclical pattern of people's earnings over a lifetime holds an important implication. Even if every person in the labor force received the same total income over their whole life, any examination of income patterns across a large segment of people at one time would evidence large variations in the income received at that time.

Black economists Walter Williams and Thomas Sowell have noted that many of the income figures for minorities fail to take into account the higher percentages of youthful and unskilled workers in that minority. If the percentage of young, uneducated, and unskilled workers is lower for one minority group than another, its pattern of income distribution will appear higher.[4] On the whole, they argue, income for working blacks compares favorably to income for working whites. But the overall statistics are misleading because there is a disproportionately high percentage of younger blacks, many of whom are also unskilled.

People's income differs also with respect to the amount of time they work. This can affect both annual income and income for an entire life. When total income *after taxes* and *after tax transfers* (cash and noncash welfare benefits) are computed *per hour worked,* the differences between high-income and low-income people is surprisingly small.[5] About 12 percent of Americans are viewed as living below the poverty line. This segment of the population is helped considerably by such noncash or in-kind transfers as food stamps and assistance for medical treatment and housing. Official poverty figures do not take such transfers into consideration, which means that even though someone may be receiving considerable aid in the form of in-kind transfers, such aid does not *officially* reduce the poverty of the recipients. When such in-kind transfers are added to cash transfers and other income (often unreported) received by the poor, the number of people living in poverty is reduced to something betwen 3 and 6 percent.[6]

Recent studies have also begun to show how much fluctuation there is on the income ladder. According to one such study, the evidence shows

that economic well-being fluctuates markedly for individuals over time, with many shifting upward from the lower end of the family income distribution and others shifting downward from the top. By far the most important cause of change is change in family composition—births, deaths, children leaving home, and especially divorce and marriage.[7]

This particular study began in 1968 and was conducted by the Survey Research Center of The University of Michigan. Its ten-year study

> shows that the popular conception of 'the poor' as a homogeneous stable group is simply wrong. Although the series of snapshot pictures of poverty provided by the Census Bureau surveys show fairly constant numbers and characteristics for poor families each year, actual turnover in the poverty population is very high. Only about two-thirds of the individuals living in families with cash incomes below the poverty line in a given year were still poor in the following year, and only about one-third of the poor in a given year were poor for at least eight of the ten prior years. Although the living standard afforded by a poverty level income may be unrealistically low, and although many individuals climbing out of poverty may not go very far, it is clear that persistent poverty characterizes a considerably smaller fraction of our population than the one-year figures would suggest. The addition of in-kind (noncash) benefits from the government would decrease the estimates of persistent poverty still further. . . .[8]

Income fluctuation also exists at the top of the income ladder. Less than one-half of the children of parents in the top 20 percent of the population are able to reach that level of income themselves.

The Extent of America's Assistance to Its Poor

While we often hear how little America has done and is doing for its poor, the fact is that our nation has been extremely generous in making money and other forms of assistance available to its poor. In 1965, all means-tested benefits (that is, benefits for people below specified income and wealth levels) including both cash and noncash benefits amounted to 19.3 billion dollars (measured in constant 1980 dollars).[9] In 1965, income transfers were 9 percent of personal income. By 1975, income transfers had increased to 18 percent of personal income or a total of 57.7 billion dollars (in constant 1980 dollars). This was an increase of 300 percent.

During the same decade when means-tested transfers were rising 300 percent, personal income in the U.S. rose only 42 percent (in constant dollars). Even though cash transfers began to decline after 1975, the slack was more than met with continuing increases in noncash transfers. By 1980, the total of means-tested cash and noncash aid had reached 62.7 billion dollars.

When the Food Stamp program began in 1965, it served 424,000 people. At the end of Johnson's presidency, recipients totalled 2.2 million. The number doubled during Nixon's first two years as president. By the end of Nixon's first term (1972), the number of food stamp recipients had quintupled. By 1980, more than twenty-one million people were receiving food stamps, fifty times more people than were covered during the Johnson presidency.

In 1982, the total U.S. welfare bill at all levels of government (federal, state, and local) came to 403 billion dollars.[10] If we take figures from the Bureau of the Census (August 1984) which state that the number of people living in poverty in the U.S. was 15.2 percent of the population or 35.3 million people, an amazing fact emerges. Had we simply divided the 403 billion dollars this nation spent on poverty at every level of government among the estimated number of poor people, each poor person could have received $11,133. For a family of four, this would have totaled $44,532. Since the official poverty level per family for that year was $9,287, it is clear that America's fight against poverty involves enormous overhead costs. Most of the tax dollars collected to fight poverty end up, Thomas Sowell notes, "in the pockets of highly paid administrators, consultants, and staff as well as higher-income recipients of benefits from programs advertised as anti-poverty efforts."[11] Clearly, the bucket used to carry money from the pockets of the taxpayer to the poor is leaking badly. Many think the real beneficiaries of liberal social programs are not the poor and disadvantaged but the members of the governmental bureaucracy who administer the program.

Two things are clear: (1) America has been spending more than enough money on poverty; and (2) it has not spent that money very wisely. In the words of James Gwartney and Thomas McCaleb, "The problem of poverty continues to fester not because we are failing to do enough, but rather because we are doing so much that is counterproductive."[12]

Have Antipoverty Programs Hurt the Poor?

As we have seen, America has been spending more than four times as much on poverty than would be necessary to raise every poor family in the country above the poverty level. But much more is at stake than the enormous waste of resources. A number of recent studies have shown how well-intended but economically unsound governmental policies have helped poverty become more entrenched in our society. These studies document how the very War on Poverty programs that were supposed to end poverty have in fact made the plight of the poor worse. Only now, twenty years after the start of the War on Poverty programs, are we gaining access to enough data to see the shocking truth about the real effects of social welfare programs.

It is easy to forget that before the War on Poverty began in the mid-1960s, people at the bottom of the economic ladder were making rapid strides towards improving their economic situation. Between 1950 and 1965, the percentage of poor Americans was cut in half (from about 30 percent to less than 15 percent). This remarkable decline took place during the fifteen years prior to the start of the War on Poverty. Poverty in American fell most rapidly during the Eisenhower-Kennedy years when welfare assistance was only a fraction of what it became during the 1970s and 1980s.[13]

The most rapid growth of poverty programs began, then, about the time when poverty in America reached its lowest level.[14] When the War on Poverty programs were just beginning in 1965, the percentage of poor families in the U.S. had dropped to 13.9 percent. This decline occurred without any help from any Great Society programs. The common wisdom in the mid-1960s was that the massive aid to the poor that started flowing under the War on Poverty programs would continue the reduction in poverty. But just the reverse took place. Soon after huge increases in tax transfers began, the progress against poverty slowed, then stopped, and then went into reverse. As Charles Murray documents in his book *Losing Ground: American Social Policy 1950-1980,* progress in reducing poverty stopped abruptly at the very time when federal spending on social-welfare programs began to climb astrononmically.[15]

Many people believe that significant progress against poverty did not begin until the programs of the Great Society got into high gear. But the truth is that once those programs did get started, the improvement of poor people in America began to stop. While poverty had declined from 1947 to 1968, it stood in 1980 at the same percentage as 1968 even though social-welfare spending had multiplied 400 percent between 1968-1980. Even the constancy of the poverty level throughout that period hides some important information. Poverty rates for poor people over the age of sixty-five did decline during the 1970s. But the poverty rate for families under the age of twenty-five jumped dramatically and has continued to climb. In 1968, the poverty rate for families under age twenty-five was 13.2 percent. In 1982, this figure had doubled to 26.1 percent. This climb took place during the decade when the most aid was being given.

In the two decades since the advent of the War on Poverty programs, we have spent over a trillion dollars to end poverty. However, the very social-welfare programs that were supposed to eliminate poverty have increased it and institutionalized it. The millions presently living under the poverty line are much greater than the numbers in this class prior to the start of the War on Poverty. The poor today suffer from less education, higher illegitimacy rates, and more unemployment—all traceable to the very programs that were supposed to improve the lot of the poor. The quality of life among America's poor is far worse today than before the advent of Great Society programs; the likelihood of the poor escaping from the poverty trap is much less.[16]

In the view of Charles Murray, what our nation did in the name of humanitarianism was create a system that has institutionalized poverty and entrapped millions who along with their children may never be able to escape. While our goal was giving the poor more, what we really did was create more poor. We thought we were breaking down barriers that would help the poor escape from poverty, but what we ended up doing was building a poverty trap from which little escape seems likely.[17]

James Gwartney relates the failure of poverty programs to the political concerns of the Christian Left:

Seeking to promote the welfare of the poor, the disadvantaged, the unemployed, and the misfortunate, well-meaning citizens (including a good many evangelical Christians) have inadvertently supported forms of economic organization that have promoted the precise outcomes they sought to alleviate. For too long, socially concerned Christians have measured policies by the intentions of their advocates, rather than the predictable effectiveness of the programs. Put simply, in our haste to do something constructive, we have not thought very seriously about the impact, particularly in the long-run, of alternative policies on the well-being of the intended beneficiaries.[18]

One of the more surprising things about proponents of tax-transfer approaches to helping the poor is their failure to recognize how tax-transfer programs give people incentives to alter their behavior. These adjustments to governmental programs defeat the purposes of the program and often result in the program's being counterproductive.

The harm done by poverty programs to America's poor has been especially hard on American blacks. Nothing did more to focus the nation's attention on the crisis of the black family than Bill Moyers's courageous CBS documentary "The Vanishing Family" (January 25, 1986). At this stage in our history, 60 percent of all black births are illegitimate. The actual percentage of illegitimate births in America's inner cities is obviously even higher than this. Fifty percent of all black teenage females get pregnant. Close to 50 percent of all black children are supported to some extent by one or more levels of government. As the black family disintegrates, the surrounding society falls into moral chaos. More black males are murdered in America each year than the total number of blacks that died during the entire Vietnam War.

What has the crisis of the black family got to do with America's poverty programs? Glenn C. Loury, a black professor of political economy at Harvard's Kennedy School of Government, gives the answer. He writes: "I am persuaded by the argument of George Gilder and Charles Murray that the easy availability of financial support for women with children without fathers present has helped create a climate in which the breakdown in the family could be accelerated."[19] Robert Woodson, another prominent American black and president of the National Association of Neighborhood Enterprises, also sees the welfare state implicated in the crisis of the black family.[20] As black author Joseph Perkins declares:

> I lay the blame for the disintegration of inner-city families wholly on the welfare state. What we have is a welfare system which creates incentives to dissolve existing family unions. . . . I think it is difficult for anyone to argue that the burgeoning welfare state did not bring about the dissolution of black families. Essentially, the state has supplanted the family among disadvantaged blacks. Young black mothers turn to the paternalistic federal government for support instead of looking to the fathers of their children. And young black males eschew their social and moral responsibilities because they too know that the state will act as their surrogate. Be-

cause of the multiplier effect, we have increasing numbers of black children born into single-parent households. And with so many children growing up in female-headed households, the importance of a husband-wife household is inevitably devalued. Thus, marriage doesn't hold the lustre among black youth in today's inner city that it did for their pre-welfare state counterparts.[21]

In the words of Warren T. Brookes, nothing "can begin to match the systematic degradation, dehumanization, and cultural genocide that has been wreaked on black Americans." The American government, he continues, has in the past twenty years, with the best of intentions, "seduced blacks out of the rigors of the marketplace and into the stifling womb of the welfare state."[22] An earlier chapter noted the complicity of liberal economic policies in high rates of black unemployment. This chapter has recognized the role of liberal welfare programs in high rates of black illegitimacy and the dissolution of the black family. While the politics and economics of the Left are justified in the name of compassion, they are speeding us down the tracks to the destruction of the black family and the disintegration of society. And yet representatives of the Christian Left assure us that what the Bible demands is more of this "humanitarian" statism.

Reforming the Welfare System

James Gwartney and Thomas McCaleb have suggested several reforms of the present welfare system.[23] First, the system should be altered so as to reinforce and not subvert such traditional norms as work, intact families, and childbearing within marriage. As they state, "The welfare system must recognize the importance of the family, church, private charity, and community action in the alleviation of poverty."[24] A similar suggestion emerged from a New York conference sponsored by The Center on Religion and Society on "Moral Obligation in America." In part, a published consensus that grew out of the conference stated: "In strengthening and restoring [important social values], the most critical factors are work and family, and these are mutually dependent. . . . The most obvious measure to be taken is to remove existing subsidies and incentives that undermine the nexus of family and work."[25]

Second, Gwartney and McCaleb argue that the welfare system should be reformed so as to give proper recognition to the importance of such voluntary organizations as churches and private charity. In their words, "The welfare system should be structured to reinforce certain traditional values that encourage individual, parental, and family responsibility."[26] Interestingly, The Center on Religion and Society conference affirmed the same point: "The key institutions [in dealing with poverty] are the mediating structures of family, church, voluntary associations, and neighborhoods. Through these institutions, people are empowered to meet their own needs as they best understand their own needs. . . . Policies that strengthen the mediating structures are good; policies that weaken them are bad."

Third, welfare recipients "should not be allowed to use children as hostages in order to blackmail society."[27] It is clear that many welfare mothers use pregnancy as a means of fostering the continued support of the welfare state. Ways should be sought to alter the incentives that encourage such activity.

The Center on Religion and Society conference issued what amounts to a fourth set of reforms.

> New approaches are needed to enforce existing laws regarding child support. Within the existing welfare administration, programs such as "workfare" should be strengthened. Nothing will change without a new sense of obligation backed by law and social sanction. . . . The element of risk in economic activity and in life generally must be frankly affirmed. This means transcending the mentality of entitlements and guarantees. This is required for full participation in this kind of society. Poor people should not be deceived into thinking that, in this respect, the society is going to be changed. They should rather understand that special provisions that make sure they cannot fail also make sure that they do not really belong in this society.

Many of us can already hear the wailing and gnashing of liberal teeth as they denounce such cruel measures against the poor and downtrodden. There is nothing at all cruel about these recommendations. They are made with the conviction that poverty is evil and with the added recognition that many have been induced into perpetual poverty by the false promises and easy support of the welfare state. To quote economist Walter Williams once more: "[I]t is clear that we do not help the less fortunate person by destroying his *best* alternatives, no matter how unattractive that alternative may seem to more affluent observers. . . . Many assume that just because a policy *intends* to help the disadvantaged it will in fact have the intended effect."[28]

The Political Use of the Poor

Since Christians ought to take the poor seriously, they should be among the first to condemn any who use the poor for personal or partisan gain. There may be merit then in heeding the words of Joseph Sobran in this regard. According to Sobran,

> Any politician who is rash enough to challenge the dependency programs can be put back in his place by a spate of fearful demagogy calculated to terrify and enrage dependent voters. He will be accused of "lacking compassion." If he tries to represent the interests of taxpayers against these programs . . . he will be accused of representing "greed" and "favoring the rich." Liberalism, of course, professes to speak for "the poor," even though, given a choice between the poor themselves and a program whose real effect is to hurt the poor, it will choose the program.[29]

Sobran continues:

> "The poor" are to liberalism roughly what "the proletariat" is to Communism—a formalistic device for legitimating the assumption of power. What matters, for practical liberals, is not that (for example) the black illegitimacy rate has nearly tripled since the dawn of the Great Society; it is that a huge new class of beneficiaries has been engendered—beneficiaries who vote, and who feel entitled to money that must be taken from others.[30]

Black scholar Walter Williams expresses his outrage at what such people have done to his own race by calling them "poverty pimps." They profit by trading on the misery of the poor.

To this point, the representatives of the Christian Left have been largely silent about the accumulating evidence that their beloved poverty programs have caused enormous harm among the poor. All one can hear from their direction are echoes of the past—namely, that those who refuse to support such programs lack proper Christian compassion. The evidence is in, however, and it reveals still one more sordid side to the Christian Left's war against economics.

17
Third-World Poverty

reat disparities exist among nations with regard to their present economic status. In 1980, the per capita income of developed nations was about five times that of less developed nations. For the 25 percent of the world that lives in North America, most of Europe, Japan, Oceania, and the Soviet Union, per capita income exceeds what is needed for bare subsistence. Living conditions in these areas are the best in history. But almost 60 percent of the world has an income at or below the level of bare subsistence.

Two hundred years ago, poverty was much more widespread than now. Even though there were nations that could be regarded as rich in the mideighteenth century, the per capita income of the rich in those nations was often just two times that of the poor. By 1850, economic development was taking place at a much more rapid rate. Significant economic development began in Europe and North America and then spread to Russia, Japan, and many nations in Oceania. This concentrated economic growth produced residual benefits for other nations.

A century ago, per capita income in developed nations averaged about two times that found in less developed countries. Today per capita income in developed nations averages five times that for less developed countries. The present level of affluence in the developed nations is the highest in history.

The enormous improvement of the developed nations relative to that of less developed countries is not a result of exploitation and oppression. The disparity is a result of some nations growing while others stagnate or decline. The important role that the market system has played in this growth cannot be exaggerated.

It is a mistake to think of the world as forever divided into rich and poor nations, with the position of nations in one group or another being a condition immune to change. Nations differ greatly with regard to their rates of economic development or decline.

Lesser developed countries exhibit significantly different rates of economic growth. One way of measuring economic growth is real (inflation-adjusted) per capita income growth. This figure is approximated by starting with the nation's real gross national product growth[1] and then subtracting the country's annual population growth. For example, between 1970 and 1979 the growth of Bangladesh's real GNP averaged 3.3 percent. During the same period, the annual growth in population for Bangladesh was 3.0 percent. This left Bangladesh with an average growth rate in real per capita income between 1970-1979 of approximately 0.3 percent. Zaire is an example of a nation whose real GNP actually declined during the 1970s; its annual average decline was 0.7 percent. When combined with Zaire's annual population growth rate of 2.7 percent during the same decade, it is clear that Zaire was moving backwards rapidly.

There is an important lesson in all this. A nation's rate of population growth will have as much effect on its overall economic growth as will any increase in the total value of the goods and services it produces. Mexico is a good example of this. During the 1960s and 1970s, Mexico's annual growth in real GNP averaged 6 percent. But its annual population growth averaged 3 percent which, of course, had the effect of reducing its annual increase of per capital real income to 3 percent. If a number of nations in the world could get the rate of population growth under control, they could begin to emulate the growth rate of nations like Japan.

Those nations that experienced a more rapid growth in per capita income were helped by their low population growth plus a rapid growth in gross national product. For example, during the decade of the seventies, South Korea experienced an annual average real growth rate of 8.4 percent. Other poor countries that experienced rapid growth rates in per capita real income during the 1970s were Brazil, Egypt, Singapore, Indonesia, Nigeria, and Hong Kong.

An important distinction must be made between a nation's extensive and intensive economic growth. Any real growth (against inflation) of a nation's gross national product will constitute extensive growth. But if that nation is also experiencing too rapid a growth in population, the benefits of any extensive growth may result in little if any real benefits to the people. For intensive economic growth to occur, there must be growth per person. There must be a broad improvement in the standard of living across the whole range of a nation's population; this improvement must also help the people at the bottom of the nation's income ladder.

Many of the fastest growing economies in the world are found in eastern Asia. They include Hong Kong, Singapore, Taiwan, South Korea, Malaysia, Thailand, and Indonesia. One important implication of these nations' impressive growth rate is that easy access to natural resources is *not* a condition of economic development. If the major difference between being a rich or poor nation were easy access to natural resources, countries like Japan and Taiwan would be poor while the nations of South America would be rich.

The Charge of Exploitation

The Left's favorite explanation of why some nations are rich while others are poor is the charge that all poverty results from exploitation. If some person or nation is poor, it must be because some other person or nation is guilty of exploitation. If any nation is poor, its poverty must be the result of malevolent actions by some more powerful nation. This leads to the charge that the Third World[2] is poor because it has been exploited by First-World capitalism. The high standard of living in the West is supposed to be a result of its taking raw materials, agricultural products, and goods manufactured by cheap labor. Evangelical theologian Ronald Sider has written of the "stranglehold which the developed West has kept on the economic throats of the Third World." Sider has accused the West of participating "in a system that dooms even more people to agony and death than the slave system did."[3] Sider obviously has an antipathy to understating his case.

While the Third World has a number of legitimate complaints against the First World, it simply is not true that the poverty of the Third World can be blamed on the West. The exploitation charge was first raised by First-World intellectuals who borrowed it from Marx. Third-World politicians have been quick to exploit the charge for their own purposes. The exploitation thesis is grounded on the assumption that economic exchange is a zero-sum game, a claim that I offered reasons to reject earlier in this book.

The economically superior position of the West is not an effect of colonialism. The European nations that did establish colonies were already rich by comparison with the areas they colonized. Some of the richest and most advanced nations (including Norway, Sweden, Denmark, and Switzerland) were never involved in the establishment of colonies. Some of the most economically advanced nations in the world (such as Canada, Australia, and the United States) are former colonies.

Instead of the West being the cause of Third-World poverty, the truth is just the reverse. The major reason for Third-World economic progress has been its contact with the West. Economic advancement in the Third World declines in proportion to the degree that contact with the West declines. The most economically advanced areas in the Third World happen to be the ones that have had the greatest amount of contact with the West.

It was such contacts with the West that introduced the ideas, skills, and resources that helped the Third-World nations which have developed. Several years ago, a student group at Cambridge University in England published a pamphlet that claimed that the British "took the rubber from Malaya, the tea from India, raw materials from all over the world and gave almost nothing in return." The reply of P. T. Bauer to this charge is a classic.

> This is as nearly the opposite of the truth as one can find. The British took the rubber *to* Malaya and the tea *to* India. There were no rubber trees in Malaya or anywhere in Asia . . . until about 100 years ago, when the British took the first rubber seeds there out of the Amazon jungle. From these sprang the huge rubber industry—now very largely Asian-owned. Tea-plants were brought to India by the British somewhat earlier.[4]

One hundred years ago, the area now known as Malaysia was composed of small fishing villages and hamlets. Because of the advent of the rubber and tea industries, large cities had been established by the 1930s. By now, of course, the region is one of the fastest growing economic areas of the world. Bauer objects to claims that colonial powers like Britain have done nothing but drain wealth from Third-World countries. "Far from draining wealth from the less developed countries," he writes, "British industry helped to create it there, as external commerce promoted economic advance in large areas of the Third World where there was no wealth to be drained."[5]

Western contacts have resulted in significant contributions to the development of many areas of Africa through the adoption of the rule of law, public security, modern means of communication and transportation, increased literacy, advances in public health, reduced infant mortality, increased life expectancy, as well as the elimination of slavery inside Africa.[6] It is not necessary to defend the entire record of colonialism to recognize that colonialism fails as an explanation of Third-World poverty. The Third-World countries that have experienced the greatest economic development happen to be those that have had the most extensive contact with the West. The poorest Third-World countries such as Afghanistan, Tibet, and Nepal were never colonies. (Afghanistan is a colony now, but was poor even before Soviet takeover.)

The ease with which many accept the exploitation thesis illustrates how often Third-World poverty is explained in terms of *external* causes—that is, factors external to the nation itself. Nations are supposed to be poor or become poor because of what other nations have allegedly done to them. What I plan to show in the rest of this chapter is that important causes of national poverty are *internal,* not external. The answers to why most nations are poor are to be sought inside that nation and not in its external relations to other nations. Moreover, I will argue, the internal causes of national poverty are often noneconomic in nature.

Since I know firsthand how easily one's views on such subjects can be misunderstood or misrepresented, it may be helpful to make explicit several claims that have certainly been implicit throughout this book. (1) *Some* poverty *is* the result of external conditions. (2) *Some* poverty *is* the result of exploitation and oppression. I do not know anyone who denies (1) and (2). What I have been arguing against is the simplistic thesis that all or most poverty is a result of external conditions, of exploitation and oppression. It is also true that (3) Some businessmen and some bankers have acted in ways that are morally reprehensible. But so have many political functionaries, including those in centrally controlled or public sector economies. There is no shortage of people to point fingers at external causes of poverty and to offer remedies for poverty that results from such causes.

What I am saying is that there are *also* important internal causes of poverty. They are internal to nations in the sense that they did not have external conditions as their necessary and sufficient causes. And there are other causes of poverty that are internal (rather than external) with respect to individuals. In this latter case, the remedy does not lie in changing anything external to the persons involved; the remedy rests in individual people changing such things as their values, their motivation, their orientation towards the future (Banfield's future time horizon), and their incentives.

Instead of offering a simple panacea for poverty, I am actually suggesting that the problem is more complex than many on the Left seem to realize. It follows therefore that there is no single or simple solution to poverty in less developed nations.

Two Popular External "Solutions" to Third-World Poverty

Two of the most popular recommendations for relieving poverty in less developed countries exemplify what I have called the external approach. Both approaches begin by focusing on alleged external causes of poverty in that nation and move easily to the conclusion that any answer to that nation's poverty must also be external.

The Redistribution of Wealth

Many people believe mistakenly that the major step that must be taken before Third-World proverty can be eliminated is redistributing the wealth *within* that nation. A major problem with this view is that there is not enough wealth to go around. Even if a particular undeveloped nation does have a class of wealthy people, it is so small that poverty would continue to exist even if all that wealth were confiscated and distributed among the entire nation.[7]

Nor can the problem of Third-World poverty be eased by including the wealth of the West in any redistribution plans. Such a plan, if enacted, would succeed only in impoverishing everyone. For one thing, as Brian Griffiths points out, "a good deal of wealth in the West is embodied in a highly skilled labour force, so that it is impossible to transfer high-technology industry to less developed countries without at the same time transferring high-technology personnel as well."[8]

Moreover, it is unlikely that any transfer of wealth from more developed to less developed nations of the required magnitude would occur voluntarily, even if it made economic sense. Efforts first to confiscate the wealth and redistribute it by such coercive means as taxation would have serious negative effects on economic activity in the developed nations. It would so alter people's incentives that instead of ending or easing misery in some nations, it would only spread the misery around. Griffiths also draws attention to the fact that

> redistribution through the coercive power of the state breeds dependence. The creation of the welfare state in developed countries has bred a new class which is to a greater or lesser extent dependent on the state for employment, education,

health, housing, benefits, security and status. In Third World countries, the same dependency syndrome has appeared. If food is brought in, why produce it? If bureaucracy can profit from handing out aid, why encourage domestic production? If personal wealth can be obtained through holding political office, why bother to set up new enterprises? If agricultural output must be sold to a government monopoly buying agency, why bother to innovate and seek out new markets?"[9]

Griffiths also urges that more attention be paid to questions about the mechanisms that would be required to effect the kind of coercive transfer of wealth between nations. "A global welfare state would require a global coercive government with powers to enforce taxation measures akin to those now exercised by nation states, assuming (not unreasonably) that the West would be unwilling to surrender its 'surplus' wealth voluntarily."[10] Griffiths finds the political and spiritual implications of this scenario troubling, to say the least. It is clear, he concludes, that "The redistribution of wealth is not an adequate solution to the problem of world poverty. Continued emphasis on redistribution can only exacerbate the world's economic problems."[11]

Foreign Aid

Foreign aid is another external approach to easing poverty in lesser developed nations. While transfers of wealth through redistribution are justified on the grounds of *justice*, foreign aid is usually viewed either as a matter of *charity* or a necessary cost of one's nation's pursuit of a particular goal. Whatever reasons may be offered to support it, foreign aid has become an accepted feature of the relationships between more-developed and less-developed nations.[12]

Many believe that the future development of the Third World and the easing of Third-World poverty depends upon the West's provision of foreign aid. P. T. Bauer has objected to the use of the word "aid" in connection with official transfers of wealth from one government to another. For one thing, much of this alleged "aid" turns out to be aid for little more than the private bank accounts of well-placed officials and politicians in Third-World nations. As Bauer sees it, foreign aid "is much more likely to obstruct than to promote . . . the development of the Third World and the relief of poverty there."[13]

Foreign aid was not a necessary condition for the economic development and progress of nations in the West. Why then should it be regarded as indispensable for the development of Third-World nations? As Bauer argues:

> Large parts of the Third World made rapid progress long before foreign aid was invented. Witness Southeast Asia, West Africa, Latin America, which were practically transformed in the century before the 1950s, long before the advent of foreign aid. Emergence of hundreds of millions of people both in the South and in the West, from poverty to prosperity has not depended on external gifts. Economic achievement has depended and still does depend on people's own faculties, motivations, and mores, their institutions and the policies of their rulers. In short, economic achievement depends on the conduct of people, including governments.[14]

There are many unfortunate consequences of foreign aid. It often hinders economic development, frequently subsidizes destructive national policies, encourages consolidation of political power at the expense of individual freedom, reinforces the myth that the reason some countries are rich is because they have exploited poor countries, and deceives people into thinking that benefits are available without the need to pay for them. Because so much can be gained by acquiring political power in a situation where millions of dollars of foreign money are channeled through the government, foreign aid can also lead to greater politicization in nations receiving it. Pursuit of the prize of political control that in turn provides access to foreign aid dollars has produced much internal strife and conflict.

Foreign aid has damaged its recipients further, Bauer explains, by encouraging governments

> to implement policies detrimental to living standards and material progress. Examples include under-payment of farmers, which discourages the output of food and export crops and emergence from subsistence production. As well there is forced collectivization, and suppression of trading activities. This has aggravated the effect of crop failure in famine areas in Africa. Then, too, there is discrimination against productive minorities and their harrassment, or worse. Witness for instance, the Asians in East Africa.[15]

Some governments have adopted bizarre methods of enhancing their prospects of receiving official aid. Some have discovered that by expelling economically successful ethnic minorities, they can produce statistics that make the level of poverty in their nation appear higher, thus qualifying them for many times more aid.

Official aid neither relieves poverty nor promotes development, Bauer argues.

> In fact, harmful policies buttressed by aid usually damage the poorest, most notably the rural poor. This is the result of the urban bias of Third World economic policies. Aid goes to government, that is, to the ruler, not to the pitiable figures familiar in aid publicity. To give money to Third World governments on the ground that most of their subjects are poor, differs completely from giving money to the poor themselves. The policies of aid-recipient governments, including their patterns of public spending, are rarely governed by the needs of the very poor.[16]

For example, the governments of such nations as Nigeria, Tanzania, Pakistan, and Malawi have used official aid to build, at huge costs, new cities to serve as their capitals. These huge expenditures provided no relief for the very poor.

Much of the so-called foreign aid to Third-World countries has been sent under conditions which raise questions about the sanity of the West. For example, the West continued to send foreign aid to Uganda while Idi Amin was killing tens of thousands of people. It sent aid to Pol Pot's Kampuchea even though it knew about the atrocities that resulted in the murder of millions. The West sent aid to India while it was engaged in the forced sterilization of thousands of Indians. Tanzania continued to receive aid even as it was setting up its own version of Stalinism. Ethiopia got aid while its government was slaughtering thousands. Iraq and Iran continued to get aid even while they were expropriating the assets of companies belonging to the nations sending the aid. The West sent aid to oil-producing countries aligned with OPEC during the 1970s even though some of those nations had average incomes higher than some of the nations sending the aid. If one is seeking actions of Western nations to condemn on moral and economic grounds, one could easily begin with their practices of foreign aid.

Conclusion

There is little reason then to get excited about suggestions that relief of Third-World poverty depends on the adoption of such external measures as foreign aid or the redistribution of wealth. If any serious attempt were to be made at redistribution, it would result only in the impoverishment of all. In the case of foreign aid, the evidence is clear: the approach is clearly counterproductive and results in far more harm to the poor of those nations that receive official aid.

Internal Causes of Poverty

Nations are poor primarily because of internal factors and not because of such external factors as exploitation. A list of the more obvious internal factors would include poor education. Most of the people in lesser developed countries are illiterate. The lack of proper health services is another contributing factor to national poverty. Poor health has an obvious negative effect on a worker's productivity. There is often a shortage of tools and capital needed for production. The tools that are available are often crude. What production of food and goods occurs is inefficient and wastes human capital.

More attention needs to be given to the important role that personal and societal values and attitudes play with regard to poverty. For example, several years ago several groups of concerned Christians attempted to establish new businesses in the Caribbean. It was their plan to invest the money needed for capital, train a group of poor men and women to make the goods that the businesses would sell, and eventually allow those workers who demonstrated management skills to assume leadership positions. Eventually, it was thought, the whole operation would simply be turned over to the workers. On paper this certainly looked like a good idea. Had anyone asked me, I'd have been glad to make a donation toward a project that appeared to be a meaningful approach to helping some poor people achieve economic independence. But there was one drawback that no one anticipated—namely, the culture and morals of the workers. Even though the workers were told that the business would someday be theirs, even though this would have provided sufficient incentive for different workers in a different setting, these particular workers lacked important personal characteristics needed to turn the experiment into a success.

For one thing, the workers lacked ambition. Even though they were told that any success would benefit them, they showed up for work when they felt like it. They often stole which, under the circumstances, meant that they were stealing from themselves. In short, they evidenced what Edward Banfield called a short time horizon. They were unable to think beyond the present and recognize how present sacrifices (which meant nothing more than productive work) would benefit them and their families in the near future. Regrettably, these noble efforts to help the poor of at least one underdeveloped country to rise out of poverty failed.

Brian Griffiths comments on the importance of culture, morality, and religion in this regard.

> Why is it that in some societies individual human beings have the view of the physical world, of the importance of work, and the sense of self-discipline which they do? Why is it that in other societies they do not? Why is it that in some societies the institutions of the society are conducive to economic development while in others they are not? Personally, I find it impossible to answer these questions satisfactorily in purely economic terms.[17]

Some poverty—perhaps a great deal of poverty—is not explicable in exclusively economic terms because it has a cultural, moral, and even a religious dimension. If a people, for example, do not have a moral aversion to stealing, they will have no respect for private property. As our example shows, the lack of respect for any private property creates an environment in which poverty cannot be eased in a nonviolent way.[18]

Cultural conditions are relevant in other ways. If a society chooses, for whatever reasons, not to kill cattle, this will have an obvious effect on their material well-being. If a society discourages women from seeking employment outside the home, this will result in a lower per capita income than nations where women are permitted to work outside the home. A culture may hinder the ability of people to move upwards in society. For example, a caste system not only hinders upward social mobility but has a negative effect on business where people in one class are prohibited from economic exchanges with people in other classes.

In many instances, the wealthiest people in the nations of Southeast Asia are Chinese and others who entered those countries as penniless slaves. The economic advancement of such people in that region of the world reflects a simple economic fact of life: ambitious people end up better off economically than those with less ambition. As P. T. Bauer argues:

Economic achievement depends on people's attributes, attitudes, motivations, mores and political arrangements. In many countries the prevailing personal, social and political determinants are uncongenial to material progress: witness the preference for a contemplative life, opposition to paid work by women and widespread torpor and fatalism in certain countries.[19]

While emergence from poverty does not require external actions such as foreign aid, it does require changes in the internal conditions that we have noticed. The morals and the motivation of a people along with the institutions and policies of their country are crucial if the problem of poverty is to be challenged. Economic development within a nation will depend on how individuals and their rulers conduct themselves.

I have mentioned the importance of the attitudes, attributes, morals, and motivation of individuals. Another essential factor in a nation's economic well-being concerns the conduct of its rulers. One necessary condition for the easing of poverty is political stability. Political instability undermines the security of property rights which in turn discourages investment. It is not hard to see why foreign investors will be more interested in risking their resources in a nation where a stable political situation makes their investment safer. Entrepreneurs need a strong legal system that will minimize the possibility of acts of fraud, theft, and violations of contracts. They also need assurances that the government will not act capriciously against their persons or possessions. Wise entrepreneurs have to calculate their expected future gain against present and future risks. Political instability increases their risks, often to the extent that some projected investment is judged to be unwise.

The economic stability of a nation is also an important factor in the easing of poverty in lesser developed countries. Obviously, economic stability is impossible without political stability. Secure property rights in a nation encourage private investment from foreign sources. Different rates of investment reflect appraisals of a nation's economic stability, especially with respect to such factors as inflation, controls over foreign exchange, the nation's past record with respect to the nationalization of private company assets, and the tax structure.

Latin American economist Manuel F. Ayan suggests that a

lack of understanding about economics is another internal cause of poverty. He writes:

> My first inclination, in looking for the source of poverty, was to look for evil people who were intent on making us poor. I have since forsaken this inclination. The problem is much more serious: We are kept poor by well-intentioned people who are largely ignorant of sound economic logic and who operate in a nonmarket environment. For example, with very few exceptions, government officials entrusted with designing policy in [debtor-problem countries] deny that there is a connection between the exchange rate and the level of employment, or that overvaluing or undervaluing foreign exchange perpetuates production patterns that are inconsistent with a country's comparative advantage.[20]

If First-World countries are serious about helping lesser developed nations develop economically, it is important that they help the present and future leaders of such countries to understand

> the mechanisms that coordinate people's endeavors in society. In my studies in three different countries, I was never exposed to explanations of the constraints of the marketplace, of the price system as a system of communication, and of how under voluntary exchange one man's gain is not another's loss. This ignorance, which I shared, is the reason why the market is discarded as chaotic and unjust, and why government-planned economic solutions are invariably adopted. This educational abyss is, in the end, the cause of the debt problem.[21]

It is interesting to note that the economic lessons Ayan thinks are so essential for the future economic development of Third-World nations are precisely those presented in this book.

Economic ideas have consequences. Nations that give greater place to a market system exhibit much greater rates of economic growth than those that have controlled economies or public sector economies. Consider the following figures taken from the *Economic Handbook of the World Bank* for 1981. The figures show the average annual growth of each nation's real Gross Domestic Product.

	1960-69	1970-79
Hong Kong	10.0	9.4
Singapore	8.8	8.4
Thailand	8.2	7.7
South Korea	8.6	10.3
Ivory Coast	8.0	6.7
India	3.4	3.4
Uruguay	1.2	2.5
Ghana	2.1	−0.1
Chad	0.5	−0.2
Zaire	3.6	−0.7

One obvious difference between the five nations above the line, whose economic performance far surpassed that of the other nations, and those below the line was the greater commitment of the former nations to a market economy.

It is a fact that market economies grow more rapidly than centrally controlled economies. Third-World countries that adopt a market economy grow more rapidly than those that insist on governmental planning and control of the economy.

According to economist Alvin Rabushka,

Perhaps the single best example of the market economy model of economic development is found in the incredibly successful record of the British Crown Colony of Hong Kong. Its US $180 per capita income in 1948, reflective of Third World levels, has surpassed US $6,000, the second highest per capita income in Asia. Its policies include low tax rates (17 percent for individuals and 18.5 percent for corporations), balanced budgets, an aversion to central planning and public debt, and free trade. It has overcome a lack of natural resources, overcrowding, distance from its key markets, military indefensibility, and other handicaps.[22]

The rather incredible economic performance of Hong Kong and other Asian nations like Taiwan, South Korea, and Thailand demonstrates how a government can encourage economic growth by following a market approach. The success of such nations needs to be compared with nations that follow a state-directed approach. It is clear, Rabushka argues, that the Third World does not need more socialism; what it needs is more capitalism. It will be interesting to see how far the People's Republic of China goes in its "process of dismantling the most comprehensive system of Socialist planning and practice ever attempted in the Third World in favor of a headlong dash for freer markets, freer prices, greater emphasis on private enterprise, and replacing the rule of man with the rule of law."[23] China's turn towards a more market-oriented economy since 1978 has already resulted in significant improvements in its economic performance.

> The value of agricultural output since 1979 has grown at more than double the rate between 1953 and 1978. Rural per capita incomes increased in real terms by 98.5 percent between 1979 and 1983. Total grain harvest grew by a third, from 304.7 million tons in 1978 to surpass 400 million tons in 1984; China has switched from being a grain importer to a grain exporter.[24]

Growth rates for other crops have been even greater.

Conclusion

It is time to bring both this chapter and the book to a conclusion. In this chapter, I have argued that the most important causes of Third-World poverty today are internal, not external; many of these internal reasons are noneconomic factors such as the morals, attitudes, and motivation of the people along with relevant features of the culture. Other internal factors include the conduct of a nation's rulers with respect to providing political and economic stability. And, of course, there is the crucial matter of which economic system will be adopted. There is no easy set of answers as to why different nations are poor or what they can do to begin the alleviation of poverty. But we have certainly noticed some important signpoints along the way.

This book is a reflection of the growing Christian interest in economics. That relationship would be far more productive if Christians would improve their understanding of economics. It is both foolish and ultimately harmful to attempt to use economics without understanding it. We cannot do a very good job of improving the economic order if we do not know how it works.

There is one more thing to say before I bring this project to a close. I have agreed with those who argue that a people's morals, religion, and culture holds important consequences for its economic life. If that claim is true, what can the friends of economic freedom think when they survey the declining role that Judeo-Christian morality is playing in Western civilization.

A capitalism that is cut loose from traditional values is a capitalism that is headed for trouble. A capitalism grounded on God and Judeo-Christian values versus a capitalism grounded on hedonism, the love of money, and materialism are heading in two different directions. Brian Griffiths explains:

> One type of economy has a view of work as a calling, the other of work simply as a way of getting money; one involves responsibility for the future and hence the need to save and invest, the other is concerned with the present, with the maximising of consumption; one has abandoned all rules with respect to money creation and government deficits; one views the family as the basic unit in economic welfare, the other the state as the major engine of redistribution; one involves small government, the other large government; one believes in private property, the other state ownership; one involves trade unions remedying injustices, the other state involves labour monopolies raising their real income at the expense of fellow workers; one involves corporations concerned with more than profit in a world of conscious moral choices, the other is concerned with economic men, living in an amoral world, maximising profits.[25]

This book then has two important messages. Christians who want to help the poor need capitalism. Rational economic activity is quite simply impossible apart from a market system. But, and let all friends of a market system pay heed, capitalism needs Christianity. The West's continued movement in the direction of secularism and humanism holds disturbing implications for economic life.

Notes

1: The Christian War Against Economics

1. See Ronald Nash, *Social Justice and the Christian Church* (Milford, Mich.: Mott, 1983), Chapter One.
2. Benjamin Rogge, "Christian Economics: Myth or Reality?," *The Freeman*, December 1965.
3. See Dinesh D'Souza, "The Bishops as Pawns," *Policy Review*, No. 34 (Fall 1985), pp. 50-56.
4. An *uncritical* alliance with the political and economic Right is grounds for equal concern. It should also be obvious that a large number of people who regard themselves as conservative have no clear grasp of the theoretical foundations of their political and economic views.
5. Herbert Schlossberg, *Idols for Destruction* (Nashville: Thomas Nelson, 1983), pp. 241-243.
6. *Ibid.*, p. 241.
7. *Ibid.*, p. 242.
8. But see the distinction I draw in Chapter Two between positive and normative economics.
9. See my elaboration of this distinction in Chapter Two.

2: What Is Economics?

1. A. P. Lerner, "Microeconomy Theory," in *Perspectives in Economics*, ed. A. A. Brown, E. Neuberger, and M. Palmatier (New York: McGraw-Hill, 1968), p. 29.
2. It is customary to distinguish a third branch of economics in addition to microeconomics and macroeconomics. International economics studies economic relationships across national boundaries.
3. This view is held by most representatives of the Austrian School of economics. For an example of a textbook that plays down the role of normative economics, see Armen A. Alchian and William R. Allen, *University Economics*, 2nd ed. (Belmont, Calif.: Wadsworth, 1967), p. 5. For a textbook that affirms the legitimacy of normative economics, see James D. Gwartney and Richard Stroup, *Economics, Private and Public Choice*, 3rd ed. (Orlando, Fla.: Academic Press, 1983), p. 11.
4. Charles Murray argues that this is precisely what happened as a result of American social policy towards the poor since the start of the Great Society programs in the mid-1960s. See Charles Murray, *Losing Ground:*

American Social Policy 1950-1980 (New York: Basic Books, 1984). See also Charles Murray, "Have the Poor Been 'Losing Ground'?," *Political Science Quarterly,* 100 (1985), pp. 427-445. In his 1985 article, Murray replies to critics of his book.

5. This idea has been captured nicely in a widely used economics text. See Paul T. Heyne, *The Economic Way of Thinking* (Chicago: Science Research Associates, 1973). Heyne's text has since appeared in a number of editions.

6. Economists do draw a distinction between free goods and economic goods. The discussion in this section does not have free goods in view. The distinction between free goods and economic goods will be discussed later in the book.

7. See James Gwartney and Thomas S. McCaleb, "Have Antipoverty Programs Increased Poverty?," *Cato Journal,* 4 (1985), pp. 1-16; *op. cit.,* Charles Murray, *Losing Ground;* George Gilder, *Wealth and Poverty* (New York: Basic Books, 1981); and Thomas Sowell, *Race and Economics* (New York: David McKay, 1975).

8. James Gwartney, "Social Progress, the Tax-Transfer Society and the Limits of Public Policy," unpublished paper, Department of Economics, Florida State University, p. 3.

3: Some Basic Economic Concepts

1. It is important to distinguish between *demand* and *quantity demanded.* The word *demand* refers to a relationship that economic texts indicate by a curve showing the different quantities of some good or service that buyers will freely purchase at different prices, other things being equal. *Quantity demanded* is a specific point on that curve; it is a specific quantity that buyers will demand at a specific price. A similar distinction must be made between *supply* (another relationship indicated by a curve) and *quantity supplied,* a specific point or value on the curve.

2. The resources that people draw on in such cases include more than the supply of the desired good. A person's resources also include such things as knowledge, ability, strength, wealth, and time.

3. One important qualification is necessary. The resources that people utilize to satisfy their wants often do not involve the use of force. Economics typically studies the noncoercive means that people adopt in order to satisfy their wants.

4. Scarcity should not be confused with shortage. Scarcity exists whenever human wants are greater than the means to satisfy those wants. A shortage exists in those cases where, *at some specific price,* the quantity demanded for some good or service is greater than the quantity being supplied. A shortage can—at least in theory—be eliminated—for example, by raising the price so that quantity demanded decreases and quantity supplied increases. But because it is impossible for all humans to satisfy all of their wants at the same time, scarcity can never be eliminated from the human condition.

5. Armen A. Alchian and William R. Allen, *University Economics,* 2nd ed. (Belmont, Calif.: Wadsworth, 1967), pp. 15, 16.

6. *Ibid.,* p. 20.

7. Bettina Bien Greaves, *Free Market Economics* (Irvington-on-Hudson, N.Y.: Foundation for Economic Freedom, 1975), p. 231.

8. Armen A. Alchian and William R. Allen, *University Economics,* p. 18.

4: The Theory of Subjective Economic Value

1. For an example of one line of argument against Marx's labor theory of value, see Ronald Nash, *Freedom, Justice and the State* (Lanham, Md.: University Press of America, 1980), pp. 162-164.

2. Some interpreters find at least two objective theories of economic value in Adam Smith's *Wealth of Nations* that was first published in 1776. Smith seems to have believed that goods and services are valued at their cost of production, a view similar to the one later advanced by Marx. But Smith also held that the value of goods and services is a function of what people will exchange for them. Smith also spoke of "use value," a kind of value where personal or subjective evaluation was relevant. But he failed to see the full implications of this notion. Its complete development would not appear until more than a century later in the work of such economists as Menger, Jevons, and Walras.

3. Bettina Bien Greaves, *Free Market Economics* (Irvington-on Hudson, N.Y.: Foundation for Economic Education, 1975), p. 173.

4. *Ibid.*

5. This last sentence does not imply that human choices with regard to nonmaterial goods cannot be explained in terms of other economic theories. I am simply pointing out the extent to which the subjective theory of economic value is compatible with important Christian concerns.

6. Karen L. Vaughn, "Does It Matter That Costs Are Subjective?," *Southern Economic Journal,* 46 (1980), pp. 708, 709.

7. Israel Kirzner, "The Open-Endedness of Knowledge," *The Freeman,* 36 (1986), p. 87.

8. I must also pay some passing attention to still another way in which our language tends to confuse people on the issue before us. The word "desirable" can be used in two quite different senses. I have already referred to the fact that we sometimes use "desirable" to refer to that which people ought to desire. In this sense, something is desirable if it is worth seeking, if it merits preference. But many people use "desirable" to describe anything that arouses desire. Because things like cocaine, heroin, and pornography have the power of arousing desire in some people, they are sometimes said to be desirable. It would certainly be easier to think more clearly about these issues if we were to use two different words to refer to these quite separate cases. It should be understood that whenever the word "desirable" occurs in my discussion, it is used in the first sense—that is, in the sense of being worthy of desire.

9. Careful attention should be paid to the way I word this point. It would be wrong, of course, to think that all Christians would agree about the contents of any list of economic choices that ought to be criticized. All I am claiming is that an acceptance of the subjective theory of economic value is consistent with *any* person's criticizing particular economic choices on *moral* grounds. But having the right to make such objections is

distinct from being right in those judgments. Anyone who presumes to make such judgments should be prepared to defend his claim. Naturally, any debate that might ensue would not be a debate about economics.

10. James M. Buchanan, "Introduction: L.S.E. Cost Theory in Retrospect," in *L.S.E. Essays on Cost*, ed. J. M. Buchanan and G. F. Thirlby (New York: New York University Press, 1981), p. 14. The Letters *L, S,* and *E* in the title refer to the London School of Economics.

11. *Ibid.,* pp. 14, 15.

12. Bettina Bien Greaves, *Free Market Economics*, p. 218.

13. Israel Kirzner, "The Open-Endedness of Knowledge," p. 87.

14. *Ibid.,* p. 88.

15. A *successful* entrepreneur is one whose beliefs about an opportunity prove to be correct. Every entrepreneur takes risks based on his beliefs. Since there is no certainty in economic activity, entrepreneurs sometimes win and sometimes lose.

16. Stephen C. Littlechild, *The Fallacy of the Mixed Economy* (San Francisco: The Cato Institute, 1979), p. 74.

5: The Market

1. James Gwartney, "Social Progress, The Tax-Transfer Society and the Limits of Public Policy," unpublished paper, Department of Economics, Florida State University, pp. 3, 4.

2. Thomas Sowell, *Markets and Minorities* (New York: Basic Books, 1981), p. 4.

3. Ludwig von Mises, *Human Action* (New Haven: Yale University Press, 1949), p. 257.

4. *Ibid.,* p. 258.

5. James Gwartney, "Social Progress, The Tax-Transfer Society and The Limits of Public Policy," p. 4.

6. My discussion in the previous paragraph as well as several following paragraphs is indebted to the very nice discussion in Paul Heyne's book, *The Christian Encounters the World of Economics* (St. Louis: Concordia, 1965), Chapter One.

7. *Ibid.,* pp. 22, 23.

8. Tom Rose, *Economics* (Milford, Mich.: Mott, 1977), p. 213.

9. James Gwartney, "Social Progress, The Tax-Transfer Society and the Limits of Public Policy," p. 5.

10. James D. Gwartney and Richard Stroup, *Economics, Private and Public Choice*, third ed. (Orlando, Fla.: Academic Press, 1983), p. 61.

11. For examples of this, see the later chapters in this book that discuss economic interventionism and the Great Depression.

12. Peter J. Hill, "Private Rights and Public Attitudes: A Christian Defense of Capitalism," unpublished, Department of Economics, Montana State University, p. 6.

13. The mistaken view that voluntary economic exchange is a zero-sum game will be examined in more detail in the chapter on capitalism.

14. James D. Gwartney and Richard Stroup, *Economics, Private and Public Choice*, p. 43.

15. Israel Kirzner, "Equilibrium versus Market Process," in *The Foundations of Austrian Economics,* ed. Edwin G. Dolan (Kansas City, Kan.: Sheed and Ward, 1976), p. 116.
16. *Ibid.*
17. Stephen C. Littlechild, *The Fallacy of the Mixed Economy* (San Francisco: The Cato Institute, 1979), p. 21.

6: Capitalism I

1. José Míguez-Bonino, *Christians and Marxists* (Grand Rapids: Eerdmans, 1976), p. 115.
2. This outrageous claim is certainly one implication of the argument contained in Andrew Kirk's book *The Good News of the Kingdom Coming* (Downers Grove, Ill.: InterVarsity Press, 1985).
3. By "collectivism," I mean a system that subordinates the rights and liberties of individual people to some larger whole or collective. Socialism, as a later chapter explains, is a collectivist system.
4. The text of the Canadian bishops' statement along with several discussions of the text can be found in "Economics and the Canadian Bishops: A Symposium," *This World*, No. 5 (Spring, Summer, 1983), pp. 122-145. The quote from Heyne appears on p. 140.
5. Bonino, whose hostility to capitalism was noted earlier in this chapter and whose sympathy for Marxism will become apparent in a later chapter, is widely regarded as an evangelical.
6. Richard V. Pierard, *The Unequal Yoke: Evangelical Christianity and Political Conservatism* (Philadelphia: J. B. Lippincott, 1970), p. 73.
7. Andrew Kirk, *The Good News of the Kingdom Coming*, p. 71.
8. I do not mean to ignore right-wing extremists who have their own problems. But it seems clear that the major obstacle to a balanced, sane, and reasoned evangelical discussion of Christianity and economics comes today from extremists on the Left like Kirk.
9. I provide several examples of this procedure in another book, *Social Justice and the Christian Church* (Milford, Mich.: Mott, 1983), Chapter Six.
10. Along this line, a strange kind of reasoning shows up in some of the writings of a Dutch Christian named Bob Goudzwaard. Goudzwaard criticizes many Christians (he seems to have people of a conservative bent in mind) for their adoption of secular ideologies as grounds for dealing with the serious crises of the day. Goudzwaard, whose views are widely admired by the Christian Left, condemns this approach and urges Christians to take an entirely different approach to these crises. The first step is for Christians to repent, a recommendation that few Christians will find fault with. But after Christians have repented of their use of such secular ideologies as capitalism, Goudzwaard calls on them to take his second step, which turns out to be the acceptance of a different set of secular ideologies—namely, those he recommends. Of course, Goudzwaard tries hard to convince his readers that his own ideologies are really Christian. For an example of Goudzwaard's approach, see his article "World Crises and Their Common Roots," *Third Way*, December 1985, pp. 10-13.

11. Herbert Schlossberg, *Idols for Destruction* (Nashville: Thomas Nelson, 1983), p. 318.

12. Some have been troubled by Williams's use of "violence" in connection with the second means of exchange. It may help to note that he uses the word in a somewhat technical sense—namely, the abusive or unjust exercise of power. In many situations, the violence that Williams has in view is implicit; it functions primarily as a threat. For example, as long as one does the state's bidding, the state will not unleash the force it has at its disposal. If anyone is still troubled by references to the *violent* means of exchange, we could make essentially the same point by talking about voluntary exchange versus coerced exchange.

13. Edmund Opitz, "Socialism," in *Baker's Dictionary of Christian Ethics,* ed. Carl F. H. Henry (Grand Rapids: Baker, 1973), p. 639.

14. Compare this with the Biblical concern for just weights and measures (Deut. 25:15, 16).

15. I should add that we have a right to expect more than minimal conformity to the spirit and framework of the market system. Christians have a right to expect both buyers and sellers to go the second mile with regard to their ethical obligations.

16. Armen A. Alchian and William R. Allen, *University Economics,* second ed. (Belmont, Calif.: Wadsworth, 1967), p. 5.

17. Ronald Nash, *Social Justice and the Christian Church,* p. 82.

18. *Ibid.,* pp. 82, 83.

19. This argument against socialism is developed in a later chapter. It is this defect at the very heart of socialism that accounts for the failure of Socialist systems in the real world.

20. Neither the objection nor my answer has what are sometimes called "local monopolies" in view—for example, the person who happens to own the only source of water in the middle of a desert. For more on monopoly, see Ronald Nash, *Social Justice and the Christian Church,* pp. 142-146; Donald Devine, *Does Freedom Work?* (Ottawa, Ill.: Caroline House, 1978); and Yale Brozen, "Is Government the Source of Monopoly?," *The Intercollegiate Review,* 5 (1968-1969). Brozen's essay is also available in his book, *Is Government the Source of Monopoly? and Other Essays* (San Francisco: Cato Institute, 1980).

7: Capitalism II

1. In two earlier books I considered a more extensive list of objections to capitalism. See Ronald Nash, *Social Justice and the Christian Church* (Milford, Mich.: Mott, 1983), Chapters Ten and Eleven; and Ronald Nash, *Freedom, Justice and the State* (Lanham, Md.: University Press of America, 1980), Chapter Six.

2. See Andrew Kirk, *The Good News of the Kingdom Coming* (Downers Grove, Ill.: InterVarsity, 1985), p. 80.

3. It is clear that Andrew Kirk holds this view. He thinks that if one person maximizes his advantage, it must inevitably be at the expense of someone else. It never occurs to Kirk that society can be arranged in such a way that one person's success can produce an advantage for the other person. See Kirk, *The Good News of the Kingdom Coming,* p. 82.

4. Of course, it is still true that economic exchanges *may* be marred by exploitation. But it is difficult to imagine an example where exploitation characterizes an exchange that does not compromise the essential conditions of a *free* exchange. A free exchange is one in which force, fraud, and theft are absent. But even if such examples exist, the important question here is whether exploitation is a necessary and unavoidable feature of market exchanges. Obviously, it is not.

5. An exchange can also be regarded as beneficial if it is the lesser of two evils. A businessman may sell some product at a loss because, in the circumstances that prevail, not selling would entail even greater costs.

6. Alexander H. Shand, *The Capitalist Alternative: An Introduction to Neo-Austrian Economics* (New York: New York University Press, 1984), p. 222.

7. Brian Griffiths, *The Creation of Wealth* (Downers Grove, Ill.: InterVarsity Press, 1985), p. 70. Griffiths disagrees with the views described in this paragraph.

8. *Ibid.*

9. Peter J. Hill, "Private Rights and Public Attitudes: A Christian Defense of Capitalism," unpublished, Department of Economics, Montana State University, p. 22. Hill goes on to say: "One of the reasons why we have failed to recognize the very real improvement of the economic position of the poor through economic growth is that we have tended to concentrate on changes in the relative standing of those in poverty, rather than looking at alterations in their absolute position. Most discussions of poverty in the United States focus on the share of total wealth or income that is received by a certain portion of the population, usually the bottom 20 percent. Although such a measure may be of importance for certain policy considerations, it is feasible for those at the bottom of the economic ladder to not change their relative position, i.e., they may have the same percentage of national income over a long period of time, yet still be experiencing very substantial increases in their economic well-being as measured in absolute terms" (pp. 22, 23).

10. Walter Williams, "Free Enterprise Responses to Attacks on Capitalism," *The Presbyterian Layman*, May-June 1985, p. 6.

11. Friedrich Hayek, ed., *Capitalism and the Historians* (Chicago: University of Chicago Press, 1954). For more on this subject, see Ronald Nash, *Freedom, Justice and the State*, pp. 159-162.

12. Paul T. Heyne, *The Christian Encounters the World of Economics* (St. Louis: Concordia, 1965), pp. 92, 93.

13. Henry Hazlitt, *The Foundations of Morality* (New York: Von Nostrand, 1964), p. 325.

14. Peter J. Hill, "Private Rights and Public Attitudes: A Christian Defense of Capitalism," p. 8.

15. Michael Novak, *The Spirit of Democratic Capitalism* (New York: Simon and Schuster, 1982), p. 226.

16. Peter J. Hill, "Private Rights and Public Attitudes: A Christian Defense of Capitalism," pp. 17, 18.

17. Brian Griffiths, *The Creation of Wealth*, p. 89.

18. Peter J. Hill, "Private Rights and Public Attitudes," p. 19.

19. Wilhelm Roepke, *A Humane Economy* (Indianapolis: Liberty Fund, 1971), p. 105.

20. Arthur Shenfield, "Capitalism Under the Tests of Ethics," *Imprimis,* December 1981.
21. *Ibid.*
22. *Ibid.*
23. *Ibid.*

8: Socialism

1. Compare this to Alchian and Allen who state that socialism "is a system in which rights to the uses of a good are not assigned to specific individuals but instead are divided among various people in government agencies, who decide about uses and consequences to be borne. This is a system of 'government ownership.'" Armen A. Alchian and William R. Allen, *University Economics,* second edition (Belmont, Calif.: Wadsworth, 1967), p. 5.
2. Capital includes any good that humans make and use to produce other goods and services.
3. The reason efforts to establish small Socialistic communities failed was the inability of utopian Socialists to deal realistically with fallen human nature. On earth, at least, it does no good to set up an economic system that would work only for angels.
4. Paul Hollander, *Political Pilgrims* (New York: Oxford University Press, 1981), pp. 416, 417.
5. *Ibid.,* p. 417. See also Paul Hollander, *The Many Faces of Socialism* (New Brunswick, N.J.: Transaction Books, 1983), pp. 8, 9.
6. Mises's argument was originally published in German. For an English translation, see Ludwig von Mises, *Socialism* (New Haven: Yale University Press, 1951).
7. Giovanni Sartori, "The Market, Planning, Capitalism and Democracy," *This World,* Number 5 (Spring/Summer, 1983), p. 59.
8. Tom Bethell, "Why Socialism Still Doesn't Work," *The Free Market,* November 1985, pp. 6, 7.
9. Ludwig von Mises, *Socialism,* p. 122.
10. Thomas Sowell, *Economics: Analysis and Issues* (Glenview, Ill.: Scott, Foresman and Co., 1971), p. 83.
11. *Ibid.,* pp. 83, 84.
12. Economist Robert Heilbroner makes this very claim on behalf of socialism in his book *Between Capitalism and Socialism* (New York: Random, 1970), p. 88.
13. Friedrich Hayek, *The Essence of Hayek,* ed. Chiaki Nishiyama and Kurt R. Leube (Stanford, Calif.: Hoover Institution Press, 1984), p. 56.
14. *Ibid.* This would be a good time to reread the long quotation by Thomas Sowell belonging to Note 11.
15. David Ramsay Steele, "Lange's Theory of Socialism After Forty Years," *Austrian Economics Newsletter,* Vol. I (1978), p. 12. Lange's own views can be found in Oskar Lange and Fred Taylor, *On the Economic Theory of Socialism* (New York: McGraw-Hill, 1938).
16. Henry Hazlitt, *The Foundations of Morality* (New York: D. Van Nostrand, 1964), p. 304.

17. Tom Bethell, "Why Socialism Still Doesn't Work," p. 7.
18. Friedrich Hayek, *The Essence of Hayek,* p. 61.
19. The literature on this subject is extensive. For additional discussions see: Lancelot Lawton, *Economic History of Soviet Russia* (London, 1922); Paul Craig Roberts, *Alienation and the Soviet Economy* (Albuquerque: University of New Mexico Press, 1971); Murray N. Rothbard, "Ludwig von Mises and Economic Calculation Under Socialism," in *The Economics of Ludwig von Mises,* ed. Laurence S. Moss (Kansas City: Sheed and Ward, 1976), pp. 67-78; Robert Bradley, Jr., "Market Socialism: A Subjectivist Evaluation," *The Journal of Libertarian Studies,* 5 (1981), pp. 23-39; F. A. Hayek, ed., *Collectivist Economic Planning* (London: George Rutledge and Sons, 1935); and T. J. B. Hoff, *Economic Calculation in the Socialist Economy* (London: William Hodge, 1949).
20. Brian Griffiths, *The Creation of Wealth* (Downers Grove, Ill.: InterVarsity Press, 1985), p. 33.
21. *Ibid.,* p. 26.
22. Peter Berger, "Underdevelopment Revisited," *Commentary* (July 1984), p. 41. Subsequent quotes come from page 43 of Berger's article.
23. *Ibid.,* p. 45.

9: Christianity and Marxism

1. The story of this grim episode in the history of American Christendom is recounted in Lloyd Billingsley, *The Generation That Knew Not Josef* (Portland: Multnomah Press, 1985).
2. James L. Tyson, *Target America* (Chicago: Regnery Gateway, 1985).
3. José Míguez-Bonino, *Christians and Marxists* (Grand Rapids: Eerdmans, 1976).
4. *Ibid.,* p. 76.
5. *Ibid.,* p. 77.
6. Peter L. Berger, "Underdevelopment Revisited," *Commentary,* July 1984, p. 43.
7. José Míguez-Bonino, *Christians and Marxists,* p. 90.
8. Andrew Kirk, *The Good News of the Kingdom Coming* (Downers Grove, Ill.: InterVarsity Press, 1985).
9. *Ibid.,* pp. 44, 45.
10. Sidney Hook, *Marxism and Beyond* (Totowa, N.J.: Rowman and Littlefield, 1983), p. 27.
11. *Ibid.*
12. These manuscripts, along with a helpful introduction, can be found in *Karl Marx, Early Writings,* translated and edited by T. B. Bottomore (New York: McGraw-Hill, 1964).
13. I have offered arguments against the more recent expressions of this thesis in the work of Neo-Marxists like Herbert Marcuse. See Ronald Nash, *Freedom, Justice and the State* (Lanham, Md.: University Press of America, 1980), pp. 140-145 and Ronald Nash, *Social Justice and the Christian Church* (Milford, Mich.: Mott Media, 1983), pp. 97-102. For an earlier statement of these arguments, see Ronald Nash, "A Note on Marcuse and 'Liberation,' " *The Intercollegiate Review,* 14 (1978), pp. 55-57.

14. For a description of Socialist alienation in Communist China, see *Time* magazine, November 28, 1983, p. 45. Among other things, the article notes that since 1978, Chinese journals have published six hundred articles on alienation. It is predictable that such alienation in a Socialist society will be blamed on spiritual pollution from the West.

15. Sidney Hook, *Marxism and Beyond*, p. 46.

16. *Ibid.*

17. Daniel Bell, *The End of Ideology* (New York: Free Press, 1960), p. 344.

18. Sidney Hook, *Marxism and Beyond*, p. 46.

19. Jose Miranda, *Marx Against the Marxists* (Maryknoll, New York: Orbis Books, 1980).

20. Erich Fromm, *Marx's Concept of Man* (New York: Ungar, 1961), p. 79.

21. Sidney Hook, "Marxism in the Western World," in *Marxist Ideology in the Contemporary World* (New York: Frederick A. Praeger, 1966), p. 16.

22. Robert Tucker, *Philosophy and Myth in Karl Marx* (Cambridge: Harvard University Press, 1961), p. 235.

23. Sidney Hook, "Marxism in the Western World," p. 27.

24. Daniel Bell, *The End of Ideology*, p. 344. See also Daniel Bell, "The 'Rediscovery' of Alienation," *The Journal of Philosophy*, 56 (1959), pp. 933-952.

25. Sidney Hook, *Marxism and Beyond*, p. 48.

26. See Humberto Belli, *Breaking Faith* (Westchester, Ill.: Crossway Books, 1985). For a different perspective on Castro's use of Christianity in the furtherance of his Marxist goals, see *Time* magazine, December 30, 1985, p. 71. Even Bonino comments on the extent to which liberation theology can help overcome religious opposition to communism. See his *Christians and Marxists*, pp. 25, 26.

27. Humberto Belli, "Nicaragua: Field Test for Liberation Theology," *Pastoral Renewal*, September 1984, pp. 30, 31.

28. Humberto Belli documents such claims in his book *Breaking Faith*, already cited.

29. Humberto Belli, *Nicaragua: Christians Under Fire* (Garden City, Mich.: The Puebla Institute, 1984), pp. 84, 85. Belli's *Breaking Faith* is an expanded version of this book.

10: True and False Liberation Theology

1. Humberto Belli, "Nicaragua: Field Test for Liberation Theology," *Pastoral Renewal*, September 1984, p. 18.

2. *Ibid.*, pp. 18, 19.

3. *Ibid.*, p. 19.

4. Two good books to consult in this regard are: Emilio Núñez, *Liberation Theology* (Chicago: Moody Press, 1985) and Gerard Berghoef and Lester DeKoster, *Liberation Theology, the Church's Future Shock* (Grand Rapids: Christian's Library Press, 1984).

5. Jose Miranda, *Marx and the Bible* (Maryknoll: Orbis, 1974), p. 44.

6. Michael Novak, *Freedom with Justice* (San Francisco: Harper and Row, 1984), p. 184.

7. Humberto Belli, "Nicaragua: Field Test for Liberation Theology," p. 27.

8. Humberto Belli, *Nicaragua: Christians Under Fire* (Garden City, Mich.: Puebla Institute, 1984), p. 85.
9. *Ibid.*
10. John Paul II, "Opening Address at Puebla," in *The Pope and Revolution,* ed. Quentin L. Quade (Washington, D.C.: Ethics and Public Policy Center, 1982), pp. 53, 54.
11. Michael Novak, *Freedom with Justice,* p. 192.
12. *Ibid.,* p. 188.
13. See Michael Novak, *The Spirit of Democratic Capitalism* (New York: Simon and Schuster, 1982), Chapters Sixteen, Seventeen, Eighteen.
14. William L. Scully, "The Brandt Commission: Deluding the Third World," *The Heritage Foundation Backgrounder,* No. 182, April 30, 1982, p. 16.
15. James V. Schall, S. J., *Liberation Theology in Latin America* (San Francisco: Ignatius Press, 1982), p. 44.
16. Novak's statement appears in *Liberation Theology,* ed. R. Nash (Milford, Mich.: Mott Media, 1984), p. 245.
17. Richard John Neuhaus, *The Naked Public Square* (Grand Rapids: Eerdmans, 1984), p. 83. Neuhaus thinks that authoritarian governments like those in the Philippines, South Africa, and several Southern American countries fall into a different category from Marxist-Leninist totalitarianism. These nations deny that they are irrevocably opposed to liberal democracy. Indeed, Neuhaus observes, "they often claim to aspire to liberal democracy, asserting that their denial of democratic freedoms is only a temporary expedient on the way to that goal" (p. 83).
18. Quoted in *Newsweek,* February 22, 1982.
19. Humberto Belli, "Nicaragua: Field Test for Liberation Theology," pp. 28, 29.
20. Humberto Belli, *Nicaragua: Christians Under Fire,* p. 85.
21. Carl F. H. Henry, "Liberation Theology and the Scriptures," in *Liberation Theology,* ed. Ronald H. Nash (Milford, Mich.: Mott Media, 1984), p. 202.

11: Interventionism

1. To say that these market forces frustrate the government's intentions *spontaneously* means simply that the actions individual persons take in response to governmental intervention were not undertaken for the express purpose of frustrating the government's goals. This was an unintended consequence of actions that had other ends in view.
2. Ludwig von Mises, *A Critique of Interventionism,* trans. Hans Sennholz (New Rochelle, N.Y.: Arlington House, 1977), p. 140.
3. *Ibid.,* p. 151.
4. For another example of this form of economic interventionism using a different example, see Ronald Nash, *Freedom, Justice and the State* (Lanham, Md.: University Press of America, 1980), pp. 147-149.
5. Laws against discrimination do not make my observation irrelevant. Human nature being what it is, human beings often wish to act in unjust ways. In a market system, discrimination will often impose certain costs on the discriminator. Governmental action that reduces or eliminates that cost has the unintended effect of encouraging discrimination. This point reappears later in the chapter.

6. *Time,* October 10, 1969, p. 94.
7. This claim is not falsified by statistics that suggest that employment has increased since the last increase in the minimum wage. During a time when an economy is expanding, the negative effects of minimum wage legislation on employment will tend to be hidden. The simple fact is that whether an economy is expanding or not, more people would be employed without the minimum wage than with it. Moreover, the higher labor costs required by the minimum wage law have an additional negative effect on the performance of the economy: without the higher labor costs mandated by the law, the economy would expand even more rapidly.
8. Walter E. Williams, "Government Sanctioned Restraints That Reduce Economic Opportunities for Minorities," *Policy Review,* No. 2 (1977), p. 11.
9. *Ibid.*
10. James D. Gwartney and Richard Stroup, *Economics, Private and Public Choice* (Orlando: Academic Press, 1983), p. 521.
11. Walter E. Williams, "Government Sanctioned Restraints That Reduce Economic Opportunities for Minorities," p. 11.
12. In fact, during the same years, prior to the advent of the programs of the Great Society, blacks of all ages achieved higher rates of employment than whites. See U.S. Congress, Joint Economic Committee, 95th Congress, 1st Session, *Youth and Minority Unemployment* (Washington, D.C.: Government Printing Office, July 1977).
13. Walter E. Williams, "Government Sanctioned Restraints That Reduce Economic Opportunities for Minorities," pp. 13, 14.
14. Walter E. Williams, "Free Enterprise Responses to Attacks on Capitalism," *The Presbyterian Layman,* May/June, 1985, p. 7. See also: Walter E. Williams, *The State Against Blacks* (New York: McGraw-Hill, 1982), Chapter Three; and Warren L. Coats, Jr., "The Economics of Discrimination," *Modern Age,* 1974, p. 68; James Gwartney and Richard Stroup, *Economics, Private and Public Choice,* pp. 523, 524.
15. Walter E. Williams, "Free Enterprise Responses to Attacks on Capitalism," p. 7.
16. See Walter Williams's writings cited in Notes 13 and 14.
17. Arthur Shenfield, *Myth and Reality in Economic Systems* (Washington, D.C.: The Heritage Foundation, 1981), p. 30.

12: The Great Depression I

1. Murray N. Rothbard, *America's Great Depression,* 3rd ed. (Kansas City: Sheed and Ward, 1975), Introduction.
2. Susan Love Brown, et al, *The Incredible Bread Machine* (San Diego: World Research, Inc., 1974), p. 33.
3. Murray Rothbard, *America's Great Depression,* Introduction.
4. See Jude Wanniski, *The Way The World Works* (New York: Basic Books, 1978), p. 125.

13: The Great Depression II

1. See Benjamin M. Anderson, *Economics and the Public Welfare* (Indianapolis: Liberty Press, 1979 [1949]), p. 224.

2. Tom Rose, *Economics: The American Economy* (Mercer, Pa.: American Enterprise Publications, 1985), p. 166.
3. See Murray Rothbard, *America's Great Depression*, 3rd ed. (Kansas City: Sheed and Ward, 1975), pp. 168ff.
4. *Ibid.*, p. 168.
5. Susan Love Brown, et al, *The Incredible Bread Machine* (San Diego: World Research, Inc., 1974), p. 44.
6. See "The Morgenthau Diaries," *Colliers*, October 25, 1947.
7. For the harmful effects of the National Recovery Act on the economy, see Benjamin Anderson, *Economics and the Public Welfare*, p. 335.
8. In 1936, the Supreme Court declared that the AAA was unconstitutional.
9. The unemployment figures are taken from Benjamin Anderson, *Economics and the Public Welfare*, p. 476.
10. Lawrence W. Reed, *Unraveling the Great Depression* (Caldwell, Ida.: The Center for the Study of Market Alternatives, 1985), p. 13.
11. Benjamin Anderson, *Economics and the Public Welfare*, p. 483.
12. Murray N. Rothbard, *America's Great Depression*, p. 295.

14: Social Security

1. See J. A. Dorn, "Social Security: Continuing Crisis or Real Reform?," *The Cato Journal*, 3 (1983), pp. 335-338.
2. See Martin Feldstein, "Social Security Induced Retirement and Aggregate Capital Accumulation," *Journal of Political Economy*, September/October, 1974, pp. 905-926.
3. Peter J. Ferrara, "For Social Security, The Crisis Continues," *The Heritage Foundation Backgrounder*, Number 467, November 4, 1985, p. 6.
4. Ferrara's figure of 14.1 percent was the combined employee/employer tax rate for 1985. Both the percentage and taxable wage base increased for 1986.
5. Peter Ferrara, "For Social Security, the Crisis Continues," p. 9.
6. Peter J. Ferrara, "The Prospect of Real Reform," *The Cato Journal*, 3 (1983), p. 616.
7. Peter J. Ferrara, "For Social Security, The Crisis Continues," p. 15.
8. Peter J. Ferrara, "The Prospect of Real Reform," p. 621.
9. For obvious reasons, this chapter could not provide more detailed analyses about the future problems of the Social Security system or about recommended reforms. For more detailed discussions, see: Peter J. Ferrara, *Social Security: The Inherent Contradiction* (Washington, D.C.: Cato Institute, 1980); Peter J. Ferrara, ed., *Social Security: Prospects for Real Reform* (Washington, D.C.: Cato Institute, 1985); and Peter J. Ferrara, ed., *Social Security: Prospects for Real Returns* (Washington, D.C.: Cato Institute, 1985).

15: Money, Mammon, and Wealth

1. Jacques Ellul, *Money and Power* (Downers Grove, Ill.: InterVarsity Press, 1984).
2. *Ibid.*, p. 78.

3. *Ibid.*, p. 76.
4. *Ibid.*, p. 79.
5. *Ibid.*
6. *Ibid.*
7. *Ibid.*
8. Andrew Kirk, *The Good News of the Kingdom Coming* (Downers Grove, Ill.: InterVarsity, 1985), p. 71.
9. Jacques Ellul, *Money and Power*, p. 76.
10. *Ibid.*, pp. 75, 76.
11. For the Old Testament view on this subject, see Ecclesiastes 5:19: "Moreover, when God gives any man wealth and possessions, and enables him to enjoy them, to accept his lot and be happy in his work—this is a gift of God."
12. See Luke 16:1-3; 19:11-27; Matt. 25:24-30. These parables also commend those who demonstrate their ability to increase their wealth.
13. Brian Griffiths, *Morality and the Market Place* (London: Hodder & Stoughton, 1982), p. 92.
14. Brian Griffiths, *The Creation of Wealth* (Downers Grove, Ill.: InterVarsity Press, 1985), p. 61.
15. *Ibid.*, pp. 60, 61.
16. *Ibid.*, p. 48.
17. See Michael Novak, "Helping the Poor," *Center Journal*, 2 (Summer, 1983), p. 37.
18. Isaiah 5:7-23; Amos 2:6-9; 5:7-12; 8:4-6.
19. Brian Griffiths, *The Creation of Wealth*, p. 60.
20. *Ibid.*, p. 45.
21. *Ibid.*, p. 44.

16: Poverty in America

1. Edward C. Banfield, *The Unheavenly City Revisited* (Boston: Little, Brown and Co., 1974).
2. *Ibid.*, pp. 56ff.
3. *Ibid.*, p. 61.
4. See, for example, Thomas Sowell, *Race and Economics* (New York: David McKay, 1975).
5. See James D. Gwartney and Richard Stroup, *Economics, Private and Public Choice*, third ed. (Orlando: Academic Press, 1983), p. 584.
6. *Ibid.*
7. Greg J. Duncan, *Years of Poverty, Years of Plenty* (Ann Arbor, Mich.: Institute for Social Research, 1984), p. 28.
8. *Ibid.*, p. 60.
9. Some definitions may help. Means-tested cash benefits include Aid to Families with Dependent Children (AFDC), General Assistance, Supplementary Security Income, and means-tested veterans' pensions. Noncash means-tested aid includes food stamps, school lunches, public housing, and Medicaid. The data comes from the U.S. Department of Commerce: Bureau of the Census, *Estimates of Poverty Including the Value of Noncash Benefits: 1979-1982*, Table A.

10. See Jonathan Hobbs, "Welfare Need and Welfare Spending," *Heritage Foundation Backgrounder*, October 13, 1982.

11. Thomas Sowell, "The Uses of Government for Racial Equality," *National Review*, September 4, 1981, p. 1013.

12. James Gwartney and Thomas S. McCaleb, "Have Antipoverty Programs Increased Poverty?," *Cato Journal*, 4 (Spring/Summer 1985), p. 15.

13. For more specific information regarding these numbers, see the Gwartney-McCaleb article cited in Note 12, pp. 1-16.

14. We should not be confused by the fact that the percentage of American poor declined until it reached a 1973 low of 11.1 percent. This additional decline from the 15 percent figure cited earlier had little or nothing to do with War on Poverty programs which were just getting into high gear by 1973.

15. See Charles Murray, *Losing Ground: American Social Policy 1950-1980* (New York: Basic Books, 1984).

16. It is important to note that the total bill for poverty programs has continued to climb during the Reagan presidency. See Dwight R. Lee, "The Politics of Poverty and the Poverty of Politics," *Cato Journal*, 5 (1985), pp. 17-35.

17. Political liberals don't like books like Murray's since it challenges all of their cherished assumptions about how the poor need the help of a benevolent state. Murray's book and other studies like it serve as an indictment of liberal social policy. It is important therefore to examine Murray's careful replies to his many critics. See Charles Murray, "Have the Poor Been 'Losing Ground'?," *Political Science Quarterly*, 100 (1985), pp. 427-445; and Charles Murray, "How to Lie With Statistics," *National Review*, February 28, 1986, pp. 39-41.

18. James Gwartney, "Social Progress, The Tax-Transfer Society and the Limits of Public Policy," unpublished, Department of Economics, Florida State University, p. 1.

19. Loury's statements and several from other leading blacks that follow appear in a symposium, "Black America Under the Reagan Administration," *Policy Review*, No. 35 (Fall 1985), pp. 27-41. Loury's quote appears on page 39. Loury's mention of George Gilder is a reference to Gilder's book *Wealth and Poverty* (New York: Basic Books, 1981).

20. *Ibid.*, p. 39.

21. *Ibid.*, pp. 39, 40.

22. Warren T. Brookes, "High Technology and Judeo-Christian Values," *Imprimis*, April 1984.

23. James Gwartney and Thomas McCaleb, "Have Antipoverty Programs Increased Poverty?," especially pp. 14ff.

24. *Ibid.*, p. 14.

25. A report of the conference can be found in the October 1985 issue of *The Religion and Society Report*.

26. Gwartney and McCaleb, p. 15.

27. *Ibid.*

28. Walter E. Williams, "Government Sanctioned Restraints That Reduce Economic Opportunities for Minorities," *Policy Review*, 2 (1977), p. 7.

29. Joe Sobran, "Pensees: Notes for the Reactionary of Tomorrow," *National Review*, December 31, 1985, p. 40.

30. *Ibid.*

17: Third-World Poverty

1. A nation's real gross national product (GNP) is the total money value of that country's economic output of final goods and services produced during a one-year period, adjusted for changes in the price level.

2. I use the expression "the Third World" in this chapter with some reservations. It is a gross oversimplification to write or speak as though the world were divided neatly into three blocs. This is especially true of those who attempt to set up a black and white contrast between the "rich nations of the West" and the impoverished nations of the Third World. There is actually little uniformity among the two-thirds of the world that make up the so-called Third World. A number of Third-World countries happen to be quite wealthy—e.g., Saudi Arabia and Kuwait. A number of other nations, notably those in Southeast Asia, have experienced some of the highest rates of economic growth in the world in recent years. Many nations in Southeast Asia, the Middle East, and Latin America contain large numbers of wealthy people. It is simplistic to regard poverty as an essential feature of Third-World countries. Nor are many Third-World nations neutral with respect to East-West tensions. Even though some economists are beginning to regard the expression "the Third World" as a fiction that makes it easier for certain nations in this group to pick the pockets of Western nations, common usage makes it difficult to refer conveniently to this amorphous group of nations with some other phrase.

3. Ronald Sider, "Mischief by Statute: How We Oppress the Poor," *Christianity Today*, 20 (July 16, 1976), p. 16.

4. P. T. Bauer, *Equality, The Third World and Economic Delusion* (Cambridge, Mass.: Harvard University Press, 1981), pp. 74ff.

5. *Ibid.*, p. 68.

6. I have no wish to minimize the horrors of the Atlantic slave trade. But it was not a cause of Third-World poverty. See Bauer, pp. 72ff.

7. This is obviously a complex subject about which much more needs to be said. The paragraph that precedes this note does not address a number of different subjects which are sometimes thrown into the discussion at this point. For example, it does not address clear questions of theft, oppression, and injustice. It does not deny the need for rectification of prior injustices. Nor does it address such issues as land reform which may be justified on the grounds of prior theft and oppression. All my paragraph asserts is an obvious truth. Given particular nation A and the size of its population and the degree of its poverty, the problem of poverty in that nation would not be solved by confiscating all of the wealth of the small upper class and redistributing it.

8. Brian Griffiths, *The Creation of Wealth* (Downers Grove, Ill.: InterVarsity Press, 1985), p. 12.

9. *Ibid.*, p. 13.

10. *Ibid.*

11. *Ibid.*

12. Of course, when wealth is transferred from a nation like the United States to countries like Saudi Arabia or Kuwait, as was the case until recently, the word "aid" seems inappropriate.

13. Bauer's remarks in this quote and in several that follow were made at a conference on "Liberation Theology and Third World Development," the

proceedings of which are contained in *Theology, Third World Development and Economic Justice,* ed. Walter Block and Donald Shaw (Vancouver, B.C.: The Fraser Institute, 1985). This particular statement appears on p. 35 of the book.

14. *Ibid.,* pp. 36, 37.
15. *Ibid.,* pp. 37, 38.
16. *Ibid.,* p. 38. It is clear from this last paragraph that Bauer's criticisms are directed against official aid—that is, transfers of wealth from one government to another. He is not addressing the separate question of assistance to the poor of some nation by voluntary agencies. Herbert Schlossberg reports that the government of Bangladesh has admitted that all of the relief it received in the form of food for one year was sold in India. The profit from those sales went into the pockets of politicians and their friends. See Schlossberg's *Idols for Destruction* (Nashville: Thomas Nelson, 1983), p. 73.
17. Brian Griffiths, *The Creation of Wealth,* p. 143.
18. The qualifying phrase "in a nonviolent way" is meant to preclude efforts to ease poverty through acts of theft and fraud.
19. P. T. Bauer, *Equality, The Third World and Economic Delusion,* p. 100.
20. Manuel F. Ayan, "The Impoverishing Effects of Foreign Aid," *Cato Journal,* 4 (1984), p. 324.
21. *Ibid.,* p. 325.
22. Alvin Rabushka, *Does the Third World Need More Capitalism?,* p. 5. Rabushka is a senior fellow at the Hoover Institute of Stanford University. His essay appears in a booklet containing the 1985 Burkett Miller Lecture Series that is distributed by the Center for Economic Education of the University of Tennessee at Chattanooga.
23. *Ibid.*
24. *Ibid.,* p. 7.
25. Brian Griffiths, *The Creation of Wealth,* pp. 37, 38.

Acknowledgments

A number of people have made important contributions to the writing of this book. Dr. Charles Van Eaton, professor of economics at Hillsdale College, was present when many of these ideas first took hold. Dr. Robert Pulsinelli, professor of economics at Western Kentucky University, offered many helpful comments as the manuscript reached its final form. Dr. James Gwartney, professor of economics at Florida State University, shared many important insights both in personal conversation and in material sent through the mail. Dr. William Peterson, professor of economics at The University of Tennessee-Chattanooga, was kind enough to read the manuscript and offer suggestions. I also appreciate the willingness of Dr. Herbert Schlossberg and of Dr. John Jefferson Davis, professor of theology at Gordon-Conwell Theological Seminary, to take the time to read the manuscript. My expression of appreciation for the help of these gentlemen does not mean that they necessarily agree with everything I have said. Nor were they responsible for any errors in fact or reasoning.

For Further Reading

Readers interested in exploring the topics of this book further will find the following books and articles to be helpful places to begin. Additional sources are identified in the notes to this book and in the bibliographies of many of the books listed below.

Alchian, Armen A. and Allen, William R. *Exchange and Production: Competiton, Coordination and Control,* 3rd ed. (Belmont, Calif.: Wadsworth, 1983).

Anderson, Benjamin M. *Economics and the Public Welfare* (Indianapolis: Liberty Press, 1979 [1949]).

Anderson, Martin. *Welfare: The Political Economy of Welfare Reform in the United States* (Stanford, Calif.: Hoover Institute, 1978).

Bauer, P. T. *Equality, The Third World and Economic Delusion* (Cambridge, Mass.: Harvard University Press, 1981).

Friedman, Milton and Rose. *Free to Choose* (New York: Harcourt Brace Jovanovich, 1979).

Gilder, George. *Wealth and Poverty* (New York: Basic Books, 1981).

Greaves, Bettina Bien. *Free Market Economics* (Irvington-on-Hudson, N.Y.: Foundation for Economic Education, 1975).

Griffiths, Brian. *The Creation of Wealth* (Downers Grove, Ill.: Inter-Varsity Press, 1985).

Gwartney, James and Stroup, Richard. *Economics, Private and Public Choice,* 4th ed. (Orlando, Fla.: Academic Press, 1986).

Heyne, Paul T. *The Economic Way of Thinking,* 4th ed. (Chicago: Science Research Associates, 1982).

———. and Johnson, Thomas. *Toward Understanding Macroeconomics* (Chicago: Science Research Associates, 1976).

——— and ———. *Toward Understanding Microeconomics* (Chicago: Science Research Associates, 1976).

Johnson, Paul. *Will Capitalism Survive?* (Washington, D.C.: Ethics and Public Policy Center, 1979).

Littlechild, Stephen C. *The Fallacy of the Mixed Economy* (San Francisco: The Cato Institute, 1979).

Miller, Roger Leroy and Pulsinelli, Robert W. *Understanding Economics* (St. Paul, Minn.: West, 1983).

Murray, Charles. "Have the Poor Been 'Losing Ground'?" *Political Science Quarterly,* 100 (1985), pp. 427-445.

————. *Losing Ground: American Social Policy 1950-1980* (New York: Basic Books, 1984).

Nash, Ronald. *Freedom, Justice and the State* (Lanham, Md.: University Press of America, 1980).

————, ed. *Liberation Theology* (Milford, Mich.: Mott Media, 1984).

————. *Social Justice and the Christian Church* (Milford, Mich.: Mott Media, 1983).

————. "The Christian Debate Over Economic Freedom." *The Journal of Private Enterprise,* 1 (1985), pp. 58-63.

Rose, Tom. *Economics: Principles and Policy from a Christian Perspective* (Milford, Mich.: Mott Media, 1977).

Shand, Alexander H. *The Capitalist Alternative: An Introduction to Neo-Austrian Economics* (New York: New York University Press, 1984).

Sowell, Thomas. *Race and Economics* (New York: David McKay, 1975).

Williams, Walter E. *The State Against Blacks* (New York: McGraw-Hill, 1982).

Woodson, Robert. "Helping the Poor Help Themselves." *Policy Review,* 21 (Summer, 1982), pp. 73-86.

Index of Subjects

Index of Persons